LEICESTERS
RUTLAND AIRFIELDS
IN THE SECOND
WORLD WAR

Martyn Chorlton

COUNTRYSIDE BOOKS
NEWBURY, BERKSHIRE

COUNTRYSIDE BOOKS
3 Catherine Road
Newbury, Berkshire

To view our complete range of books,
please visit us at
www.countrysidebooks.co.uk

ISBN 1 85306 800 4

The cover painting by Colin Doggett shows
a Lancaster returning to base after a night raid

Designed by Mon Mohan
Typeset by Textype, Cambridge
Produced through MRM Associates Ltd., Reading
Printed by Woolnough Bookbinding Ltd, Irthlingborough

CONTENTS

MAP OF THE LEICESTERSHIRE & RUTLAND AIRFIELDS IN THE SECOND WORLD WAR

I
SETTING THE SCENE

On 3rd September 1939, when Britain declared war on Germany, Leicestershire, like many other counties, was ill-prepared for the task ahead. Military aviation in the county was limited to one pre-war bomber station at Cottesmore in Rutland and one flying training airfield at Desford. During wartime, twelve additional military airfields were hastily built to support the war effort. Bottesford, Woolfox Lodge and North Luffenham, in particular, played key roles in Bomber Command operations.

Leicestershire is no stranger to aviation, with connections dating back to the early 19th century, when an intrepid balloonist called Sadler flew across the county and landed near Pickworth in Rutland. Nearly 100 years passed before the first interest in powered aviation began to filter through the county; when the Leicester Aero Club (LAC) was formed in 1909, it was initially only a gathering of aviation enthusiasts with no aircraft or flying ground.

The first real aviation event to make use of the county was the *Daily Mail* Circuit of Britain air race in 1911. One of the refuelling points was at Brentingby, near Melton Mowbray, and, when the locals heard of this, both young and old were excited. The race began at Brooklands in Surrey on 22nd July and the short first stage took the competitors only as far as Hendon in north London. Two days later, the race moved on, the second stage being considerably longer, with Edinburgh as the final destination. It was a Monday morning, but this made little difference; to observers it seemed that the entire population of

Leicestershire and Rutland was heading for the small village near Melton Mowbray. The competitors had left Hendon very early and when the first of them flew over Brentingby at 5.15 am, even by this time a huge, buzzing crowd had gathered. People did not go to work and several schools closed in Melton Mowbray because of such poor attendance. It is difficult to imagine today, but this was something very new. It was a long day for competitors and spectators alike when the last aircraft flew past at 7.45 pm, bringing to an end a novel day for the thousands of people who witnessed the race. Fifteen aircraft had left Hendon, but only three made it to Edinburgh, and the race was finally won by Jean Conneau, who was the first of only two finishers.

From 1911 onwards, several demonstration events were organised with prominent pilots of the period, including Benjamin Hucks and Gustav Hamel, who were displaying their aircraft. Pilots were commissioned to tour the country and Leicestershire and Rutland hosted several exhibitions of flying in 1912 and 1913.

This period spurred the members of the LAC into action and several members began building flying models and some full size aircraft, although no evidence of completion exists. An effort to establish aviation in Leicester was initiated in a meeting chaired by Samuel Faire at the Grand Hotel on 18th June 1913. The meeting discussed the building of an aerodrome and aircraft factory in Leicester, but, unfortunately, little came of it, and the plan was shelved with the arrival of the First World War.

The early years of the First World War were quiet for Leicestershire and Rutland, but the advent of Zeppelin raids from early 1916 onwards changed all that. On the night of 31st January, Kapitanleutnant Franz Stabbert crossed the Lincolnshire coast in Zeppelin L-20. His orders were broad: attack England, preferably in the south or the Midlands and, if the opportunity arises, bomb Liverpool. With this in mind, Stabbert headed inland and, when reaching what he thought was Sheffield, came under fire from a 'battery'. L-20 dropped six bombs and the guns fell silent, but Stabbert was not over the Yorkshire city, he was in fact over Loughborough. The bombs had fallen into the middle of the town and killed ten people outright, injured twelve and caused severe damage to many civilian homes.

Another incident happened shortly afterwards on 5/6th March 1916. Zeppelin L-13, commanded by Kapitanleutnant

Heinrich Mathy, crossed the Lincolnshire coast at North Coates. Mathy immediately encountered several severe storms and decided to head south after struggling to reach Newark. The situation did not improve when an engine failed whilst he was over Grantham. Mathy circled Belvoir Castle and assessed the situation. He decided that there was no option but to abandon the bomb load. Initially, 32 incendiaries were dropped just south of Sproxton in Leicestershire, the only casualty being a cow in the wrong place at the wrong time! L-13 continued on slowly south to where the final part of the bomb load was released. Fourteen High Explosives (HE) were released, south west of Thistleton. The explosions were said to have been heard in Norwich, over 85 miles away! L-13 continued southbound over Stamford and finally limped home via the Kent coast.

This prompted the senior staff of the Royal Flying Corp (RFC) to form an air defence squadron for the protection of the Midlands. Originally formed at Thetford in Norfolk on 1st April 1916, 38 Squadron was redesignated and re-formed on 14th July 1916 at Castle Bromwich in the West Midlands as a home defence squadron. This location gave the defending BE.2cs and BE.2es, operated by 38 Squadron, no time to gain the necessary altitude to attack a Zeppelin and so, three months later, it moved to a more easterly location.

On 1st October, the HQ of 38 Squadron moved to Melton Mowbray under the command of Major the Hon. L J E Twistleton-Wykeham-Fiennes. However, this move did not bring about the construction of any permanent airfield within the county borders. The three squadron flights were dispersed at airfields in Lincolnshire, at Stamford, Leadenham and Buckminster, of which the last village is in Leicestershire, the airfield only yards over the border. In support of 38 Squadron, seven landing grounds were constructed within Leicestershire but there is little evidence of use of the airfields by the squadron or any other military aircraft. The most used was Scalford, near Melton Mowbray, which was purposely situated as close as possible to the main HQ. The other landing grounds were at Blaston, Burton on the Wolds, Castle Donington, Peckleton, Queniborough and Welham.

38 Squadron began to receive marginally better aircraft in late 1916, but this did little to improve the success rate against the

attacking Zeppelins. BE.12s and FE.2bs still struggled to get anywhere near the high flying Zeppelins, which usually attacked at approximately 15,000 ft. There was only one recorded occasion during 38 Squadron's stay in the county when an aircraft managed to attack. On the night of 19/20th October 1917, Lieutenant G H Harrison was flying a FE.2b at 13,000ft near Leicester, when he spotted a Zeppelin, thought to be L-45, 2,000ft above him. He managed to close the gap but, after three bursts of fire, his machine gun jammed and Harrison had to give up the chase.

With nothing to show for their efforts, 38 Squadron left Melton and its three Lincolnshire airfields on 31st May 1918. Their destination was Capelle in northern France, where the squadron changed role and became a night bomber unit. The squadron left behind several personnel and aircraft, which became a re-formed 90 Squadron and which served out the end of the First World War at Buckminster.

Another attempt was made in 1919 to organize a Leicestershire and Rutland Aero Club but, once again, interest was lacking, even with many ex-service aviators now living in the two counties. It was not until 1926 that the Leicestershire Chamber of Commerce started to show an interest in aviation, and a lecture regarding the topic was held at the De Montfort Hall. The main speakers were two very influential people, the well known aviator Sir Alan Cobham and Sir Sefton Brancker, who was the Director of Civil Aviation at the time. The meeting was well attended and was such a success that it spawned the formation of the Commercial Aviation Committee. This, in turn, led to a sub-committee exploring the potential of siting an airport near Leicester.

Certain members of the Chamber showed some restraint and a sensible decision was made to form a flying club before embarking on ambitious plans to develop an airport. On 30th November 1928, the Leicestershire Aero Club was officially re-formed, the earlier attempt having petered out before the First World War. The next stage was to find a suitable location in which to conduct flying, which resulted in a visit to the old First World War landing ground at Peckleton. The field was found to be suitable and in September 1929 the new Desford Aerodrome was officially opened.

One year later, another airfield was opened, near Ratcliffe on the Wreake. Its owner, Lindsay Everard, would become a significant patron in virtually all civilian flying in the county. In the meantime, the hunt was still going on for a suitable site for Leicester's new airport and, by 1932, land had been acquired for the project at Braunstone Frith.

Braunstone, or Leicester Municipal Airport, opened in 1935 and was managed by the LAC, who moved from Desford that same year. Also in the same year, a second flying club was formed and called the Leicestershire Flying Pou Club or 'Flying Flea'. The intention of the club was to build Pous from the designer Henry Mignet's published plans and fly them from a field near Melton Mowbray. Unfortunately, the Flea was unsafe and the club purchased a Kronfield Drone instead, which, quite apart from having an inappropriate name, still needed a more suitable flying ground. Lindsay Everard came to the rescue and found the now renamed County Flying Club a new airfield near Rearsby in 1938.

In November 1938, A L Wykes, a textile machinery manufacturer based at Thurmaston, made the brave decision to begin construction of aircraft. He formed Taylorcraft Aeroplanes (England) and in April 1939 the first aircraft began to leave the factory and were test flown from Lindsay Everard's airfield at Ratcliffe. This was a significant aviation development and, although the Second World War halted all civilian production, military orders were received, and the rest is history – the Auster range of aircraft had been born.

Military aviation began to rejuvenate in the mid 1930s, in line with the RAF Expansion Scheme, which commenced in 1934. This was basically part of a re-armament programme initiated in response to the worrying activities of a certain Adolf Hitler in Germany. The first airfield to be affected by this was Desford, whose owners, Reid and Sigrist, were operating a Civil Flying Training School (CFTS). The CFTS was quickly renamed as 7 Elementary and Reserve Flying Training School (E&RFTS) to accommodate service pilots from the forthcoming RAF Volunteer Reserve, which was formed in April 1937.

The expansion scheme resulted in a large increase of squadrons, which, in turn, led to a demand for new airfields. One of these new airfields was built at Cottesmore in Rutland and

Line of bright yellow Tiger Moths of 7 Elementary & Reserve Flying Training School seen at Desford in September 1938, captured during an inspection by AOC Training Command. When war broke out twelve months later, all these civilian registered Tigers were impressed into service use and painted in camouflage.

opened in March 1938. It remains the only military airfield within the two counties that is still active.

The start of the Second World War brought to an end the very active civilian aviation fraternity which was building rapidly within the county. On 3rd September 1939, all private and club flying was stopped and a permit had to be requested for every flight undertaken, which apparently was not worth the aggravation and red tape. Hardly any civilian aviators had the chance to apply to fly as the military quickly took over civilian flying grounds and requisitioned the majority of civil-owned aircraft. Many of the Tiger Moths that operated from Desford had been privately owned machines and a few actually survived the war and were returned to their original owners.

Many potential airfield locations had already been surveyed several months before the outbreak of war. Twenty sites in all were looked at in both counties, of which ten were built in Leicestershire and two in Rutland (Cottesmore, also in Rutland was already active.) If the war had continued beyond 1945, the sites that had not been built upon may have been called into use.

The others, which had all received a survey from the Air Ministry, were at Croft, Countersthorpe, Foxton Lodge, Kilby, Ragdale and Snarestone, and a bomber station was planned at Essendine in Rutland. Ragdale was dropped in favour of Castle Donington and became a bombing range for the use of 28 Operational Training Unit (OTU). Snarestone was planned as a Fleet Air Arm airfield at which the Admiralty proposed to house an Advanced Training Unit. Essendine was to have been another heavy bomber station with two squadrons but, like in Snarestone, local opposition against the use of such prime agricultural land won the day.

The majority of wartime airfields within Leicester and Rutland were used in a training capacity. However, in the early war years, several made valuable contributions to the air offensive against Germany. All three airfields in Rutland and Bottesford, in the very north eastern corner of Leicestershire, were occupied by operational squadrons. The majority of important targets within Germany and occupied Europe were attacked and all of the units involved suffered terrible losses.

Both counties, with their central position within the country and relatively flat countryside, were well suited for the operation of training airfields. On several occasions during the Second World War, all the airfields in the two counties were involved in aircrew training in one form or another. The only exceptions were Ratcliffe and Rearsby, but even these airfields were used briefly by Air Training Corps gliding schools. Ratcliffe was a base for the Air Transport Auxiliary (ATA) for the entire duration of the war and, with the exception of Melton Mowbray, was the busiest airfield in Leicestershire and was visited by a large variety of aircraft.

Basic flying training was carried out at Desford, along with its satellite airfield at Braunstone, and the school based there gave many future RAF pilots their first insight into flying. Several pilots who had trained at Desford and Braunstone returned to continue their training at one of the many Operational Training Units (OTU) that were also located within the two counties. Thirteen of the county's airfields were used at various stages for housing OTUs, several of them moving home within the county to cater for the ever changing roles of each airfield. Woolfox Lodge, for example, started its wartime period as an OTU; it was twice a home for two different bomber squadrons and also for two Heavy Conversion Units (HCU), not to mention the brief period when it came under the 9th Air Force's control. This was typical of the continuous movement of units throughout the war years.

From the end of 1943, the planned invasion of Europe started to become a reality, with the war progressing at a good pace during the invasion of Italy. The airfields in the east of the county quickly came under American control with the arrival of the 9th Air Force Troop Carrier Command (TCC). Cottesmore and Saltby played the most significant role during the American invasion, and Bottesford, too, albeit to a lesser extent and even though it was only used briefly by flying units. American Douglas C-47s became a common sight, practising paratroop drops and towing gliders.

In the later stages of the war, the many airfields that were operating a Bomber Command OTU were transferred to Transport Command and eventually the common sight of the Vickers Wellington was replaced by the Douglas Dakota. HCUs

A scene typical of any one of the eleven airfields that operated the Wellington; on average over 50 of the Barnes Wallis geodetic bombers could be seen on a station housing an OTU.

also featured prominently in the later stages of the war, all flying four-engined bomber aircraft like the Short Stirling, Handley Page Halifax and the Avro Lancaster.

As mentioned earlier, the only active RAF station remaining today is Cottesmore, operating its high tech trio of Harrier squadrons. Civilian flying remains at Castle Donington (East Midlands Airport), Leicester East (Leicester Airport), Saltby (Buckminster Gliding Club) and, in a limited capacity, at Bruntingthorpe, where the airfield continues to receive contributions to its growing collection of ex-military jet aircraft.

Flying Training

Apart from the extreme eastern side of the county, Leicestershire's central location did not lend itself to front line operations. Flying training, however, at one point during the war

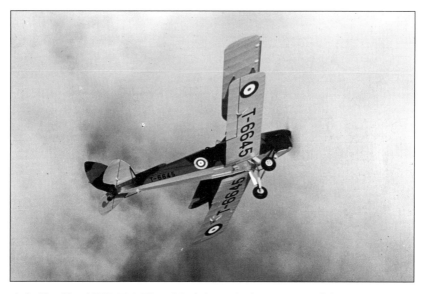

A de Havilland DH.82A Tiger Moth in typical pose – one of the RAF's most successful elementary training aircraft. During the whole of the Second World War and beyond, the Tigers of 7 EFTS filled the skies around Desford and Braunstone.

13

was making use of every airfield within the two counties, except Ratcliffe and Rearsby.

Military training began in Leicestershire at Desford in November 1935, with the formation of 7 Elementary and Reserve Flying Training School (E&RFTS) and remained there for twenty years. It was forever associated with the de Havilland Tiger Moth, which made the ideal basic trainer and in which thousands of future fighter, bomber and transport pilots gained their wings.

When the war began, Bomber Command was inundated with aircrew volunteers and it quickly had to re-organise itself in order to cope. Squadrons were initially reserved from operations and acted as training units, known as Group Pool Squadrons, under the control of 6 (Training) Group. They were renamed in April 1940 as Operational Training Units (OTUs) and these units would become the most common operated within the two counties. The units provided six-week courses, in which individual airmen were shaped into crews and converted onto a particular bomber type. The course involved 55 hours for those crews on a heavy bomber OTU and 60 hours for light and medium bombers.

Before the volunteers got anywhere near an aircraft, they needed to undergo basic theory and flying training in Training Command. Potential aircrew had to go through basic training like any other airmen, with drill, physical training and much classroom work to prepare mind and body for the next stage. Once the individual had passed the relevant psychological and aptitude tests, the successful airman was shipped overseas for flying training, with the exception of Flight Engineers, whose training was carried out at St Athan in South Wales.

Flying Training Command had schools in Canada, USA, Australia, South Africa, South Rhodesia, India, New Zealand, the Bahamas and the Middle East and many bomber crews who trained at these locations have vivid and happy memories of big friendly skies. Once the pilots, navigators, bomb-aimers, wireless operators and air-gunners had arrived from their exotic locations, it was up to the OTUs to turn fledgling airmen into fighting bomber crews.

On arrival at an OTU, the highly unorthodox, but generally successful, method of 'crewing up' was carried out. Usually

A nervous instructor looks on as he sends a pupil on his first solo in a Tiger Moth. A scene all too familiar on many training airfields throughout the country.

herded into a hangar, the new arrivals would be simply told to sort themselves out into crews; there was no science behind this and it seemed to work. Friendships were quickly formed between young men from all over the Empire and, if the crews were lucky enough to make it through the war, these friendships would last a lifetime.

By 1942, the length of OTU training had increased to 80 hours flying during a ten-week course, a time scale that was often extended because of the English weather. New crews arrived once a fortnight and averaged between eleven and sixteen crew at a time. The most common type of aircraft seen on an OTU was the Vickers Wellington, although 14 OTU at Cottesmore and Saltby was the longest user of its main predecessor, the Handley Page Hampden. At full strength the average OTU would have 54 Wellingtons and a collection of support aircraft, which included types such as the Avro Anson, Airspeed Oxford and Westland Lysander. As the war progressed, more varied aircraft included Hurricanes, Spitfires, Beaufighters and Mosquitoes. The majority of Wellingtons that arrived on the OTUs were cast offs from front line squadrons, often well past their best and always needing attention from the ground engineers to keep them flying. This led to many OTU machines still flying long after they would have

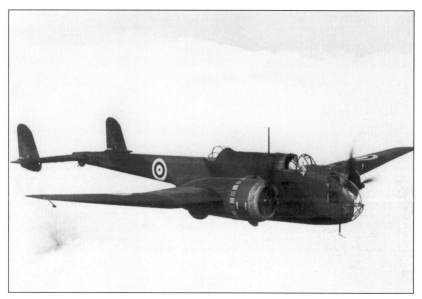

A Handley Page Hampden bomber was the main equipment of 14 OTU at Cottesmore and Saltby in the early war years, until replaced by the Vickers Wellington.

been grounded in peacetime and resulted in the needless loss of many young aircrew and their aircraft. A combination of worn out equipment and inexperienced crews accounted for an alarmingly high loss rate: some classes lost as many as 25 per cent of their strength in three or four months.

As the war and technology progressed, the introduction of four-engined aircraft presented two problems. Firstly, to convert crews from the twin-engine Hampdens and Wellingtons, the front line squadron had to be withdrawn from operations. The second problem involved the Wellington, which, in Leicestershire alone, equipped 14, 28 and 29 OTUs. The majority of aircraft had their front and mid-upper gun turrets removed and possessed no flight engineer, all of which were features and requirements of the Short Stirling, Handley Page Halifax and Avro Lancaster.

A temporary solution was introduced whereby a Heavy Conversion Unit (HCU) was assigned to each Bomber Group and a Conversion Flight (CF) was also allocated to each individual

Line of Handley Page Herefords like those operated by 14 OTU. They differed from the Hampden in that they were powered by Napier Dagger in-line engines. Compared with the Hampden's Bristol Pegasus radials, the Daggers lacked reliability, which resulted in the Herefords often being grounded.

squadron. A good example of this was 207 CF, based at Bottesford. 207 Squadron at this time was operating the twin-engined Avro Manchester and were in the process of converting to the four-engined Lancaster. Bottesford was under the control of 5 Group Bomber Command, and 1654 HCU, stationed at Swinderby in Lincolnshire, provided the main conversion training before the crews returned to their respective squadrons. By the end of 1942, all Conversion Flights were disbanded and resources were focused on the HCUs. The control of OTUs also changed, when in May and June of 1942, 91, 92 and 93 (OTU) Groups were formed in order to cope with the huge demands for bomber aircrew operational training. These three groups controlled the Midlands area of the country and, throughout the Second World War, several airfields in Leicestershire and Rutland came under their jurisdiction.

In May 1943 Woolfox Lodge was the first airfield in the two counties to receive an HCU. 1665 HCU was equipped with Short Stirling Mk.Is, and their equipment, like the OTUs', comprised worn out hand-me-downs, with poor serviceability records, and this, combined once again with an inexperienced crew, resulted in many losses. Bottesford, Cottesmore, North Luffenham and Saltby were all used by HCUs, which, coupled with all of the OTUs' flying training, made the county a major provider of new crews for Bomber Command operations.

Bomber Command

When Cottesmore opened in 1938, it became the two counties' first bomber station, and its new squadrons were equipped with the latest examples of what Bomber Command had to offer. 35 and 207 Squadrons were initially equipped with the Vickers Wellesley, but these were quickly replaced by the uninspiring Fairey Battle light bomber. When war was declared in September 1939, Bomber Command only had 280 bomber aircraft at its disposal. Air Chief Marshall Sir Edgar Ludlow-Hewitt, who was then Commander-in-Chief of Bomber Command, endeavoured to raise awareness of the command's situation at Air Staff level, highlighting the fact that Bomber Command was poorly equipped, lacked armament and, most importantly, that aircrew training was totally inadequate for the task ahead.

When the Battles left Cottesmore, they were replaced by 106 and 185 Squadrons, equipped with the Handley Page Hampden. A more potent aircraft than the Battle, it still lacked a serious bomb load and, in Cottesmore's case, was relegated to a training role with 14 OTU. However, the Hampden did equip many front line squadrons and was bravely operated by two units from North Luffenham, who lost many aircraft in the process. Both 61 and 144 Squadrons operated the Hampden from the Rutland station but, by September, 61 Squadron had re-equipped with the Avro Manchester and moved its operation to Woolfox Lodge.

When Bottesford first opened in September 1941, it became Leicestershire's one and only heavy bomber station. 207 Squadron operated the Manchester from here until it was replaced by the Avro Lancaster in June 1942. Operations performed from

The Avro Manchester, hopelessly underpowered with Rolls Royce Vulture engines. The forerunner of the Lancaster was operated from Bottesford, North Luffenham and Woolfox Lodge and all units operating the Manchester suffered losses, both mechanical and to the enemy. This example is from 207 Squadron based at Bottesford.

Bottesford were typical of the difficult task Bomber Command were faced with. The Manchester was incredibly unreliable, the squadron only managed to put up ten aircraft on two raids while using the twin-engined bomber. The main focus of the command was the German fleet during early 1942, in particular the capital ships *Scharnhorst* and *Gneisenau*, lain up in Brest Harbour. Along with 61 Squadron at Woolfox Lodge, raid after raid was flown into the heavy flak defences at the French port. Losses were high for both squadrons and, in the end, both warships escaped to the relative safety of German ports, but not before both were damaged by mines already laid by 5 Group aircraft.

With the departure of the bomber squadrons from North Luffenham and Woolfox Lodge, 207 Squadron remained as the only front line bomber squadron, now equipped with the Avro Lancaster. This did not mean that the many OTUs that were springing up around the counties were not playing their part.

Sir Arthur 'Butch' Harris was appointed Commander-in-Chief of Bomber Command in early 1942, and he immediately set to

Excellent air to air photograph of a Vickers Wellington Mk.II. Although only one example of a Mk.II was operated in either county, the Wellington generally was the most common aircraft to be seen in Leicestershire and Rutland.

work raising the profile and efficiency of the Command. One of Harris's plans was to assemble a force of 1,000 bombers and send them out in one massive raid on a German city. The plan was received with great enthusiasm by Churchill, even though Harris had only about 400 aircraft with trained crews, who were regularly used for front-line operational work. To resolve this deficit, Harris made use of the many aircraft that were used by Conversion and Operational Training Units. These aircraft, along with many more from Flying Training Command, made up the necessary amount. The aircraft from these units would be crewed by a combination of instructors, many of them ex-operational, and by men in the later stages of their training. 14 OTU's Handley Page Hampdens and 18 and 29 OTUs' Vickers Wellingtons both contributed to the 1,000 bombers raids, the first against Cologne on 30th/31st May 1942.

By early 1943, all front-line Bomber Command activity within Leicestershire was once again focused upon Bottesford, and the long suffering 207 Squadron was replaced by an Australian unit, 467 (RAAF) Squadron, also flying Lancasters. Under the leadership of Wing Commander Gomm, the Australians suffered badly during their stay at Bottesford, but still managed to make a significant contribution to the war effort. The squadron attacked a large variety of far reaching targets, including the Italian Naval base at La Spezia, which was successfully bombed, before the attacking force continued south to the safety of bases in North Africa. The squadron also took part in the first attack on Peenemunde, home of the Germans' 'secret weapons', in particular, the V-2 rocket, then being developed.

When 467 Squadron left Bottesford for Waddington on 11th November 1943, it not only brought the end of an era for the airfield but also created a temporary lull in Bomber Command activity. Aircraft from the various OTUs carried out 'Nickel'

By 1944, only one front-line bomber squadron was operating from the two counties. 218 Squadron was equipped with the Short Stirling, and flew from Woolfox Lodge until August; the veteran unit was then re-equipped with the Avro Lancaster.

21

raids, or leaflet drops, but other than this no more active operations would be carried out until the arrival of a veteran unit at Woolfox Lodge in April 1944.

218 Squadron moved in from Downham Market, flying the Short Stirling Mk III, which, by this stage of the war, was entering its twilight days in front line service. The aircraft flew many interesting raids from Woolfox, including several Special Operation Executive (SOE) sorties, which involved a detachment of aircraft operating from Tempsford in Bedfordshire. The highlight of the squadron's stay at the Rutland bomber station was a special operation called *Glimmer*, which was carried out on 6th June 1944, D-Day. The object of the exercise, along with 617 Squadron's operation *Taxable*, was to create a pair imaginary convoys using 'Window'. These ghost convoys were designed to fool the German forces into thinking that the planned invasion was approaching from a different location. Both operations were a complete success, and their importance was later expressed by Sir Arthur Harris, who could not overstate how much the two operations had contributed to the surprise element of the invasion.

When 218 Squadron left Woolfox Lodge in August 1944, it became the last wartime Bomber Command squadron to operate in the two counties. Bomber units would return, but in a new age of Canberras, Victors and Vulcans at Cottesmore – a far cry from the Wellesleys and Battles that bounced across the grass so many years before.

The United States 9th Air Force Troop Carrier Command

First activated at Cottesmore on 16th October 1943, the 9th Air Force Troop Carrier Command (TCC) was originally under the control of the 8th Air Force but, within a matter of months, the TCC expanded to three wings comprising over 8,500 personnel and 1,256 aircraft.

Cottesmore also housed the 50th Troop Carrier Wing (TCW), but this was replaced in February 1944 after a re-shuffle of units by the 52nd TCW, which made its home in Exton Hall until March 1945.

General Dwight D Eisenhower addresses the men of the 82nd Airborne Division at Leicester East on 10th August 1944. (D Wills)

Officially the 9th Air Force, TCC had three airfields made available for its use between the end of 1943 and May 1945. Cottesmore, Bottesford and Saltby were the main centres of activity, but at Leicester East and North Luffenham, also, American aircraft were no strangers. Being located conveniently close to the main camps of the 82nd Airborne Division, Leicester East was used by American Douglas C-47s, operating a daily shuttle service for the benefit of the airborne troops based nearby. Both Leicester East and North Luffenham were used for glider training by the US forces, North Luffenham in particular hosted the trials of the glider pick-ups, involving a low flying C-47, literally snatching the glider into the air. Woolfox Lodge was also allocated to the 9th Air Force, and it was even renamed Army Air Force Station 478 but, after only six weeks, and with no sign of any American flying unit moving in, Woolfox Lodge was returned to RAF control.

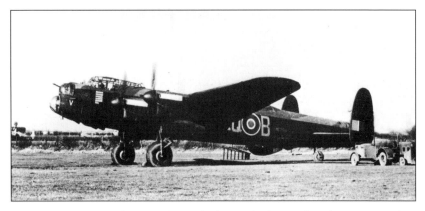

An Avro Lancaster of 1651 HCU, which was the last unit to be permanently based at Woolfox Lodge.

On 6th January 1944, the 436th TCG (Troop Carrier Group) became the first US C-47 group to be stationed within Leicestershire and was quickly followed by the 316th TCG at Cottesmore and the 314th TCG at Saltby. On average, each TCG was allocated 64 operational aircraft with sixteen in reserve, and two combat aircrews per aircraft.

The one and only reason for the existence of the 9th TCC was the forthcoming invasion of Europe, and, leading up to this, the Command organised a comprehensive series of exercises to prepare its crew for this task: exercises involving paratroop drops; glider tow-offs and landings with the American Waco CG-4A, the most used glider used by the Command; air landing of supplies; and casualty evacuation. Between January and May 1944, Command and 38 Wing exercises were carried out, culminating in Exercise Eagle, a full scale dress rehearsal held on 12th May 1944.

A unique unit was established in February 1944 at Bottesford. Initially without a title, the unit moved to Cottesmore and became the 9th Air Force Pathfinder School. The school selected the best crews from each group and put them through an intensive course of training in all aspects of day and night navigation and the use of all the available electronic devices which would enable navigators to determine their position accurately. An overcrowded Cottesmore forced the school to move out on 23rd March 1944 and settle a few miles away at North Witham in Lincolnshire.

By the time D-Day arrived on 6th June 1944, only the 316th and 314th TCGs remained, as Bottesford groups had flown south to join 53rd TCW based at Greenham Common. Preceded by the nineteen pathfinder C-47s from North Witham, aircraft from Cottesmore and Saltby joined twelve other TCGs to become part of the aerial armada carrying paratroops of the 82nd Airborne Division and their equipment into Normandy. The American paratroopers were all dropped in the Ste Mère Église area of Normandy and both groups returned to their bases to pick up more troops and perform re-supply missions.

Returning to the routine of training during the summer months, the 314th and 316th TCGs prepared themselves for action over Arnhem in the Netherlands. Operation *Market Garden* once again involved all fourteen groups, dropping British and American paratroops and later towing CG-4A and Airspeed Horsa gliders to landing zones, in an attempt to capture the strategically important bridges that crossed the Rhine. Saltby's aircraft delivered paratroopers of the 1st Airborne Division, while Cottesmore carried troops from the 82nd Airborne Division. The 9th TCC once again contributed all fourteen TCGs, and for Operation *Market Garden*, 1899 glider/tug combinations were towed from thirteen English bases.

In early March 1945, the 314th TCG left Saltby and relocated to France, for Operation *Varsity*, the crossing of the Rhine and the final push into Germany. This now left the 316th TCG at Cottesmore as the only American flying unit within the two counties, and the group would make the long flight from its Rutland home, via Wethersfield in Essex, in support of *Varsity*. The operation began on 24th March and involved 610 tug aircraft, towing 906 gliders. This unbalanced figure was reached because a large proportion of the TCGs involved were towing two gliders each. Curtiss C-46 Commandos saw active service in Europe for the first time as part of *Varsity*; a pair of these were on the 316th TCG's strength, but played no part in the operation. They did appear in number, briefly, at Saltby in March 1945, as part of a detachment of the 440th TCG, transporting 1,163 troops of the British 1st Airborne Division and delivering 1,700,000lbs of freight and supplies to Copenhagen, Oslo and Stavanger.

25

The 316th TCG returned to the United States in May 1945. Cottesmore, named by the Americans as Army Air Force Station 489, was returned to RAF control on 1st July 1945.

Transport Command

Often overlooked, Transport Command had a key role to play during the Second World War, especially in the later stages. Several airfields within Leicestershire were involved in the training of former bomber crews for the much safer task of operating transport aircraft. Bitteswell, Castle Donington, Leicester East, North Luffenham, Nuneaton and Wymeswold all housed units for such a purpose. All of them, with the exception of Leicester East, were already used to the operations of bomber OTUs, and a change to a Transport OTU or (T)OTU was a painless transition.

The RAF's Transport Command was formed on 25th March

As Transport Command began to take over several airfields within the counties, the Douglas Dakota became the most common aircraft. Like the Wellingtons before, the aircraft would perform the continuous practice of 'circuits and bumps'.

1943 and, initially, it took executive control of 44 and 45 Groups (all of Leicestershire's Transport airfields came under 44 Group). Early equipment for the (T)OTUs consisted of nothing more than Vickers Wellingtons, fitted with dual controls and all gun turrets removed. Early transport aircraft, like the training aircraft, were nothing more than converted bombers – the Halifax, Liberator, Stirling and Lancaster were all modified into limited passenger and freight aircraft. The arrival of the Douglas Dakota, however, turned Transport Command into an effective force and, operating alongside the Avro York, it became the backbone of the Command. Over 1,900 Dakotas were supplied to the RAF under Lend-Lease and 24 Squadron became the first unit to receive some, in March 1943, operating from Gibralter.

On 25th June 1943, Nuneaton became the first to be controlled by Transport Command with 105 OTU flying Wellington Mk.Ic and Mk.Xs. This particular unit was renamed 1381 (T) Conversion Unit (CU) a few months later and, like many other Transport Command training units in the county, did not begin to receive the Dakota until the middle of 1945. Post war, they became a familiar site and the last airfield to operate a Transport Command unit was North Luffenham. 1382 (T) CU started out at Castle Donington, moved to Wymeswold and then on to North Luffenham before being renamed 240 Operational Conversion Unit (OCU). Over 40 Dakotas were operated by 240 OCU, and continued to be until the unit was disbanded on 16th April 1951.

2

BITTESWELL

National Grid Reference: SP514846; 6½ miles N of Rugby

Bitteswell had been ear-marked for use as an airfield in 1938. A survey party from the Ministry of Public Buildings and Works visited the proposed site, and a satisfactory report came of it. Eighteen months later, in March 1940, construction of a grass airfield was started. Another fifteen months would pass before use could be made of the new station.

The station opened as part of 6 Group, Bomber Command, and was initially intended to serve as a satellite of 18 (Polish) Operational Training Unit (OTU), which was based at Bramcote, not too far from the county border in Warwickshire. Two officers and 105 airmen, who had travelled from Bramcote, officially opened the airfield on 3rd June 1941. Flight Lieutenant L G Bloomfield was in command of the opening up party and temporarily became the new station commander.

On arrival, the Bramcote airmen were faced with scenes of complete chaos. The airfield was in a poor state: no accommodation was finished and, on top of all that, no mains water or electricity had been connected. So it was 'under canvas' for the airmen, and for the next two months all work efforts were placed on getting the airfield into an operational condition.

The official date for 18 OTU's arrival at Bitteswell was 30th June 1941, but it was several more weeks before the airfield was ready to receive its first aircraft. At that time, the unit was only a half size OTU, with an establishment of 27 Vickers Wellington

Mk.Is and nine Avro Ansons. 18 OTU was first formed on 15th June 1940, from the Polish Training Unit in 6 Group based at Hucknall, Nottinghamshire. The unit's first task was to train light bomber crews for the Polish Fairey Battle squadrons, before moving to Bramcote on 7th November 1940.

By the end of July, work had progressed to such a level that the airfield was almost ready to receive its first aircraft. Most of the perimeter track and dispersal aprons had been finished, and runways and many technical and domestic buildings were also nearing completion. On 12th August 1941, night flying training started with 18 OTU's aircraft making good use of an extra airfield for its training programmes. A few days later, six Vickers Wellington Mk.Ics of newly formed 'D' Flight made Bitteswell their permanent home.

August and September saw the airfield achieve a more permanent and comfortable feel. Water and electricity were finally connected and many technical and administration buildings were all but finished. The control tower was operational and the officers' mess was occupied. From the airmen's point of view, a newly opened cookhouse and a move from canvas to hutments must have greatly improved morale.

September ended with the only serious accident documented by 18 OTU at Bitteswell. On the night of the 29th, R3216, a Wellington Mk.Ic, was carrying out night flying circuits and bumps. It not known exactly what caused the crash, but the aircraft came down on the airfield perimeter and burst into flames. Seven of the eight-man crew were killed instantly, the only survivor being the tail gunner, thanks to the quick actions of the first airmen to arrive on the scene. S W J Green was the duty MT driver at the time and managed to rescue the gunner from the blazing wreck. For his heroism he was later awarded the George Medal.

By April 1942, the OTU had reached full strength, with an establishment of 54 Wellingtons, eighteen Ansons, and a pair of Westland Lysanders for target towing duties. This number of aircraft was short lived as, on 11th May, 6 Group became 91 Group and 18 OTU suddenly found themselves involved in the main Bomber Command offensive. The OTU, like many others, contributed to all three '1000 bomber' raids on Cologne, Essen and Bremen, losing three aircraft operating from Bramcote in the process. On 1st September, the unit moved to 93 Group but was significantly smaller as a Polish Flight had been formed and transferred to 6 (C) OTU at Thornaby in Yorkshire.

A regular unit that made use of Bitteswell was 1513 Beam Approach Training Flight (BATF). This moved to Bramcote, to which Bitteswell was a satellite airfield, from Honington in Suffolk on 31st October 1942. Equipped with eight Airspeed Oxfords they would be very often heard, before being seen, as they suddenly appeared out the gloom and landed straight down the runway.

With winter fast approaching, it soon became apparent that the grass runways would not cope with the poor weather and continuous use put on them by the Wellingtons. On 18th December, 'D' Flight, mainly made up of Polish aircrew at this stage, was disbanded. The six Wellingtons left in early 1942 for Moreton-in-the-Marsh in Gloucestershire and Bitteswell became unserviceable. 18 OTU never returned to Bitteswell. The last of the OTU's personnel had left by 7th February and officially departed, via Bramcote, to their new home at Finningley in Yorkshire on 27th February 1943.

Work had already started on upgrading Bitteswell's facilities when the last of the OTU Wellingtons left, but the airfield would still not be open until the summertime. Three concrete runways were built, complete with connecting perimeter track and dispersal areas. The main runway was 2,000 yards in length, intersected by two others 1,400 yards in length. Twenty-seven dispersals, capable of supporting an RAF heavy bomber and a pair of hangars, were also constructed. Accommodation was classed as temporary, but still provided for 1,175 officers and airmen and over 100 WAAFs. In the south-western corner of the airfield, Armstrong Whitworth Aircraft (AWA) Company also constructed a large hangar system for their use. The company already had sites at Baginton and Whitley, both near Coventry.

Being located near the heavily bombed city of Coventry made Armstrong Whitworth eligible for a move away from the city, and Bitteswell was chosen as one of its new dispersed, final assembly factories. Armstrong Whitworth was contracted for the construction of Avro Lancasters, so a move was vitally important to continue production. Lancasters started to leave the airfield from August 1943 and this continued until late 1945. A total of

1,329 Lancasters of various marks were assembled and test flown from Bitteswell.

In May 1943, the airfield re-opened as part of 93 Group, having been transferred from 6 Group in September 1942. The station continued as a satellite for training Bomber Command crews but now was attached to 29 OTU, with Bruntingthorpe as the parent station. The OTU started its move on 24th May 1943, after an initial attempt back in October 1942, when a detachment was sent from North Luffenham and the airfield was found to be far from complete. It was many months before Bruntingthorpe was ready, but 29 OTU's move was finally complete on 1st June 1943.

'A' and 'B' Flight were to be located at Bitteswell and would carry out type conversion training while 'C' and 'D' Flight would be responsible for operational training at Bruntingthorpe. On 1st June, 30 officers and NCOs of 'A' Flight arrived from Woolfox Lodge, joined by 49 officers and NCOs of 'B' Flight from North Luffenham the same day. By 5th June, flying training had begun and both flights quickly reached an average of 45 flying hours per day, with a lot of time initially spent on getting used to the luxurious concrete runways, rather than the grass of their previous homes.

On 9th June, the aircraft strength increased when 29 OTU's flight of Avro Ansons flew in. These aircraft were mainly used for training bomb aimers in the art of aerial map reading. It was not long before the first accident involving a 29 OTU Wellington occurred. Sergeant A G G Johnson was practising night circuits and landings in Z1668, a Mk.III, on 29th June 1943 when the starboard engine failed. Johnson managed a successful forced landing near Glebe Farm, Lutterworth with no-one on board injured. Bitteswell's safety record was building quite a reputation for itself, with only two more Wellingtons written off in accidents before the year's end. Most importantly, no aircrew were injured in either incident.

The majority of OTUs were first equipped with the Westland Lysander and Boulton Paul Defiant for target towing and fighter affiliation duties. Neither aircraft was designed for this role and, in response to an Air Ministry directive, a purpose-built aircraft was sought. Miles won the contract and produced the RAF's first purpose-designed target tug, the Miles M.25 Martinet. Based on the Miles Master trainer, 1,724 were built before the war's end, serving with many OTUs, training units and gunnery schools. 29 OTU had several Martinets on strength, most remaining with the unit until Hawker Hurricanes replaced them in 1945. The only recorded incident at Bitteswell involving a Martinet occurred on 11th April 1944, when Flight Lieutenant E A Loos DFC was returning from a fighter affiliation exercise. On its final approach to the runway, the Martinet's engine failed and the aircraft stalled and crashed short of the runway, injuring Loos and his observer. Despite this, the safety record remained high throughout 1944, with only one more Wellington lost in an accident.

Because of Bitteswell's Midland location, it was not common for it to receive unexpected visitors. But, on the morning of 5th October 1944, a group of Handley Page Halifaxes were low on fuel after being diverted from their fog-bound Yorkshire stations. A single 427 RCAF Squadron Halifax Mk.V from Leeming was one of many aircraft that was returning from a successful raid on Frankfurt. The Halifax just made it into Bitteswell with far too much air in the fuel tanks! It returned to its Yorkshire home later that day.

An early indication of a change of ownership at Bitteswell occurred on 5th April 1943, with the formation of 105 (Transport) OTU at Bramcote. The unit was introduced to train crews for transport squadrons and was initially equipped with Wellington Mk.Is and Mk.Xs fitted with dual Vickers Warwick controls. These were replaced in September 1944 by the Douglas Dakota, a much more appropriate transport aircraft. As priority towards transport rather than bomber crews increased, 29 OTU was obliged to shrink in size and flew its last sortie from Bitteswell on the night of 28th/29th October 1944.

Within a few weeks, the airfield was active again, returning to its previous role as satellite to Bramcote, but by now under the control of 44 Group Transport command. On the surface, operations at Bitteswell showed no change as the unit's aircraft were still Wellingtons, but the sharper eyed would have spotted them to be the more powerful Mk.Xs. 'B' Flight, of the 105 (T) OTU, moved in on 22nd November from Bramcote's other satellite airfield at Nuneaton. 'D' Flight followed them a few days later, also from Nuneaton. Both flights used the Wellington Mk.X for conversion training.

From December 1944, an unusual unit began to make use of

Bitteswell as a satellite airfield. The Power Jets Unit was formed on 12th May at 65 Maintenance Unit, which was based at Blaby Wharf, south of Leicester. The unit was formed specifically for RAF personnel who were working with Power Jets Limited, a company formed by the legendary jet pioneer, Frank Whittle. A disused foundry in nearby Lutterworth, called the Ladywood Works, had been used for Whittle's early experiments since 1938 and, as development of the jet engine was rapidly advancing, a permanent airfield was needed for continuing flight testing. The Power Jets Unit initially based itself at Bruntingthorpe, and Bitteswell was only used by the unit's single Hawker Hurricane, Miles Master and de Havilland Dominie. But, in the near future, Bitteswell would become one of the main centres in the country involved in jet development.

In the early hours of 4th March 1945, the Luftwaffe launched an intruder campaign over England, named 'Gisela', in a final attempt to disrupt the Bomber Command offensive. Enemy aircraft followed the bomber streams back to their home bases, choosing only to strike when the unsuspecting aircraft entered the airfield's circuit. Between the hours of 00.20 and 02.14, the Luftwaffe night fighters shot down 25 aircraft, resulting in 70 aircrew killed and 21 injured. Airfield lights were extinguished all over the east of England, with hundreds of aircraft diverted to safer airfields in the Midlands. Bitteswell was one of many airfields that provided a safe haven for Bomber Command aircraft that grim morning. Nine Lancasters of 5 Group, belonging to 44, 57 and 106 Squadrons, were all safely down by 01.00 hrs.

105 (T) OTU's safety record was marred for the first time at Bitteswell on 17th April 1945, when Wellington Mk.X NC667 force landed near the airfield after the port engine failed. Fortunately, the crew suffered only minor injuries, but the aircraft was completely destroyed by fire before the crash tender arrived. This was followed a few weeks later by a more serious incident on 16th May. Whilst carrying out night circuit training, Wellington Mk.X, NC713 reported to Bitteswell tower that they were having engine problem and were attempting to land. On final approach, at only 200ft, the starboard suddenly burst into flames and the Wellington nose-dived into the ground, killing all on board instantly.

With the war at an end, a re-organisation of airfields was carried out on 1st June 1945. The station became part of 4 Group Transport Command and the OTU began to re-equip with the Dakota. Conversion to the new aircraft was swift, but they only remained at Bitteswell for a few weeks. On 17th July 1945, two flights of 105 OTU departed Bitteswell for their old home at Nuneaton, with a third flight moving to Crosby-in-Eden in Cumberland. Bitteswell then became a satellite for No.1381 (Transport) Conversion Unit (ex-105 OTU) from 10th August 1945 to 19th November 1945.

The airfield was officially closed on 30th June 1982; this was marked with a flying display in which a Vulcan, Shackleton and the Red Arrows gave one final performance. In February 1984, the airfield was up for sale – all 567 acres plus half a million square feet of potential industrial buildings. Bought by Douglas Arnold for £3 million, there were big plans to turn the airfield into a centre for vintage aircraft but, although Arnold did fly his extensive collection into Bitteswell, they were rarely seen, much to the disappointment of local enthusiasts. This occupation was short lived, as the airfield once again changed hands on 22nd January 1986, when Gazeley Properties purchased the airfield with plans to develop the site into a distribution centre. The group's takeover resulted in the systematic destruction of the airfield and, today, all evidence of its existence has gone.

3

BOTTESFORD

National Grid Reference SK819415; 7 miles NW of Grantham

Bottesford witnessed some of the toughest Bomber Command operations ever performed during the Second World War, housing two bomber squadrons which were at the forefront of 5 Group. The airfield was the last sight of England for far too many young aircrew and the raids flown from this Leicestershire base typified the early struggle that Bomber Command faced, although thousands of airmen from all over the Commonwealth, and later the United States, would have only happy memories of Bottesford.

In early 1940, a site was surveyed for a new airfield between the Lincolnshire village of Long Bennington and the Leicestershire village of Bottesford. Situated on the western side of Normanton Lane, the airfield straddled the Leicestershire-Lincolnshire border, with the Nottinghamshire border joining at Three Shire Oak, a few hundred yards north. The Air Ministry called the airfield Bottesford, although locally it was named Normanton after the smaller village located at the south-western corner.

Work started in November 1940; the contractor was Grantham-based George Wimpey & Company. Bottesford was unusual for an early wartime station as concrete runways were laid from the outset. The main runway ran parallel with Normanton Lane and, after alterations, was nearly 2,000 yards in length. Two other runways of approximately 1,500 yards crossed the main runway in a standard triangular pattern. Thirty-six dispersal pans and initially just one T2 hangar were built, but this increased to seven by the war's end. The main technical site and living areas were constructed on the north-eastern side of the airfield and extended towards the Great North Road. This area contained eleven domestic and two communal sites along with the station sick quarters. On its completion, the site could house 2,373 airmen and 462 airwomen. A bomb dump was built in Moss Plantation and this, along with the majority of the buildings, was located on the Lincolnshire side of the county border.

During the early war years, it was traditional to allocate major airfields with decoy or 'Q' sites. These sites were effectively dummy airfields, complete with mock-up aircraft and lighting to mimic the real airfields, the idea being that the Luftwaffe would bomb the decoy. Three decoy airfields were built for the protection of Bottesford. One was located south-east of Foston, a second west of Belvoir Castle and a third at Tithby, which was shared with RAF Newton in Nottinghamshire. None of Bottesford's decoy sites had reported being attacked by the Luftwaffe and by the beginning of 1942 many had closed down. After initial success, the brightly lit 'Q' sites became a navigation tool to the German airmen.

The station was officially opened on 10th September, and Group Captain W G Cheshire became the airfield's first Station Commander. Bottesford was then included as part of 5 Group Bomber Command, whose HQ was based at St Vincent's in nearby Grantham, Lincolnshire. It was a large house at the foot of Spittlegate Hill, which was bought by the Air Ministry in 1923 and remained in military use until its sale in 1978.

While waiting for its first Bomber Command unit, a training unit made brief use of the airfield. 3 Operational Training Unit (OTU) was lodging at Cranwell, the home of the RAF College near Sleaford in Lincolnshire. Several airfields in the area were used by 3 OTU to relieve congestion at Cranwell. It was a Vickers Wellington of 3 OTU that became the first aircraft to land at Bottesford on 22nd September 1941, to test the new runways. Although the main contractor had completed its task, Bottesford was still a few weeks away from receiving an operational squadron. A taste of things to come did arrive on 27th September in the shape of a lone Avro Manchester. 207 Squadron's 'A' Flight

Commander, 'Penny' Beauchamp, was given the job of air testing a newly arrived aircraft from the squadron's home base of Waddington, south of Lincoln. He performed several landings before returning to Waddington but unfortunately the port undercarriage failed to lower and Beauchamp performed a textbook emergency landing on the big grass airfield. A few days later, on the 3rd October, Wing Commander K P Lewis, the Officer Commanding 207 Squadron, flew a fully laden Manchester into Bottesford. At an all up weight of 45,000 lbs, this was the final test of the airfield's runways and also confirmed that 207 Squadron would become Bottesford's Bomber Command unit.

While work continued in preparation for 207 Squadron's arrival, the neighbouring airfield at Spitalgate, near Grantham, was seeking more space for its aircraft. 12 Service Flying Training School (SFTS) was formed at Spitalgate in 1938 and by the end of 1941 they had over 100 Airspeed Oxfords on strength, which were shared with Spitalgate's satellite airfield at Harlaxton. Compared with these small grass airfields, Bottesford's large runways must have seemed quite intimidating to the student pilots. 12 SFTS used Bottesford throughout October 1941, and to a lesser extent 3 OTU aircraft used the airfield until the end of the year. A new unit was formed at Bottesford during the month: 24 Blind Approach Training Flight (BATF) was equipped with eight Airspeed Oxfords and remained at the station until at least March 1944, when it moved to Tollerton in Nottinghamshire. The BATF, later renamed Beam Approach Training Flight, would very often be seen operating around the airfield in weather conditions no other aircraft would attempt to fly in. Several weeks overdue, Bottesford was ready for its new bomber squadron by mid-November.

207 Squadron's long history began on 1st April 1918, on the same day that the RAF was formed from the Royal Flying Corp (RFC) and the Royal Naval Air Service (RNAS). Many of the RAF squadrons in the 200 range descended from the RNAS and 207 Squadron was formed from 7 Squadron, RNAS. Unlike many other squadrons after the First World War, 207 Squadron was not disbanded and continued to serve in many minor conflicts between the wars. These included the Chanak crisis in Turkey, and the squadron was based in Sudan during the Abyssinian

crisis. 207 was sent to France at the beginning of the Second World War, now equipped with Fairey Battle light bombers. This move was short lived, as in April 1940 the squadron was dissolved into 12 OTU, only to be re-formed at Waddington on 1st November 1940. The squadron was also re-equipped with a new aircraft, the Avro Manchester.

Born from a 1936 Air Ministry specification for a twin-engine medium bomber, the Avro's design was in competition with the Handley Page H.P.56. The scrapping of the planned H.P.56 paved the way for Avro to produce the Manchester, while Handley Page concentrated its efforts on designing the four-engined Halifax. The prototype Manchester first flew from Ringway, near Manchester, on 25th July 1939. Its performance was disappointing and there were problems with the Rolls Royce Vulture engines throughout the short flight. Despite this, the RAF placed an initial order for 200 aircraft, this was later doubled.

207 Squadron was chosen as the first recipient of the Manchester and was specifically reformed within 5 Group Bomber Command for this task. The first aircraft arrived at Waddington on 8th November, but it was not until February 1941 that the first operational raid took place.

An advance party of 207 Squadron arrived at Bottesford on 15th November 1941 and two days later the main party followed. By now, the squadron was a well organised and experienced fighting unit. The move to Bottesford did nothing to disrupt operations and the first raid from the airfield took place on 23rd/24th November. Only two aircraft took part in a raid on the docks in Lorient. Joined by 51 Handley Page Hampdens, the raid caused many fires at the docks and no aircraft were lost. The squadron lost its first Manchester, L7300, on a transit flight to Waddington on the afternoon of 23rd November. Pilot Officer Bill Hills suffered an engine failure at low level, a relatively critical situation, which only deteriorated when the other engine failed. Luck was on his side, a forced landing straight ahead was the only option and the ground was flat and clear. The Manchester hit the ground tail first as Hills pulled back on the control column. The rear fuselage and tail were ripped off, fortunately with no crew inside. The Manchester ploughed on at 100 mph and headed for a popular fishing spot called Fiskerton

Avro Manchester Mk.I was on a local flight to Waddington when it experienced engine problems and crashed into Fiskerton Lake, east of Lincoln. Much to the annoyance of the local fisherman!

Lake. A fishing match was going on at the time and the tranquil scene was almost comical as Hills' out of control Manchester appeared over the bank and plunged into the middle of the lake. The resulting wave sent the fisherman running up the bank as the Manchester started to settle on the lake floor. Amazingly, everyone on board escaped with just cuts and bruises and all gained a great story to tell in the bar that night.

Throughout the Manchester's career, the Vulture engines had caused problems and Rolls Royce engineers were a familiar sight at Bottesford. The crews had been complaining that with a full bomb load, they could only climb to about 7,000 ft. The engineers asked for 207 Squadron to perform an air test for them. Flying Officer Dave Green was ordered to simulate a full war load climb in L7486 on 5th December 1941. Typically, with the engineers around the Manchester appeared to perform exceptionally well, actually reaching 17,000ft with little difficulty. But, while Green was going through his visual checks, he spotted that the engine cowlings were coming loose. With instruments showing everything to be normal, he made the wise decision to descend and make a precautionary landing back at Bottesford. As they entered the bumpy air nearer to the ground, Green was alarmed to see one of his engines moving up and down on its mounts. After landing, an inspection revealed that Green and his crew had come within minutes of losing the whole engine – the supercharger had overheated, almost melting the mounts. Green's skill and experience had saved the aircraft and the crew from disaster.

Poor weather and aircraft serviceability had limited the squadron's operations at the end of 1941. Six aircraft contributed to a raid on Aachen on 7/8th December and seven more were the only Manchesters to take part in a raid on Dusseldorf on 27/28th December. One Manchester was lost en route to Dusseldorf and Squadron Leader 'Penny' Beauchamp could only manage 4,000ft before his starboard engine failed. He jettisoned his bombs off the Suffolk coast and made an emergency landing at Martlesham Heath.

There was no let up in operations for the squadron in January 1942. Bomber Command continued to send Manchester units on dangerous daylight raids, even though losses continued to be high. 207 Squadron shouldered much of this work, with efforts now being concentrated on targets in northern France, particularly on the German capital ships at berth in Brest harbour. The squadron was not unfamiliar with attacking the *Scharnhorst, Gneisenau* and *Prinz Eugen* (see North Luffenham and Woolfox Lodge chapters), and their first trip from Bottesford came on 8/9th January 1942. Bad weather and strong defences around Brest made the crew's task very difficult. The enemy flak claimed Bottesford's first operational loss, when Flying Officer Bayley's Manchester crashed into the sea off Crozon, a few miles south of Brest. There were no survivors.

The following night, two more of the squadrons joined a raid on Brest, but on this night, 61 Squadron made their first serious contribution, also flying Manchesters. The Woolfox Lodge based squadron would, from now on, begin to relieve the pressure that had been placed on 207 Squadron for so long.

During September 1941 at Waddington, the personnel of 207 Squadron had witnessed the arrival of a four-engine bomber. The aircraft was the new Avro Lancaster, which, annoyingly for

207 Squadron, had arrived to re-equip 44 Squadron, who shared the airfield. To the untrained eye, the Lancaster was a Manchester with two extra engines bolted on! But with a new wing, systems and four powerful Rolls Royce Merlin engines, there was no comparison to its older brother. Performance also was not to be compared: it cruised 30 mph faster, flew an average of 10,000ft higher, could travel 1,000 miles further and eventually would carry bomb loads of up to 22,000lbs! The development of the poorly performing Manchester created one of the greatest bomber aircraft of all time.

The good news finally arrived that 207 Squadron was to re-equip with the Lancaster and was, not surprisingly, well received by air and ground crew alike. 207 Conversion Flight was formed at Bottesford on 16th January 1942 and was initially equipped with two Manchesters and two Lancasters, the first of which arrived on 25th January. It would be several weeks before all the crews were retrained and sufficient aircraft had arrived to replace the Manchester. Replacement crews were also required to pass through the conversion flight before joining the squadron on its main operations.

In the meantime, the Manchester continued to soldier on, with small contingents joining larger operations. The squadron contributed four Manchesters on another raid to Brest on 31st January / 1st February 1942. After receiving a constant stream of intelligence that the German capital ships were on the move, Bomber Command stepped up a gear in an attempt to cripple the *Scharnhorst* and *Gneisenau*. Up to this point, over 300 separate RAF raids had failed to damage the ships and on this night 75 aircraft were once again sent into the hornets' nest of Brest harbour. The night was also a 'Maximum Effort' for the Manchester part of the force; nineteen aircraft took part from 61 and 83 Squadrons and Bottesford's own complement. This, unbelievably, was a Manchester record, which probably brings into context how Bomber Command struggled in the early years of the Second World War. All of 207 Squadron returned safely from Brest, 61 Squadron having taken the brunt of the losses, losing three of the nine aircraft sent.

A few days later, on 6th February, 207 Squadron was called upon to join a mine-laying operation off the Dutch coast. Resources dictated that the operation be performed both in daylight and without fighter escort, either one a dangerous option. Six of the squadron's Manchesters joined eight others from 61 and 83 Squadrons for the operation. One of the squadron's aircraft aborted take off at Bottesford with engine problems, while the rest continued, joining a formation of 33 Hampdens over the North Sea. The weather was solid cloud down to 1,400ft, but all but one of 207 Squadron's Manchesters dropped their mines where they were supposed to. German fighters were very active in the area and the thick cloud saved many aircraft from attack. One Hampden of 455 Squadron was shot down; Flying Officer Kneil saw it go down with two Messerschmitt Me.109s, giving chase. Kneil's own Manchester, like several others, was attacked by enemy aircraft, but luckily all managed to return home safely. The mines laid on this operation may have contributed to delaying the escape of the *Scharnhorst* and *Gneisenau* when they finally made their exit from Brest Harbour.

Before 207 Squadron's aircraft could cool down, they were refuelled and re-armed in readiness for another attack on the German battle cruisers at Brest. For the next three days, the squadron was on tenter hooks but no call came and, in frustration, Bomber Command decided upon a raid into Germany. A joint raid on Mannheim and Bremen by a force of 49 aircraft was planned for the night of 10th/11th February. 207 Squadron would bomb Mannheim, while 61 Squadron would raid Bremen. Only two of Bottesford's aircraft managed to bomb the primary target, with two others bombing Dunkirk and Saarbrucken. The rest had to abort the raid with a variety of mechanical problems, but all returned safely home to a variety of English airfields. Only one Manchester actually landed back at Bottesford before weather conditions caused the rest to divert. Bomber Command's resources had been stretched to the limit, all for an ineffectual raid. While Bomber Command re-organised its squadrons, the German naval forces began their escape from Brest.

The 'Channel Dash' of the German battle cruisers *Scharnhorst* and *Gneisenau* and the smaller cruiser *Prinz Eugen* had been a well-planned operation. The ships had slipped out of Brest in the early hours of 12th February in the worst weather imaginable, perfect for the concealment of such a large convoy. Little did the

Germans know that Bomber Command was in the worst possible position to respond – 207 Squadron alone was ill prepared, with half of their aircrew sleeping off the previous night's debacle over Germany. Bomber Command had 'stood down' for the day with 5 Group on four hours' notice. It was not until late morning that a Fighter Command Spitfire reported seeing the convoy off Le Touquet, well on their way through the Channel.

At Bottesford, frantic phone calls were being made to all the crews who had diverted the night before. By 12:00, all the crews had returned and their aircraft were immediately refuelled and re-armed ready for the daunting task ahead. Six of 207 Squadron's Manchester were ready to depart at 15:00, as part of the long planned Operation *Fuller*. The squadron's contribution to the operation was to be smaller than anticipated as two of the Manchesters became unserviceable on the runway and were cancelled. A third aircraft experienced total hydraulic failure and, after completing a circuit of the airfield, landed back at Bottesford. The remaining three aircraft joined a disorganised collection of Bomber Command aircraft, all trying desperately to locate the fleet through the poor weather. Out of the 207 Squadron group, only one aircraft, flown by Flight Sergeant J C Atkinson, actually located the battle cruisers. After circling around above the fleet at only 800ft, Atkinson managed to line up with a ship and drop his load of 12 x 500lbs. As they climbed away into the safety of the cloud, the tail gunner observed a line of explosions beside one of the German ships. At that very moment their aircraft was struck in the tail by a flak burst. Luckily no serious damage was done and they made it safely home to Bottesford.

The following day, in a final attempt to sink the German ships, four of 207 Squadron's Manchesters were prepared for a mining operation in the mouth of the River Elbe. Mechanical failings once again put paid to the success of this operation. Three aircraft returned with their mines after hydraulic failures and a fourth did manage to drop its mines, but failed to arm them.

Bomber Command had put 242 aircraft into the largest daylight operation of the war so far, but it was not a total loss. Even though aircraft on Operation *Fuller* did no damage, mines laid by 5 Group damaged both the *Scharnhorst* and *Gneisenau* before they made it to the sanctuary of ports in Germany.

As the Manchester was now entering its final weeks of operation with Bomber Command, serviceability and availability actually rose. The daily number of serviceable Manchesters available to Bomber Command at the end of February 1942 was 31 aircraft, whilst the Stirling and Halifaxes never had more than 21 and 23 respectively. This was very evident on the Billancourt Renault Factory raid on 3/4th March 1942. 26 Manchesters from 61, 83 and 207 Squadrons took part in the highly successful raid, albeit at the cost of many French civilians. Only one aircraft of 207 Squadron had to abort when it encountered engine trouble.

The final three raids for 207 Squadron were all to Essen and none of them left pleasant memories of the Manchester. The first raid, on 8/9th March, involved four Manchesters, with a fifth sent on a mining operation off Lorient. Flight Lieutenant P Birch had Bottesford's Station Commander for company, Group Captain 'Ferdie' Swain OBE, AFC. Unfortunately, Birch experienced a whole host of problems and had to turn back before reaching the Dutch coast. The other three aircraft all managed to attack the target, but all returned with serious flak damage. It was a similar story the next night – once again, aircraft returned with engine problems. The final Manchester operation by 207 Squadron was on the night of 10/11th March 1942 and they experienced the same old engine problems right to the bitter end. Four out of six either failed to take off or returned home early.

207 Squadron had been equipped with the Avro Manchester for nearly eighteen months and were now happily converting to the Lancaster. The never-ending catalogue of engine problems tormented the squadron all the way through its service. The casualty figures reveal an unenviable total of 25 Manchesters lost, the highest in any unit.

Focus at Bottesford was now on the Lancaster and during the next few weeks 207 Squadron were excused from operations while they got to grips with their new charges. The first operational outing for the squadron's Lancasters was on 24/25th April 1942. The target was Rostock and the Heinkel factory it harboured. Four Lancasters from Bottesford joined 125 other aircraft, gaining valuable experience. More Lancasters had arrived during May, putting the squadron in a stronger position to take part in major Bomber Command operations.

207 Squadron began to re-equip with the Avro Lancaster from early 1942 onwards. The Lancaster raised the squadron's ability to wage war against Germany, but unfortunately raised the squadron's loss rate as well.

On the night of 30/31st May 1942, Cologne was the target. Bomber Command broke all records by putting together a '1,000 bomber' raid for the first time. The squadron was able to dispatch twelve Lancasters on this ground-breaking raid, all returning unscathed after successfully bombing the main target. 207 Squadron joined another large raid two nights later against Essen. The squadron managed to provide fourteen Lancasters on this occasion but, unfortunately, four returned early with engine trouble. The weather was against the rest as, despite a good Met Office report, low cloud covered the target. The bombing was so scattered that eleven other towns reported being bombed. Once again, though, all the Lancasters made it home safely.

Two nights later, on 3/4th June, a much smaller force of 170 aircraft proved the point of safety in numbers. 207 Squadron suffered its first operational Lancaster loss during a raid on Bremen. Warrant Officer C Wathey's crew were on their way home over Holland when they were shot down by a Dornier Do.215 of II./NJG2, flown by Major Gunter Radusch.

45

The contribution of aircraft to raids into Germany steadily increased through the summer months. Fifteen Lancasters joined over a thousand other Bomber Command aircraft on a raid to Bremen on 25/26th June 1942. Different parts of the attacking force were allocated specific targets to attack within the city. All 142 aircraft of 5 Group taking part were tasked with bombing the Focke-Wulf factory. Although the target was covered by cloud by the time 5 Group got there, fires caused by a previous part of the raid helped the crews navigate to the German aircraft factory. One assembly shop was destroyed and several parts of the factory were damaged, but this did little to halt production.

207 Squadron's Lancasters' commitment to raids on Germany continued through June and July, with losses mounting. Flying activities were equally dangerous on and around their home base; an accident at Bottesford on 6th August 1942 highlighted this. Sergeant A S Pearson in Manchester L7385 of the Conversion Flight was returning from a night navigation exercise when, without warning, a squadron Lancaster taxied onto the runway. The limited power of the Manchester prevented an overshoot and Pearson's aircraft crashed on top of the Lancaster, both aircraft ending up in a heap of twisted metal. Two of Pearson's crew were killed instantly, with three others fatally injured in the Lancaster. The local villagers also experienced the dangers of living near an operational bomber base a few weeks later, on 19th August. Sergeant W D Fordwych was practising overshoots on three engines in his Lancaster, R5863. When climbing away from Bottesford's main runway, he suddenly lost control and the Lancaster dived straight into the middle of Normanton village. Fordwych's crew stood no chance but, incredibly, there were no civilian casualties.

Focus on German industrial targets was the main priority throughout August; they included two trips to Mainz, both of which claimed squadron aircraft. The month culminated with a successful attack on the German city of Kassel, although night fighters were out in force and they eventually claimed ten per cent of the attacking bombers. On many occasions during August, repairs had to be carried out on Bottesford's runways. Sometimes this work disrupted operations, which was unacceptable from 207 Squadron's point of view. So as not disrupt training, the Conversion Flight was sent on detachment to Swinderby in Lincolnshire on 22nd August.

The main squadron continued to operate from Bottesford's slowly deteriorating runways until a decision was made to move the squadron to a new airfield. On 20th September, 207 Squadron departed for the nearby airfield at Langar in Nottinghamshire. 207 remained a bomber squadron until it was disbanded on 1st May 1965, flying the original V-Bomber, the Vickers Valiant. Re-formed as a communication squadron four years later, 207 Squadron finally ended its long career in 1984.

RAF personnel were replaced with civilian contractors, who repaired the runways and taxiways. 5 Group had no immediate plans for Bottesford, but 3 Group were looking for an airfield to re-form one of their bomber squadrons. 90 Squadron had been disbanded in February 1942, after becoming the first RAF Boeing B-17 Flying Fortress unit in Bomber Command. The squadron was re-equipped and personnel started to arrive at Bottesford on 1st November 1942. Two weeks later, brand new Short Stirlings began to arrive, all flown by Air Transport Auxiliary (ATA) pilots. Eleven aircraft were eventually delivered and the squadron flew many training sorties, quickly getting used to their new aircraft in preparation for joining the bomber offensive.

90 Squadron were joined at the end of November by 467 Squadron, Royal Australian Air Force (RAAF). Formed only a few weeks earlier on 7th November at Waddington, the squadron was equipped with the Avro Lancaster and flew the type throughout their wartime service. Only the third Australian Squadron to be formed, they were commanded by an RAF officer, Wing Commander C L Gomm DSO, DFC, a popular CO who spared no time in getting the squadron up to scratch. The first of the squadron's Lancasters arrived on 24th November and the first few weeks at Bottesford were taken up with training and familiarisation with their aircraft and the local area.

90 Squadron's stay at Bottesford was only ever going to be a temporary one and in mid-December HQ 3 Group informed the Stirling unit that they were to be moved. Ridgewell in Essex had just been completed and the squadron flew out of Bottesford on 29th December 1942. However, all but one returned the same day! As the first Stirling touched down at Ridgewell, it bounced and careered into a ditch, closing the runway immediately. All the remaining Stirlings returned to Bottesford and finally left for Ridgewell the next day.

467 Squadron were now ready for operations and were introduced gently to them on 2/3rd January 1943, when four Lancasters successfully took part in a sea mining operation. The tempo quickly increased for the Australians as, by the end of January, ten major industrial targets were attacked without loss. This honeymoon period had to come to an end and the law of averages dictated that it be the night of 19/20th February. 338 aircraft took part in the raid on the German port of Wilhelmshaven, led by Pathfinder aircraft that would mark the target with flares. Unbeknown to the Pathfinder crews, the maps they were using were out of date and their flares fell nowhere near the target. The result was that none of the main force's bombs fell in the town; in fact, a post-raid report commented that only three people had been injured. Twelve aircraft were lost on this fruitless raid, including two from 467 Squadron with all crew lost. U-boat pens along the French coast occupied most of 467 Squadron's attention through February. Bomber Command had already turned Lorient into a ghost town earlier in the month, and now raids on St Nazaire would achieve the same result. Another squadron Lancaster was brought down over Nuremburg on 25/26th February, the fifth aircraft to be lost after the completion of 24 major operations.

The night of 5/6th March 1943 was the first raid of Sir Arthur Harris's 'Battle of the Ruhr', and signalled the start of his 'Main Offensive', which continued until the spring of 1944. Having skilfully brought Bomber Command out of the Dark Ages, Harris had been carefully conserving and building up his forces in preparation for another major effort against Germany. 467 Squadron took part in nearly all of the big raids on cities such as Essen, Nuremburg, Munich, Stuttgart and Berlin, all with mixed results. The squadron came through March 1943 relatively unscathed, with only one aircraft lost over Stuttgart on 11/12th March. Five out of eight crew survived and became POWs.

April continued in the same vein but a significant raid on the Italian port of La Spezia by Bomber Command on 13/14th April led to 467 Squadron being involved in very long range attacks. With military successes in North Africa came the liberation of airfields within range of Bomber Command aircraft. Rather than making the dangerous journeys home in European skies, bombers could now continue on to North Africa and carry out a

A happy, all-Australian crew of 467 RAAF Squadron, glad to be home at Bottesford in the early hours, after another night raid on Germany.

separate bombing raid on their way home. It was on this particular raid that three Lancasters diverted to North Africa, highlighting the usefulness of these airfields.

The first long range raid for the squadron came on the night of 20/21st June 1943 when 60 Lancasters, including eight from 467 Squadron, attacked the Zeppelin works at Friedrichshafen, on the shores of Lake Constance. The factory was heavily involved in the production of the Wurzburg radar sets, which helped to control the German fighters that were shooting down so many British bombers over Germany. The Lancasters involved were nearly all from 5 Group, apart from four Pathfinder Lancasters from 97 Squadron, based at Bourn in Cambridgeshire, which were part of 8 Group. Like the previous months' dams raid, a single nominated pilot was detailed as a 'controller', later known as 'the Master Bomber'. After the Master Bomber's aircraft had to return early with engine problems, the deputy, Wing Commander Gomm, found himself in this new position. The plan was to bomb the small factory at the relatively low altitude of between 5,000 and 10,000ft but, on arrival, Gomm found that the flak and searchlight defences were more active than expected. The Lancasters now had to climb much higher over the target before commencing their bombing runs, Gomm quickly recalculating the new time to begin dropping the bombs, as the wind speed at the higher altitude was much greater. After the Lancasters dropped their bombs, the German night-fighters were congregating over Germany and France in readiness. But the Lancaster force turned south, confusing the German aircraft, and headed for bases in North Africa, thus becoming the first shuttle raid of the war. The raid was a total success, with very accurate bombing taking place; reconnaissance photography showed a large number of bombs had hit the factory, causing considerable damage.

Three days later, seven of the squadron's aircraft returned to England via the Italian Naval base at La Spezia. Fifty-two Lancasters bombed the port and many of its installations, but the target was shrouded in haze and a very effective smoke screen. With very little flak and no fighters on the way back to England, all returned to their home bases unscathed. On arrival back at Bottesford, the Australians proceeded to unload fruit, vegetables and wine to prove that they had not been enjoying themselves too much in Africa.

For ten days from the end of July 1943, Sir Arthur Harris launched the Battle of Hamburg, also known as Operation *Gomorrah*. Europe's largest port and the second largest city in Germany, Hamburg, had already been attacked 98 times by Bomber Command but, up until now, it had never been really seriously bombed, like Cologne and many of the Ruhr communities. In the Battle of Hamburg the city was bombed on four separate occasions during the ten night battle, each of the attacks using an average of 770 aircraft. A total of 3,091 sorties were flown and nearly 10,000 tons of bombs were dropped, although not all of these came down in Hamburg. The infamous 'firestorm' developed after the second raid. It was not a deliberate plot to raze the city to the ground; the attacking aircraft were carrying no more incendiaries than on other normal raids. The fire's devastating effect on the city was caused by an unusual combination of events. The normal air temperature was high, humidity was low and, as there had not been any rain for quite a while, everything was very dry. The majority of Hamburg's fire vehicles were tied up in the western part of the city, fighting fires from the first raid, three nights earlier. Only a few vehicles managed to get through to the latest fires as rubble had blocked the main routes across the city. The situation was now out of control and fires started to join up across the city, competing with each other for oxygen. The fire raged for about three hours, consuming every flammable item in its path. The third attack caused considerable damage to residential areas, but no firestorm. The weather spared Hamburg from a fourth serious attack; several of the 30 aircraft lost were victims of severe icing. 467 Squadron took part in all four raids, losing three more Lancasters.

August 1943 was a very grim month for the Australian squadron, by now a seasoned and experienced unit. The inevitable losses were always hard to bear. After completing two very successful raids to Milan in northern Italy, the squadron took part in a third on 15/16th August 1943. Ten squadron Lancasters made up a force of nearly 200, which, once again, hit the Italian city very hard. Over France, the German night fighters were ready for the returning bomber stream and claimed four of the seven Lancasters lost that night, two of them from Bottesford. Devastatingly for 467, Wing Commander Gomm and Flight Lieutenant J McD Sullivan, a deputy flight commander, were lost, both their aircraft crashing near Chartres in France. Gomm had turned the squadron into an efficient fighting unit and was much respected by all ranks in the unit; he was one raid away from completing his second tour of operations.

A new target was brought to Bomber Command's attention for the first time on 17/18th August when Peenemunde was the target. Home of the Germans' 'secret weapons' research centre, Peenemunde was located on the Baltic coast, not far from the Polish border. Photographic reconnaissance had revealed that the German scientists' rocket development was advancing rapidly. Five hundred and ninety six aircraft were despatched in three waves, all controlled by 'Master Bomber' Group Captain J H Searby. Unfortunately for the 5 Group aircraft involved, they were in the last wave and by the time they had attacked, German night fighters had arrived in the area in force. It was the first time the German fighters had used a new weapon called *Schrage Musik*, twin upward-firing cannons fitted behind the pilot, initially in Messerschmitt Me.110s. The German pilots would simply fly under the bomber aircraft and fire into the belly. Forty aircraft were lost that night and a pair of Me.110s fitted with the new *Schrage Musik* claimed six of them. Despite these high losses, the raid was classed as a success, reports claiming that the raid set back the rocket programme by two months and reduced its eventual effectiveness. Two more experienced crews were lost from 467 Squadron: first, Pilot Officer F W Dixon with 21 operations under his belt and, secondly, Squadron Leader A S Raphael DFC, the acting squadron commander, who also had the squadron's bombing leader Flight Lieutenant Parry on board.

Like many other stations in the area, Bottesford played host to 32 Airspeed Horsa of 30 Heavy Glider Maintenance Unit from 16th August 1943. Belonging to 2 Heavy Glider Maintenance Unit at Snailwell in Cambridgeshire, the Horsas were stored in the open all over the airfield. The heavy gliders were being stored in anticipation of the various airborne operations that were already being planned for the following year.

At the beginning of September 1943, an aircraft arrived at Bottesford that would become one of the most famous individual Lancasters of Bomber Command. R5868 was a Mk.1 and was transferred from 83 Squadron, based at the Pathfinder station at Wyton in Cambridgeshire. She had already completed 68 operations with 83 Squadron and would continue this trend of good fortune with 467 Squadron until her retirement following the war. Affectionately known as 'Sugar' after her code letter the aircraft steadily reached mythological status as she repeatedly returned unscathed from raid after raid. One of R5868's many ex-crew members once commented that she could find her own way home from any target in Europe, but carried a navigator just in case! Sugar went on to complete 137 operations and, although this was disputed as twelve too many, it was still an incredible war record. Sugar, unlike many others, was saved after the war

Avro Lancaster B.I, R5868 ('Sugar') flew from Bottesford with 467 RAAF Squadron. The veteran aircraft now takes centre stage in the Bomber Command Museum at Hendon. (Author.)

as a museum exhibit and, after several moves, was placed in the RAF Museum at Hendon in March 1972. Today, she stands proud as one of the main exhibits in the RAF Bomber Command extension of the museum.

467 Squadron operations from Bottesford were drawing to a close and October was their last full month. It was not a good one for the Australian crews. Two aircraft were lost on a raid to Munich, two returning from Kassel; another was lost outbound to Hannover; and a Lancaster Mk.III crash landed at Wittering during a training exercise. Squadron Leader W J Lewis DFC and his crew were in the last 467 Squadron aircraft to be lost on operations from Bottesford; his Lancaster Mk.III was shot down by a night fighter near Antwerp while outbound to Dusseldorf on 3rd/4th November 1943. Out of the crew of eight, four were killed, two became POWs, and two managed to evade capture.

The Australian squadron was destined to return to the home of its formation, Waddington, south of Lincoln. On 8th November, an advance party left Bottesford to begin preparations for the arrival of the main unit but, in the meantime, the squadron was getting ready for one final raid from Bottesford. Eighteen Lancasters helped to make a force of 313 aircraft from 5 and 8 Groups to attack railway yards on the main line into Italy at Modane on 10/11th November 1943. Pathfinder marking was good and over 200 aircraft (fourteen of them from 467 Squadron) brought back photographs to show that their bombs had fallen within one mile of the target. The raid was a total success and, because flak and fighters were non existent, not a single aircraft out of the entire force was lost.

November 11th was the official moving day for the squadron and, first thing that morning, ground equipment started to leave the station on its way to Waddington. But the day was thrown into chaos when 467 Squadron was ordered to take part in an operation. Ground crew were tearing their hair out trying to recover the necessary ground equipment! By 14:00 hours, the move was still on and the Lancasters were flown out, followed the next day by ground crew and equipment. 467 Squadron had suffered terrible losses flying from Bottesford, but left many happy memories behind and were much missed by the locals.

The airfield was about to enter a new phase of the Second World War and receive new occupants. The Americans were coming! In readiness for the forthcoming invasion of Europe, a new command, the 9th Troop Carrier, was formed in October 1943 within the US 9th Air Force. The 9th Troop Carrier Command (TCC) was to be responsible for the dropping of troops and supplies for all forthcoming airborne operations over Europe. The HQ of the TCC shared St Vincent's in Grantham with the 5 Group HQ and moved there from Cottesmore on 1st December.

The 9th TCC was broken down into three wings: the 50th, 52nd and 53rd Troop Carrier Wings (TCW), and on 18th November the 50th TCW moved into Bottesford from Cottesmore, where it had been located for only a few weeks. Each wing was assigned four Troop Carrier Groups (TCG) and the 50th TCW looked after the 434th TCG at Fulbeck in Lincolnshire, the 435th TCG at Langar in Nottinghamshire, the 436th TCG at Bottesford and the 437th at Balderton, also in Nottinghamshire.

When the 9th Air Force took over Bottesford on 18th November, the airfield was redesignated Army Air Force Station

481 and would remain so during the Americans' tenancy of the station. The 436th TCG did not arrive at Bottesford until 6th January 1944, bringing with it nearly 60 Douglas C-47 Skytrain twin engined transport aircraft and as many Waco CG-4A assault gliders. Under the command of Colonel Adriel N Williams, every TCG was made up of four squadrons, which all displayed individual code letters. The 436th was made up of the 79th Troop Carrier Squadron (TCS) (coded S6), the 80th TCS (7D), the 81st TCS (U5) and the 82nd TCS (3D). The 436th was destined to stay at Bottesford for only a few weeks as the TCGs in the 50th TCW had been extensively training in glider towing techniques, which would mean a move to more southerly bases for all of the Wings units. On 3rd March the 436th TCG moved to Membury in Wiltshire, where it continued its glider towing training and went on to participate successfully in the Normandy landings.

The 50th Wing was quickly re-organised and, within a few

The 50th TCW's Glider officer, Captain H J Nevins, in the cockpit of a C-47 of the 436th TCG. (USAAF.)

days the 439th, 440th, 441st and 442nd arrived to occupy Balderton, Bottesford, Langar and Fulbeck respectively. The 440th TCG, complete with its four C-47 equipped squadrons, arrived at Bottesford on 11th March 1944 and was commanded by Lieutenant Colonel Frank X Krebs. Their training programme began immediately, with emphasis placed on formation flying. The Group also took part in several glider and parachute dropping exercises, most of which involved the Leicestershire based 82nd Airborne Division.

Another re-shuffle of the American units occurred in April, when the RAF made more southern airfields available to the 9th Air Force TCGs in readiness for Operation *Overlord*, the planned invasion of Europe. On this occasion, the 50th TCW was to move with the groups. The 440th TCG was the first to move to Exeter in Devon on 18th April. It was joined by the 50th TCW on 26th April, leaving behind only the 442nd at Fulbeck, which became attached to the 52nd TCW until 12th June 1944, when it moved to a southern airfield at Weston Zoyland in Somerset.

Bottesford remained in American hands until early July. During this time, the only US unit present was the 33rd Mobile Repair and Reclamation Squadron, who were tasked to look after the Horsa gliders, which had been transferred to the 9th Air Force in February 1944.

Handed back to 5 Group Bomber Command, Bottesford was found to be in a serious state of disrepair, with all the major buildings in need of attention. The station was quickly brought up to scratch in readiness for its new occupant, 1668 Heavy Conversion Unit (HCU). Originally formed a few miles to the north, at Balderton in Nottinghamshire, in August 1942, it was dissolved in 5 Lancaster Finishing School (LFS) on 21st November 1943. The HCU was reformed at Bottesford on 28th July to provide conversion training on the Avro Lancaster, which, along with the Handley Page Halifax, had by this stage of the war, become the main aircraft type operated by Bomber Command. Initially, the unit was equipped with all three marks of the Lancaster and this included the Hercules radial powered Mk.IIs, which were less common than the more familiar Merlin powered Mk.Is and IIIs. Thirty-six Lancasters were on strength in a matter of weeks and, rather than disappearing for ever on operational sorties over Germany, the HCU's aircraft embarked on a variety of training exercises and the usual endless 'circuits and bumps'.

Fighter affiliation exercises were also part of the HCU's training programme and, to perform this, 1321 Bomber Defence Training Flight (BDTF) was formed at Bottesford on 1st September 1944. The unit was first equipped with eight Hawker Hurricanes and carried out its duties in support of 1669 HCU at Langar in Nottinghamshire, as well as the Bottesford based aircraft.

Bottesford was no exception when it came to the constant re-organisation of its controlling group, and the roles and titles of its resident units. On 20th September 1944, 7 (Training) Group was re-formed at St Vincent's in Grantham to control the growing number of HCUs that were previously looked after by the Bomber Command groups. Bottesford fitted this criterion and on 7th October it came under the control of 7 Group and became the main airfield of 72 Base. The base system was introduced in an effort to centralize the administration of a group of airfields. Bottesford now looked after Langar and neighbouring Saltby,

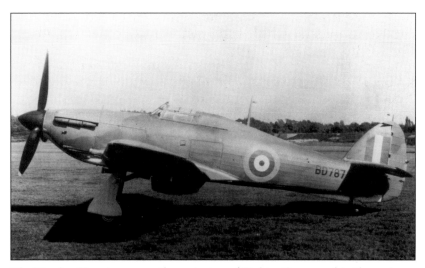

The Hawker Hurricane was the mainstay of Fighter Command in the early years of the Second World War but later on it was relegated to operate with OTUs and HCUs. This Hurricane MK.IIc is representative of a pair that were operated by 1668 HCU for fighter affiliation duties. (Via author.)

both responsible to a new station commander, Group Captain C H Flinn.

1321 BDTF was also affected by the changes and, on 1st November, was disbanded. From now on, each individual HCU was responsible for its own fighter affiliation training. A few days later, on 11th November, a 7 Group Communications Flight (Gp Com Flt) was reformed at Bottesford and was equipped with a variety of liaison aircraft which included a pair de Havilland Dominies (one of which was borrowed from 12 (P)AFU at Spitalgate near Grantham), two Percival Proctors and a single Miles Magister. The aforementioned aircraft ferried many senior officers around the 7 Group airfields, including the Air Officer commanding 7 Group, Air Commodore L H Cockey and his successor, Air Vice Marshall E A B Rice. 7 Gp Com Flt operated from the airfield until 24th March 1945, when it made the short move to Spitalgate.

During November, the HCU lost the first of many aircraft – three Lancaster Mk.IIs were wrecked at Bottesford and a fourth was written off after belly landing at Carnaby in Yorkshire; fortunately none of these incidents caused loss of life. A visiting 1669 HCU Halifax Mk.II was practising three-engined approaches on 5th November when the bomber crashed onto the airfield, injuring several of the crew.

In January 1945, the HCU still had 16 Lancaster Mk.IIs on strength. They were intending to replace all of them and to provide more continuity to the crew's training by operating only Mk.Is and IIIs. The disbandment of 1669 HCU at Langar helped to make this change, as all their Lancaster Mk.Is and IIIs were placed on Bottesford's strength. The final Mk.II had left the airfield by the end of March 1945. The fighter affiliation aircraft were also replaced, the Hurricanes had by now served their purpose and Supermarine Spitfire Mk.Vs and Bristol Beaufighters took their place, the latter for night fighter affiliation.

On the night of 20th/21st March 1945, the Luftwaffe carried out one final attack on Bomber Command's aircraft and the many airfields in the East Midlands, Bottesford included. At 20:30 hours, an imminent air raid warning was received from HQ 7 Group at Grantham and, 20 minutes later, Bottesford's tannoys ordered a full black out. This was followed at 22:00 hours by an air raid siren on the airfield and the arrival of a Junkers Ju.88 twin engined fighter bomber, which approached the airfield from the north west at 1,000 ft, dropping several anti-personnel bombs as it passed. The Junkers was not fired upon by the station defences, so took its chance and made a second pass over the airfield, firing a 20 mm cannon into several hangars and buildings. The Junkers then fired at a train which was standing in Bottesford station. Fortunately the German attacker missed it, and managed only to shatter some windows in a nearby house.

Damage at Bottesford was limited to a few buildings, but a single Lancaster was struck by a cannon shell, which passed through the aircraft's main spar, rendering the aircraft useless. Although raids of this kind did little to inhibit Bottesford's activities, it did highlight that the Luftwaffe was still a force to be reckoned with.

With the disbandment of 1669 HCU, 72 Base virtually ceased to exist and was disbanded on 1st April 1945. Bottesford was incorporated into 73 Base the same day, controlled by North Luffenham in Rutland. It was downgraded to a sub-station and made up the new base system along with Woolfox Lodge and Langar. 32 Lancaster Mk.I & IIIs, two Spitfire Mk.Vbs and two Beaufighter Mk.VIs made up 1668 HCU at the end of April and six more Lancasters fitted with 'Gee-H' bombing radar systems were introduced a few weeks later from Lindholme in Yorkshire.

One final unit was established at Bottesford in June 1945. 1 Bomber Defence Training Flight, operating three Beaufighter NF.VIs and three Spitfires, was formed within 1668 HCU as a 12 Group unit, but served Bomber Command.

Flying accidents were becoming less frequent at Bottesford. The penultimate incident involved a Beaufighter Mk.VIf, MM883, of 1651 HCU based at Woolfox Lodge. The last aviation related accident to occur happened on 13th July 1945 to an 11 OTU Wellington Mk.X, LN844, from Westcott in Buckinghamshire. Piloted by Flying Officer J W Heames, the Wellington was on a night cross-country exercise when its starboard engine failed. The aircraft was diverted to Bottesford and as the crew approached the runway the port engine also failed. The Wellington crashed short of the main runway and all seven crew managed to scramble clear before the bomber was destroyed by fire.

On 15th August 1945, the war against Japan came to a final, abrupt end, and demand for bomber crews dramatically subsided. 1668 HCU was about make its final move and Bottesford's busy flying activities were drawing to a close. On 17th September, the HCU left the airfield for the short flight south to Cottesmore in Rutland, and transfer to 91 Group, only to be disbanded in March 1946. Bottesford was relegated to a Relief Landing Ground for Spitalgate-based 17 Service Flying Training School (SFTS). The School's Airspeed Oxfords, North American Harvards, Supermarine Spitfires and the occasional Bristol Beaufort made use of Bottesford's runways until 18th June 1947, when 17 SFTS became 1 Flying Training School. Bottesford was then closed to flying.

Still retained by the RAF, the airfield played host to an Equipment Disposal Depot sub-site of 256 Maintenance Unit (MU), who were based at Barkston Heath, north-east of Grantham in Lincolnshire. 256 MU were resident at Bottesford from May 1947 to 31st December 1948, making good use of the ten hangars that remained on the airfield.

Airspeed Oxfords could be seen at Bottesford almost uninterrupted throughout the war years. (Via author.)

Aerial photograph of Bottesford taken in 1995. The airfield is generally still intact and many hangars and original wartime buildings have been restored and are still in use. (Crown Copyright.)

The post-war problem of storing and disposing of thousands of tonnes of unused munitions and bombs left over from the war saw Bottesford take on its final military task. 93 MU, whose HQ was at the wartime bomber station at Wickenby in Lincolnshire, used several airfields in Lincolnshire and the East Midlands for the open storage of bombs. The MU took over Bottesford on 17th January 1949 and quickly covered the runways, taxiways and dispersal with stacks of bombs. Any available hangar and hut was used to store ammunition and a variety of pyrotechnics. Over a ten year period, lorry after lorry removed the redundant weaponry, much of it being disposed of on ranges like Donna Nook, off the Lincolnshire coast. The airfield was finally taken over by 92 MU, based at Faldingworth, also in Lincolnshire, on 31st January 1959. Bottesford by now was almost devoid of its wartime stores, 92 MU closed down the site and the airfield closed on 4th March 1960.

Since 1954, the airfield has been systematically sold off by the Air Ministry at auction. Even though the airfield was being used to store bombs, this did not stop large areas of the site returning to agriculture. Much of Bottesford was bought by John Rose, who managed to acquire much of the old technical site and several hangars and establish the Newark Storage Company, which is now part of the Roseland Group.

Today, almost all the runways still exist, all ten hangars have been reclad and are still in regular use. Many technical buildings remain, several of them have been restored and used for business, and the control tower now houses the offices of the Roseland Group. The site is a superb example of how wartime airfield buildings can live on and serve as memorial to the many crews who perished.

4

BRAUNSTONE

National Grid Reference SK540040; 2 miles W of Leicester

What was for many people of Leicester a dream – having its own municipal airport – became reality in January 1930, when a site was chosen at Braunstone Frith, on the eastern side of the town. The area at that time was very different from now, with open fields on three sides and the potential for expansion as demand from larger aircraft increased. The location was also excellent. The A47 provided good road access, and a London, Midland and Scottish (LMS) railway branch line was within walking distance.

Some would say that strong council involvement delayed the start of the new airport. This would seem to have been the case as it was not until August 1932 that tenders were invited for the construction of the landing ground. The Leicestershire Aero Club (LAC) was approached, with a view to managing the new airport and, after negotiating a £200 per year fee towards management expenses, the club accepted.

The Syston-based construction company En-Tout-Cas Limited won the contract to build the landing ground: a good choice, considering the excellent work they had already carried out at Desford. By the middle of 1934, the landing ground was completed and various buildings were in the early stages of construction. A clubhouse, flight office, hangar and re-fuelling point were among the many facilities that would make Braunstone a modern airport. There was no terminal building in terms of the modern concept , but Braunstone had a waiting room, ticket and booking office, an HM Customs office, and additional rooms for the use of potential airlines, all in one central building. This was topped with a large restaurant on the first floor, and a small control tower on the second.

On 27th March 1935, Braunstone received from the Air Ministry a licence to operate. By the 31st, the LAC had moved in with their aircraft; the club, however, had been using the completed clubhouse since November 1934. From a sluggish start, the airfield quickly became active and, as planned, a pair of commercial airlines began to move their operations to Braunstone.

First to arrive was Crilly Airways Limited, which operated a fleet of de Havilland Dragons, later complemented by the General Aircraft Monospar ST-25 Jubilee. Services began to a variety of destinations, from early April 1935. Operations first began with flights to Bristol and Norwich, followed by extra routes to Nottingham, Northampton and Skegness. Provincial Airways were the second commercial company to arrive, moving from Desford, where they began their services in March. Provincial offered routes further afield, that included

A de Havilland DH.84 Dragon of Crilly Airways, awaiting passengers at Braunstone in 1936. (A.J. Jackson Collection.)

Southampton and Croydon, and, from July, they provided an air service to Le Touquet and Paris for a return fair of ten guineas, or £10.50 in new money!

The airfield was officially opened on 13th July 1935, and the day was blessed with good weather for a full day of activities, including demonstrations of new civilian aircraft, and flying displays by several military aircraft. Formation flying was performed by a quartet of Gloster Gauntlet biplane fighters of 19 Squadron, from Duxford, near Cambridge. A mock aerial battle was also demonstrated by three Hawker Fury fighters from 1 Squadron who 'attacked' a Boulton Paul Overstrand bomber of 101 Squadron.

At 2.30 pm, the opening ceremony was carried out by Sir Phillip Cunliffe-Lister, who was the Secretary of State for Air. He was supported by several local dignitaries including the Mayor of Leicester and Lindsay Everard, MP. The day was a total success and set the tone for Braunstone, or Leicester Airport, providing great prospects for the future.

Crilly Airways continued to expand its routes, but the winter of 1935/6 disrupted their services and the company had to look at more overseas services to develop their business. Crilly purchased four Fokker F.XII twin engine airliners from the Dutch airline KLM and planned to use these larger, more capable, aircraft between Croydon and Lisbon. In hindsight, this purchase was the beginning of the end for Crilly and, although visits to Braunstone were planned for these larger aircraft, none of the fleet ever arrived. By the autumn of 1936, the airline was in serious financial trouble and the receivers were called in. The promise of a permanent airline at Braunstone went with it. Provincial Airways had also reduced their operation and, by the beginning of 1937, they used Braunstone for a limited service only.

Despite these setbacks, the airport continued to expand and equipment improved. This included a new commercial complex, which was built on the eastern side of the airfield. A large hangar, several workshops, a new terminal building and a number of administration buildings were all available to a new tenant by the summer of 1937.

Not a single airline showed any interest in the development, but enquiries were received by two companies wanting to

Crilly Airways offered 'Fast, Comfortable and Safe' daily services to a variety of locations from Braunstone in the mid 1930s. The small airline operated a single example of the de Havilland DH.83 Fox Moth. (A.J. Jackson Collection.)

manufacture aero engines and by the aircraft instrument maker Reid and Sigrist (R&S). The latter were successful in their bid to lease the new buildings and took over the site from December 1937. This was not exactly the kind of occupant the owners of Braunstone were hoping for, as R&S brought no increase in aircraft activity to the airport. It did, however, bring an extra £400 a year into the airport coffers for the next five years, with an option to extend the lease for another five years at £450 per annum.

Flying at Braunstone by the end of 1938 was limited to the occasional visiting airline and the LAC's club activities, which included the odd air show. Efforts continued to encourage more use of the airfield at the beginning of 1939. The Air Ministry was contacted, with the suggestion that Braunstone could house a Royal Auxiliary Air Force Squadron. After much deliberation the Air Ministry decided that the small airport was unsuitable for a number of reasons. Its location was too far north for such a unit, it was too close to the already established flying school at Desford and, finally, it was the second smallest licensed airfield in the country, Barton near Manchester being the smallest. Land was available for expansion, but in June 1939, with the Second World War looming, it was decided that no more money could be spent on Leicester's Airport.

The military did plan to house 58 Elementary & Reserve Flying Training School at Braunstone in mid 1939 but, like so many other proposals, it was cancelled when war was declared on 3rd September 1939. On this day, all civilian aviation activities were brought to a close, aircraft were requisitioned, and Braunstone, along with many other civilian airfields, closed.

This did not stop yet another company, Napier & Son Ltd Aero Engines, from requesting 50 acres of land on the edge of the airport for a factory in which to build its aircraft engines. A quick decision by the Aerodrome Committee approved the sale of the land and all the extra construction work involved. But the country was now under wartime conditions and requests of this nature had to pass through the Air and Labour Ministries. They considered that employment within Leicester at that time was at a satisfactory level, and requested that Napier look for at least two other alternative sites before considering Braunstone. Much against Napier's better judgment, preferring the Braunstone location above all others, the company found an alternative in early 1940 at Luton in Bedfordshire. Once again, disappointment reigned and it was a case of 'what could have been'! Braunstone's fate was now in the hands of the Air Ministry.

A few weeks later, on 27th October 1939, Braunstone was requisitioned by the Air Ministry. It was to be used as a relief landing ground (RLG) for nearby Desford. From 13th November, the airfield was used by the Tiger Moths of 7 Elementary Flying Training School (EFTS) and it would remain in this role until after the war. Blister hangars were erected on the north side of the airfield and several huts were erected near the clubhouse, but other than this Braunstone was little changed from its pre-war appearance.

Braunstone now provided the students and instructors with an alternative circuit as Desford's was becoming somewhat overcrowded. During the first year of 7 EFTS' operations from Braunstone, the accident rate for a training unit of this kind was remarkably low. Only one accident was recorded during 1940 at Braunstone and that involved a 7 EFTS Tiger Moth. Sergeant

Ardley was the pilot of a Tiger Moth which crash-landed onto the airfield; little is known as to what went wrong but Ardley survived the crash and spent some time in sick quarters before being transferred to Leicester Royal Infirmary.

The following year was a different story. Two aircraft in March 1941 contributed to the mounting accident rate of the EFTS. Leading Aircraftman (LAC) Davies, a student pilot, crashed while practising forced landings on 6th March and LAC Watts stalled and spun into the ground whilst trying to go around on 27th March. Two more Tiger Moths were lost at Braunstone before the end of 1941. On 3rd November, the student pilots and instructors of two Tiger Moths were lucky to survive a mid-air collision over the airfield. The collision happened between BB858 and N6666 and it was both the skill and quick reactions of the instructors that saved the aircraft. The Tiger Moths were landed safely at Braunstone, and, following repair the two aircraft survived the war intact.

As no extension work had been carried out at Braunstone, the airfield was totally unsuitable for larger, more powerful wartime aircraft. The longest runway was only 780 yards long, which was all well and good for a Tiger Moth, but the pilots of two Hawker Hurricanes in January 1942 found this a little inadequate.

On 8th January 1942, the pilot of a Hurricane Mk.IIb, Z3262,

Braunstone was a satellite airfield for neighbouring Desford and 7 EFTS made good use of the small airfield with their de Havilland Tiger Moths.

thought he was approaching Rearsby (which was big enough to take such an aircraft). On touchdown, the pilot realised his mistake and attempted to go around but, lacking airspeed and any room to manoeuvre the aircraft, stalled and crash landed. The pilot was uninjured and the aircraft could not have been seriously damaged as it was repaired, and later lost, en route to Russia, when the ship that was carrying it was sunk by a German U-Boat. A similar incident happened on 31st January, when a Hurricane skidded on Braunstone's grass and overshot the runway. Once again, the aircraft was repaired and, this time, made it safely to Russia on 15th May 1942.

The Tiger Moths of the EFTS continued to be involved in a whole host of accidents ranging from tipping over whilst taxiing to mid-air collisions, but on 3rd March 1942 an unusual ground collision occurred. Flight Lieutenant Newberry was bringing Tiger Moth N7089 in to land when he struck a soldier named Private Sykes, who had appeared from nowhere. Neither Newberry nor his student, LAC Allen, were injured, but the soldier was in a serious condition and was rushed to the Leicester Royal Infirmary. Unfortunately Private Sykes died on 16th March and, owing to the nature of this accident, a court martial was held at Desford on 28th May. After investigation, Flight Lieutenant Newberry was cleared of all blame for the incident.

From December 1942, the EFTS was looking for more efficient ways of teaching its student pilots and increasing their throughput. A new type of training programme was tested out on a group of student pilots at Braunstone. The scheme consisted of dividing the pupils into two groups, for alternate hourly instruction in flying and lectures. This intensive form of training was deemed a success by the EFTS instructors and remained in place for several months after the trial was completed.

1943 passed without a single Tiger Moth being lost, although another large aircraft made a hash of getting into the small airfield. Sergeant Horton of 10 Air Gunnery School from Barrow-in-Furness was delivering a Boulton Paul Defiant TT.III, N3505, to Desford on 2nd July 1943. It is possible he mistook Braunstone for Desford, which was easily done if you were new to the area. Once again, the airfield was not big enough to take such an aircraft and the Defiant crashed on the edge of the airfield. Sergeant Horton escaped serious injury, but his aircraft was later dismantled and transported by road to Desford, where it was struck off charge on 30th September 1943.

Spitfires were a common sight in the skies around Braunstone as they were test flown by Vickers Armstrong pilots from Desford under the charge of Alex Henshaw. The majority performed without incident, but on 4th May 1944, Flight Lieutenant Phillips lost power to his engine near to Braunstone. With no option but to attempt a landing, Phillips left the undercarriage up and belly landed onto the Braunstone's longest runway. Phillips managed to save himself, but the Spitfire was a total loss and never flew again.

The following year, on 1st February 1945, Flying Officer Stevens of 29 OTU set a record in attempting to get the largest aircraft into Braunstone. His Vickers Wellington MK.X LP399 had just set out from Bruntingthorpe on a cross-country exercise when it suffered an engine failure. Fully loaded with fuel, the Wellington could not maintain height, and so an airfield was sought for an emergency landing. This was always a better option than crash landing into a field, as the emergency services could take a long time to reach a crashed aircraft. Stevens was taken by surprise when he realised exactly how big, or not, as the case may be, Braunstone was. The Wellington raced across the airfield and careered through a boundary hedge before coming to halt in a neighbouring field. Stevens' landing can certainly be classed as a successful one, as all the crew, bar one, escaped without injury. The Wellington also escaped serious damage and, after being dismantled and returned to Bruntingthorpe, it was back in the air, remaining in RAF service until 11th March 1948.

With the war at an end, the training activities of 7 EFTS declined rapidly and Braunstone was no longer required as a RLG from 9th July 1945. Personnel and aircraft disappeared almost overnight and the once busy grass airfield fell into disuse.

In 1947, a Mr E H G Brookes announced that he would like to use Braunstone for charter flying. Brookes was the RAF officer in charge of the airfield during the war and so knew the site and its still untapped potential very well. The LAC also expressed an interest in returning to their old home, but were advised to continue their flying activities at Ratcliffe. Like so many other proposals and ideas, both attempts to revive the airfield failed. By the middle of 1947, the airfield was de-requisitioned by the

Air Ministry, but by this time several major house building projects were well underway on the western side of the city. This building work would restrict any future flying and brought to an end any dreams of expanding the site into Leicester's first airport.

Braunstone became relegated to being used as a golf club and playing fields until it had to make way for one of the many new industrial estates that were sprouting up around the city. Today, the site is unrecognisable as an airfield and many people now would laugh at the suggestion. But the keen eyed enthusiast will find the original LAC club hangar still standing, hidden amongst the steadily expanding industrial estate. The last real indication of any aviation past, the Airmans' inn, located on Kirby Lane, was, sadly, demolished while this book was being written and has now become only a memory.

5

BRUNTINGTHORPE

National Grid Reference SP590885; 10 miles S of Leicester

'Rolling Thunder' conjures ideas of power, noise and excitement as great jet aircraft of the past open their throttles and blast down Bruntingthorpe's incredible two-mile long runway. Since 1996, twice yearly, the many aviation groups that occupy the airfield dust off their charges in an attempt to keep the ex-military jets in a taxi-able condition. A Handley Page Victor, a Blackburn Buccaneer, an English Electric Lighting can all be seen in action, the last always on the verge of take-off. More famously, Bruntingthorpe is the resting place of the RAF's last airworthy Avro Vulcan, XH558. She was flown into the airfield on 23rd March 1993, and hopes still run high that the great V-Bomber will return to the skies; and speculation continues as to whether it will be this flying season or the next. But in the meantime, the aircraft is kept in 'as new' condition while the chase for the necessary funds to fly such an expensive aircraft continues. If the day comes when XH558 flies again, there is no doubt that it will be a show stopper.

In 1940 the Air Ministry requisitioned over 700 acres of land between the villages of Gilmorton and Bruntingthorpe. Originally intended as an operational bomber station, the site was inspected in July 1942 and re-allocated for use by 92 Group for training.

It was officially allotted this task on 7th August 1942 and HQ Bomber Command proposed that 29 Operational Training Unit (OTU), flying the venerable Wellington, should be stationed there.

29 OTU was first stationed at North Luffenham with a satellite

The end of an era? Avro Vulcan B.2 XH558 taxiing along Bruntingthorpe's runway after its last flight on 23rd March 1993. Over 5,000 Vulcan fans greeted the famous delta winged bomber and hopes still run high that she will return to the sky one day. (Crown Copyright.)

at Woolfox Lodge, both in Rutland. The OTU was formed at North Luffenham in April 1942 to train bomber crews for night operations and was originally intended to be a Armstrong Whitworth Whitley unit but, owing to equipment shortages, the Wellington was chosen instead. The unit was no stranger to Bruntingthorpe, as it was also used by North Luffenham as a satellite from 6th November 1942.

The OTU made Bruntingthorpe its new home the following year. All forty-four aircraft left North Luffenham and Woolfox Lodge on 1st June 1943. Bruntingthorpe had become an independent station on 1st February, and Bitteswell became the new airfield's satellite. Two conversion flights operated from Bitteswell, while two operational training flights trained at Bruntingthorpe. After some initial hiccups with airfield lighting, a full flying programme started on the 6th June, with night flying commencing from both stations a few days later. Wardley in Rutland and Grandborough in Warwickshire ranges were also brought into use for practice bombing sorties and Holbeach Range was made available for target towing exercises.

To increase the capabilities of 29 OTU, a new unit was formed at Bruntingthorpe on 5th June. 1683 Bomber (Defence) Training Flight or BDTF was to carry out target towing and fighter affiliation duties for the crews of 29 OTU and units at Market Harborough, Husbands Bosworth and Desborough in Northamptonshire. A full complement of personnel did not arrive until 25th June and its first aircraft arrived on 1st July.

Their equipment included the Westland Lysander, Miles Martinet and Curtiss Tomahawk, which had been removed from front line fighter operations the previous year. The Tomahawk was a development of the Curtiss Mohawk and differed mainly in the fact that it was powered by a liquid-cooled engine rather than the air-cooled radial. It first entered service with the USAAC in 1940 as the P-40A and remained in production until December 1944, with the ultimate variant, the P-40R, or, as the RAF, knew it, the Kittyhawk.

The Curtiss Tomahawk was a rare aircraft in RAF service, and a troublesome machine it turned out to be. It served with 1683 BDTF, and soldiered on at Bruntingthorpe until replaced by the Hurricane in early 1944.

74

The BDTF received six very early Mk.I, Mk.IIa and Mk.IIb Tomahawks and by mid 1943 they were past their best. The flight suffered many problems with the American fighters, and in the first few weeks spent considerably more time on the ground than in the air. The Flight lost five of its Tomahawks by the year's end, the worst of these accidents happening after only a few weeks. Flight Sergeant Merrett was returning on 23rd July 1943 from a fighter affiliation exercise when his aircraft, AH864, suffered an engine fire. Merrett managed to bail out at very low level and survived, but suffered terrible injuries as a result. His Tomahawk plunged into a field near Arnesby, a few miles north-east of Bruntingthorpe village.

The BDTF settled down after their initial teething problems, the flight's Martinets providing targets for air to air firing practice for the OTU crews and the Tomahawks testing the crews in simulating enemy aircraft attacks. After only a few weeks, 29 OTU was assigned the first of many 'nickel' raids, or leaflet drops, over occupied Europe. Four Wellingtons were detailed to deliver their propaganda payload over Paris on 16th June. Heavy cloud covered most of France that night, and one Wellington turned back as it could not climb above it. The remaining three dropped their 'nickels' through the cloud. On their return one of the group landed at Aldermarston, Berkshire through shortage of fuel. 'Nickels' became part of the routine for the OTU, the majority of them being flown over France; targets included Versaille, Dreux, Chartres and Etampes.

The first month of training flights from Bruntingthorpe had resulted in the usual mishaps, involving aircraft from both the BDTF and the OTU. However, the dangerous reality of training was realised on the night of 2/3rd July. Sergeant W R Willard RCAF and Pilot Officer Harland were both flying night cross-country exercises when the weather deteriorated, resulting in their Wellingtons being diverted to Wellesbourne Mountford in Warwickshire. Unfortunately, the visibility around Wellesbourne was no better; the unforgiving high ground that surrounded the airfield claimed Sergeant Willard's aircraft first, killing five of the crew instantly, a sixth being severely injured. A few minutes later, Pilot Officer Harland's Wellington Mk.III followed, crashing only a mile away from Willard's aircraft. Fortunately, Harland and his crew of four survived, but all spent many weeks in hospital recovering from their injuries.

Training continued unabated at Bruntingthorpe until 31st July, when the country was struck by a heat wave. The temperature rose so high that the concrete in the runways expanded, resulting in huge sections rising up and cracking. Disruption was minimal, with many of the unit's Wellingtons continuing their training at other airfields. Bruntingthorpe based aircraft were involved in the first of a series of small raids in which OTU crews bombed ammunition dumps hidden in forests in northern France. On the night of 30/31st August 1943, six Pathfinder Mosquitoes and Halifaxes led 33 Wellingtons from various OTUs against such a target. The purpose of this raid was to get OTU crews accustomed to dropping their bombs on the markers dropped by the Pathfinder aircraft. The target on this occasion was a dump in the Forêt d'Éperlecques, just north of St Omer. Although the ammunition dump was successfully attacked, it was not without loss. A Wellington of 26 OTU from Wing was lost over France, and a 29 OTU Wellington III, piloted by Sergeant T A Wilder, ditched on the way to the target. Wilder managed to put his aircraft in the sea off Newhaven on the Sussex coast, after the Wellington suffered a fire in the starboard engine. Only Wilder managed to board the aircraft's dinghy. His less fortunate crew were drowned and an Air Sea Rescue Supermarine Walrus rescued Wilder twelve hours later.

Many of the instructors on the OTU were from Canada and two of them, Flight Sergeant Wright DFM and Flight Sergeant Browell, had been selected in July to be part of a unique crew. They were flown to Canada to collect the first Canadian built Avro Lancaster. KB700, a Lancaster Mk.X, was the first of 430 aircraft built by Victory Aircraft Ltd based at Malton, Toronto. After completing a propaganda tour, the crew ferried the Lancaster across the Atlantic and delivered it to 405 Squadron in late September 1943. KB700 was given the name 'Ruhr Express' and served with two Canadian Squadrons before coming to grief at its home airfield at Middleton St George on returning from a raid on Nurnberg on 2nd January 1945. The Lancaster bounced heavily on landing and when it tried to gain the perimeter track, it struck a mechanical digger and caught fire. The crew managed to clamber away from the burning bomber, but after 49 operational sorties this was to be KB700's last.

Work on the airfield continued throughout September and

October and included the fitment of a full lighting system for all three runways and, even though the station had been active for only had a few months, the perimeter track and dispersals were resurfaced. This did little to disrupt the flying programme and the pressure was always on the Maintenance Wing to keep the aircraft in the air. Out of the 55 aircraft that were on the OTU's strength, during October alone 32 of them received the attentions of the engineers.

In the early hours of 5th October 1943, a pair of RCAF Handley Page Halifaxes descended upon Bruntingthorpe. They were returning from a successful raid on Frankfurt and were unable to make their home bases of Leeming and Middleton St George owing to lack of fuel. The aircraft were from 427 and 428 RCAF Squadrons and they left Bruntingthorpe later that day.

In a move to centralise the operations of the BDTF, it was decided that the Flight would operate from Market Harborough, which was only eight miles to the east. The BDTF flew out of

Bruntingthorpe's original wartime control still survives today, even though it has been modified since this picture was taken in 1986. A second tower was built for the Americans, but this was demolished in 1973 as part of the disposal of the airfield. (J.N.Smith.)

77

Bruntingthorpe on 3rd February 1944 and for a short while continued to serve 29 OTU in the fighter affiliation role. By May, however, a reshuffle within the OTU resulted in its having a Hurricane flight of its own, which solely served the unit.

In the early hours of 28th May 1944, the peace at Bruntingthorpe was shattered with the arrival of five Avro Lancaster Mk.IIs. The Hercules powered Lancasters were all from 408 Squadron based at Linton-on-Ouse in Yorkshire. They had returned from a raid on the Bourg-Leopold military camp and had to divert from their Yorkshire base, as it was closed because of fog.

Bruntingthorpe played host to another new unit, which was formed there on 5th July 1944. The Bombing Analysis School was an autonomous unit which gave instruction in bombing theory and techniques and served 92 Group. Their stay was to be short as changes were afoot with the resident OTU. Following a signal received on 17th October, it was announced that Bruntingthorpe's satellite airfield at Bitteswell was to be transferred to 44 Group Transport Command on 1st November. This meant 29 OTU would have to reduce in size and drop to three flights of Wellingtons with a fourth flying the Hurricanes.

Night flying ended at Bitteswell on 28/29th October and all flying training was transferred to Bruntingthorpe, but a few weeks later doubts as to the OTU's future were raised after a visit by officers from 44 Group. The airfield was being viewed for its suitability to operate 105 (T) OTU, which was based at Bramcote in Warwickshire. The findings of the Transport Command visitors were not favourable and, mainly because of its lack of technical accommodation, Bruntingthorpe was not selected for this purpose.

In the meantime, the Bombing Analysis School left Bruntingthorpe on 5th December 1944, and, merging with the Night Bomber Tactical School from Hemswell, formed the Bomber Command Instructor's School at Finningley in Yorkshire. The school's move could have been perceived as being slightly premature, as its departure may have been the result of a potential take over by Transport Command. One month later, as a result of Transport Command's earlier visit, it was decided that 29 OTU would remain at Bruntingthorpe and continue to train crews for Bomber Command.

The OTU continued its training programme until the end of May 1945, by which time only ten serviceable Wellingtons remained on strength. The RAF maintained a presence at Bruntingthorpe with the arrival of 11 Aircrew Holding Unit. One of many holding units, its task was to process the hundreds of redundant aircrew who were waiting to be de-mobbed or transfered to an alternative trade. In the meantime flying continued at Bruntingthorpe with aircraft of a different nature.

The Power Jets Unit was formed on 12th May 1944 at 65 Maintenance Unit at Blaby near Leicester, specifically for RAF personnel who would work with Power Jets Limited, under the watchful eye of jet pioneer Air Commodore Frank Whittle. Since September 1944, Power Jets had established a flight of aircraft in connection with the testing of early jet engines. By June 1945, the flight was made up of an Avro Lancaster Mk.II, a Wellington hybrid Mk.II/VI and early marks of the twin jet powered Gloster Meteor. It was at Bruntingthorpe that Whittle first flew a jet; he had only planned on taxiing the aircraft, but temptation overtook him and the designer became its pilot. He carried out a short flight in Meteor F.1 EE221.

Whittle carried out another, more official, flight a few days later. This time, he was up for nearly 45 minutes and pushed EE221 to greater speeds. Testing of Armstrong Siddeley jets was

Parked in front of Bruntingthorpe's only B.1 hanger not long after its arrival in September 1944, the Power Jets Limited Avro Lancaster Mk.II awaits another test flight.

also carried out at Bruntingthorpe, in the bomb bay of a specially converted Lancaster Mk.III. Jet operations came to end at the airfield in mid 1946 when Power Jets was taken over by the National Gas Turbine Establishment (NGTE) and a move to Bitteswell was proposed. All aircraft, with the exception of the Meteor EE221, left Bruntingthorpe for the short flight to Bitteswell on 14th May, followed by the Meteor on 25th May 1946. Placed under Care and Maintenance from October 1946, the following year it was announced that the airfield would be retained as a satellite for Cottesmore. In 1953, the USAF were searching for suitable airfields for Strategic Air Command (SAC) units and they found Bruntingthorpe ripe for development. The base reopened on 15th February 1957. Two years later, it was taken over the 7542nd Air Base Squadron, and control of the airfield passed from the SAC to the Headquarters USAF in Europe (USAFE). On 28th September 1962, the US flag was lowered for the final time and Bruntingthorpe reverted to the RAF, becoming a statellite airfield of Wittering in Northamptonshire.

From 1965, the airfield systematically began to be sold off until in 1983, the entire site was purchased by C. Walton Limited. Twenty years later, the family-owned company still owns Bruntingthorpe. They retained the right to operate a vehicle proving ground and over the years (being keen aviation enthusiasts) have introduced various aviation groups and innumerable aircraft to the airfield. Many aircraft that are resident were flown into the airfield and include a Boeing 747, Super Guppy, Victor, Vulcan, Comet, Tristar and many other ex-RAF jets now cared for by the Walton owned British Aviation Heritage, Lightning Preservation Group and Phoenix Aviation.

6

CASTLE DONINGTON

National Grid Reference SK454262; 9 miles SE of Derby

East Midlands airport has become one Leicestershire's great success stories since it was opened in April 1965 as Britain's first municipal airport since the Second World War. The present day airport actually conceals two airfields, both of which are hidden by development. Now the home of BMi (formerly British Midland Airways), here Airbus A320s, Boeing 737-500s and a host of modern-day airliners perform their daily peaceful tasks and millions of passengers travel to exotic destinations that airmen of the Second World War could only dream of.

The first airfield was a 20 acre site selected in early 1916 as a landing ground for 38 Home Defence Squadron, whose HQ was situated at Melton Mowbray. The squadron at the time was operating an assortment of BE.2s, BE.12s and FE.2s but little recorded evidence exists today of the great activity at the small landing ground. By the middle of 1918, the airfield was abandoned and left in peace for 25 years.

A new airfield situated at Castle Donington was initially selected in 1941 to be a satellite for Wymeswold. However, a conflict of opinion between the Air Ministry (AM) and the Ministry of Agriculture and Fisheries (MAF) nearly put paid to the idea before a brick was laid. Discussions began when the MAF became concerned about the amount of good quality productive land that would be taken by Castle Donington. Approximately 465 acres of land were affected, of which 308 acres were arable, some of which were under crop ready for

81

harvest. The AM argument was always the same with MAF: 'With a strong air force we could import food, but we could never import airfields!'

With no objections from the MAF to the construction of Wymeswold, which, in their view was being built on land of poor quality, discussions continued on the location of the satellite airfield. Derby (Burnaston) and an emergency landing ground at Ragdale were both looked at, but both were unsuitable. Derby was ruled out, as the commitment increased in the airfield's role as an Elementary Flying Training School, and a long established army range restricted expansion of Ragdale's landing ground. The future of an airfield at Castle Donington was finally secured after the AM claimed that there was no acceptable alternative. MAF had to relent and construction began in early 1942.

The airfield was built as a standard 'A' Class bomber station with the traditional three-runway layout, the main runway measuring 2,000 yards. Twenty-seven heavy bomber hardstandings and two hangars were also built. All satellite stations had a very limited technical site, a control tower and emergency services. Castle Donington was no exception; with Wymeswold as the parent station, construction was restricted mainly to living accommodation. The communal sites built could accommodate 916 officers and airmen and 190 WAAFs.

28 Operational Training Unit (OTU) was formed at Wymeswold on the same day that the airfield officially opened, 16th May 1942. Equipped with the Vickers Wellington, the OTU was restricted to half size while it waited for the completion of Castle Donington. However, as completion drew closer in late 1942, the OTU reached three-quarter status, with 40 Wellingtons on strength by November. A planned opening of Castle Donington in mid-November was stalled when all the runways were condemned as unfit for aircraft. It was another six weeks before the OTU Wellingtons could use the new satellite airfield. Space at Wymeswold was becoming congested and when it was announced that Castle Donington would open on 1st January 1943, a relieved 28 OTU began to re-organise itself in anticipation.

A typical bomber OTU at full strength was equipped with 54 type training aircraft plus target tugs and various other 'hack' aircraft. The OTU was also broken into four flights, designated A to D and all tasked with different parts of the training programme. 'A' and 'B' Flights were formed at Wymeswold and were tasked with operational training while new 'C' and 'D' Flights were formed to carry out type conversion training at Castle Donington. 'C' Flight arrived at Castle Donington on 2nd January, followed by 'D' Flight a few days later. Several sections of the runways were still in need of attention and this delayed the flying programme until 11th January, when at long last the first training sorties were flown from Castle Donington.

Apart from the constant 'circuits and bumps' that were performed at Castle Donington, cross-country exercises were the next most common practice. They were designed to give the crews experience of navigation and build up the necessary flying hours to complete the course. The first incident to involve a Castle Donington based aircraft happened on the afternoon of 15th February 1943. Sergeant J Andrew and his crew of four were instructed to fly a cross-country exercise in Wellington Ic N2809. After flying for several hours without incident, the Wellington was only a few minutes away from landing back at Castle Donington when Andrew flew into a severe snowstorm. Out of control, the bomber plunged into the ground close to Hermitage Farm near Whitwick, two miles north-east of Coalville; the crew stood no chance of surviving.

Another way of building up valuable experience for the trainee crews was 'nickelling' or leaflet dropping. Several 'nickels' were flown from Castle Donington, usually to drop propaganda leaflets on French towns. These trips were still a dangerous occupation, with many trainee crews lost to enemy flak and fighters. Sergeant J W Shearek was detailed to carry out a Nickel raid in the Paris area on 3/4th June 1943. After successfully dropping his leaflets and managing to evade the attentions of flak and fighters, he headed for home. With only a few miles to run before reaching the English south coast, one of the Wellington's Bristol Pegasus radial engines failed. Shearek had no option but to ditch and made a textbook landing on sea, 35 miles south-south-east of St Catherine's point on the Isle of Wight. Posted as missing back at Castle Donington, the crew was rescued eight hours later, with only one crew member suffering an injury – a broken leg.

On 21st June 1943, Airspeed Oxfords of 1521 Beam Approach

Training Flight (BATF) arrived from Wymeswold. The unit was equipped with eight Oxfords and they were distinguished by bright yellow triangles in various positions on the fuselage sides and wings to warn other pilots. Often flying in very poor conditions, they could land and take off using any airfield that was equipped with beam equipment. Most flights were affiliated to a parent unit; in 1521 BATF's case it was 11 (P)AFU stationed at Shawbury in Salop.

The serviceability and reliability of the OTU's ageing fleet of Wellington Mk.1s was beginning to cause concern. Many of the Wellingtons had very high flying hours, and had already served on front line squadrons and other OTUs. Engine failures were the most common problems; during July and August alone, four aircraft were lost through engine failure, resulting in ten fatalities. These problems could not be overlooked, and replacement Wellington Mk.IIIs and Mk.Xs began to arrive on 28 OTU from November 1943 onwards, although it would be several months before the last Mk.I would leave. A more powerful Bristol Hercules, producing 1,500 hp, powered the Mk.III, but more significantly it was capable of carrying Bomber Command's 4,000lb HC parachute bomb, the heaviest yet carried by a British bomber. The Mk.X was introduced into service with even more powerful Hercules XVIII engines that produced 1,675hp and finished the Second World War having served with 29 different RAF squadrons. A total of 3,803 Mk.Xs were built, many of them converted to trainers that continued to serve the RAF into the 1950s.

In the meantime, 'C' and 'D' flights continued training crews in the old Mk.Is until April 1944. Sergeant A R Harris unwittingly made Bomber Command history on the 1st April, when his Wellington Ic DV444 was written off after yet another engine failure. While cruising at 9,000ft, the port engine failed and the crew returned early to Castle Donington. On arriving in the circuit, the undercarriage failed to lower, which, along with the flaps, was a significant way, of slowing the aircraft down. Despite reducing power, DV444 floated above the runway and crashed 200 yards beyond it. This was the last Wellington of its mark to be written off in Bomber Command service.

Both flights at Castle Donington were now operating the Wellington Mk.X and training accidents were significantly lowered. Nickels continued as part of the training programme, during which Flying Officer H J Brennan RCAF, flying Wellington X LN896 over northern France, ran into trouble on the night of 20/21st April 1944. It is not known what happened, but the crew were last heard from over Brest with very little fuel remaining. Lost and over enemy territory, the crew bailed out and took their chance, hoping to meet up with the Resistance. Luck was definitely on their side – five of the crew, who were all Canadians, successfully made contact with the local Resistance. Unfortunately one crew member died of his injuries a few days later, maybe from a bad landing after jumping from the Wellington. The surviving Canadian group all managed to evade capture and reached allied forces on their arrival on mainland Europe following the successful D-Day landings: quite an achievement.

At the beginning of July 1944, plans were in place to introduce RAF Pathfinder crews into the training programme. Despite high aircraft losses, 28 OTU's course pass rate was much higher than the average, a testament to the quality of the instructors on the unit. Unfortunately, these plans were shelved as the demand for bomber crews subsided and aircrew requirements changed.

Change was on the horizon for the OTU, and a signal received at the parent unit of Wymeswold on 1st October 1944 confirmed this. Both Castle Donington and Wymeswold were to be transferred to 44 Group, Transport Command and 28 OTU was to be disbanded. It makes for grim reading but, sadly, during their stay at Castle Donington the OTU lost eighteen aircraft in accidents. Only three were lost on operations and only one of those was lost to enemy action. The cost in aircrew from training units has always been overlooked but 38 aircrew were killed and eight injured. All of these statistics are more appropriate for a front-line squadron. However, many more aircrew who passed through 28 OTU went on to accomplish distinguished careers with Bomber Command and lived to tell the tale, despite the odds, which were always stacked against them.

On 10th October, 108 Transport (T) OTU was formed at Wymeswold and five days later 28 OTU disbanded to make way for the new unit. Castle Donington and Wymeswold were simultaneously transferred to 44 Group, Transport Command control but it would be several weeks before the 108 (T) OTU aircraft arrived. The new OTU's equipment was the Douglas Dakota Mk.III and Mk.IV – effectively a C-47A and a C-47B respectively. Almost 1,900 Dakotas served the RAF in 25 squadrons, the first joining 31 Squadron on the Burma front in June 1942. It continued in RAF service until 1950, when it was replaced by the Vickers Valetta.

As the Allies made good progress through Europe, demand was high for trained Dakota crews, especially with the amount of airborne operations and general logistical needs of an army on the move. The first of 40 Dakotas began to arrive in mid November and, once again, Castle Donington would host 'C' and 'D' Flights for conversion training. The first course of conversion flying was completed by 13th December 1944, the Wellingtons now well and truly replaced in the circuit by the Dakota.

Accidents at Castle Donington had shifted from an alarming regularity to an occasional mishap, such as occurred on 28th February 1945. Dakota IV KJ806 was carrying out some routine 'circuits and bumps'. When the exercise was complete, the

Castle Donington was taken over by Transport Command in October 1944. The Douglas Dakota took over as the main aircraft type in December and remained until May 1946.

Dakota overshot the runway and was written off. No crew members were injured, but KJ806 was relegated to spend the rest of its career with the RAF as an instructional airframe.

The longevity of wartime runways was also limited, and Castle Donington's had taken some serious punishment during 28 OTU's stay. A harsh winter and shoddy materials were also blamed when the main runway started to break up – over 500 yards became unserviceable at the beginning of March 1945 – and it was not until July that the runway was finally repaired.

A Transport Command reshuffle on 10th August 1945 meant that 108 (T) OTU was redesignated to 1382 (T) CU and moved to 4 Group Transport Command. Other than a name change, this had little effect on the training programme at Castle Donington; the only physical change being different code letters on the aircraft.

On 14th August, the second of only two Dakota accidents occurred: KG611, a MK.III, also overshot the runway and tipped on its nose. The main damage caused was to the trainee pilot's pride and no-one on board was injured.

This Douglas Dakota IV is representative of the type flown by 1382 (T) CU at Castle Donington until the airfield's closure in late 1946. (A.J. Jackson Collection.)

With the war at an end, many bomber stations closed immediately, but there was still a requirement for transport crews, although the course numbers were steadily decreasing. By 1946, the RAF was being reduced rapidly and, as Wymeswold was still the parent airfield, it was obvious that it would be retained in favour of Castle Donington. The Dakotas left Castle Donington on 31st May 1946 for the last time and all ground equipment was removed by September, when the airfield was officially closed to flying.

Castle Donington now lay abandoned and it was not long before runways and buildings fell into disrepair.

The years continued to roll by until it suddenly dawned on the local authorities that the region's only airport was Burnaston, south-west of Derby. By 1960, the small grass airport was

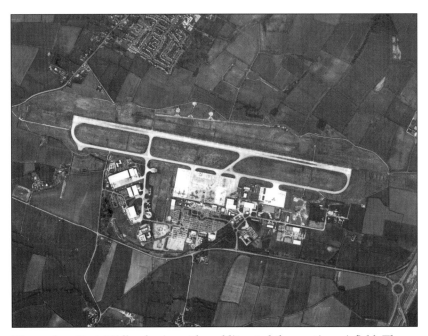

The modern East Midlands airport has obliterated the wartime airfield. The main runway follows the line of the original and, apart from a section of the northern perimeter track and a few old dispersals here and there, both the First and Second World War airfields are committed to memory. (Crown Copyright.)

handling over 35,000 passengers per year, but a rapid increase in air traffic would put too much demand on the airport. A joint committee was formed, which included borough and city councils from Derby, Nottinghamshire and Leicester. The authorities then employed a group of consultant engineers to travel the area in search of a more suitable airfield site to expand into an airport. The consultants did not have to look far – Castle Donington was the obvious choice, as the location was excellent.

Work began to develop the old airfield in 1964 at an initial cost of nearly £1.4 million. A contract was given to Richard Costain Ltd, to build a new runway, taxiways, terminal building and a large parking apron. The majority of the wartime airfield was swept away, although the main runway was laid on top of the original one at a length of 5,850ft. This was extended in 1970 and its current length is nearly 7,500ft.

The airfield re-opened on 1st April 1965 and was named East Midlands Airport. This was followed by an official opening by the Duke of Edinburgh on 21st July. In its first year of operation, approximately 100,000 passengers passed through the airport, almost three times more than Burnaston at its peak. Today, the airport caters for over two million passengers per year and continues to grow (and supports 90 tenant companies). In February 2001, East Midlands was bought for £241 million by Manchester Airport Plc and, with its future secure, passengers will continue to pass through one of Leicestershire's great avaition success stories.

7

COTTESMORE

National Grid Reference SK910158; 5½ miles NE of Oakham

Cottesmore is the only surviving RAF flying station that is active within the borders of Leicestershire and Rutland. Expanded and modified over the years, the layout of the airfield bears very little resemblance to the original site which first opened in 1938. The gentle note of a 1,000hp Rolls Royce Merlin engine has long been replaced by the sound of a Rolls Royce Pegasus, which develops over 21 times more power that its wartime predecessor. BAe Harrier GR.7s of 1, 3 and 4 Squadrons are the latest of a long line of aircraft and units that have been stationed at this Rutland airfield. Cottesmore has housed 33 different units; admittedly two were pre-war and 23 were post-war, which means that the Second World War period is only a snapshot of one of the RAF's most important airfields.

Located north of Cottesmore village, with Market Overton to the north-west and Thistleton to the north-east, the airfield was planned during the RAF's 1930s expansion period. Originally know as the 'Thistleton site', it was not until 1st May 1936 that the Air Ministry announced their intentions to start construction of an airfield. Work started in July, with initial focus on clearing the hedgerows and grading the land ready for the grass runways. The other main task was the construction of four large 'C' Type hangars and, as Cottesmore is 425ft above sea level, making it the second highest military airfield in the country today (Lyneham in Wiltshire is the highest), these hangars are still very visible on the skyline. They were typical of pre-war construction. Built of concrete and steel, they were 150ft wide, approximately 300ft long and were designed to house several bomber aircraft. Pre-war stations of the expansion period were all built with brick and had centrally heated H-block accommodation and messes for officers and airman alike. All technical buildings were also built in brick and any officer or airman posted to such a station in wartime would know that their tour would be comfortable, if nothing else.

In March 1938, the Air Ministry declared that Cottesmore would operate within 2 (Bomber) Group, whose HQ was at Andover in Hampshire. By the end of the month, the first service personnel began to arrive and Cottesmore also received its very first station commander, Wing Commander H V Drew OBE, AFC.

The airfield was ready to receive its first aircraft by April, but many technical and accommodation buildings were still to be finished. Cottesmore was planned to house two light bomber

A C-Type hangar at Cottesmore today is occupied by Harrier Gr.7s of 4 Squadron, and one of the unit's previous aircraft, a Hunter, is on display in the foreground. (J Molyneux.)

squadrons and both 35 and 207 Squadrons arrived from Worthy Down in Hampshire on 20th April 1938. Both units were equipped with the Vickers Wellesley, but 35 Squadron was in the process of re-equipping with the Fairey Battle, one example arriving with the squadron.

The Wellesley was a single-engined bomber and was unique in that it was the first RAF aircraft to employ geodetic construction, pioneered by Barnes Wallis. This construction was more famously used on its younger brother, the Wellington, and provided the fuselage with great strength and resistance to battle damage as well as being easy to repair. The Wellesley was an unusual design: the pilot was located forward of the wing in his own cockpit with the bomb aimer/observer behind the wing. Performance was good for a 1930s design, aided by a large wing of over 74ft in span which gave aircraft a good range and an excellent ceiling of 33,000ft. This performance made it the ideal

Technologically advanced for the 1930s, but obsolete by the beginning of the Second World War, the Vickers Wellesley was one of the first aircraft types to arrive at Cottesmore in early 1938. This example is K7758, which briefly served with 207 Squadron at Cottesmore before being replaced with the equally obsolete Fairey Battle. (A.J. Jackson Collection.)

choice of aircraft for the newly formed Long Range Development Unit, stationed at Upper Heyford in Oxfordshire. On 5th November 1938, three Wellesley's set out on a record-breaking flight from Ismailia in Egypt to Darwin in Australia. Led by Squadron Leader R Kellet, two aircraft made it to Darwin, setting a new world record flight of 7,157 miles in just over 48 hours – an amazing achievement. Although the Wellesley was obsolete by the start of the Second World War, it remained in service, flying reconnaissance sorties, until August 1943.

The aircraft that was to replace the Wellesley, the Fairey Battle, held no such distinction and was a quite unremarkable aircraft. Designed in response to a 1933 Air Ministry specification, the Battle was to become the main light bomber available to the RAF in the late 1930s. A clean looking low wing monoplane, its only advantage over its predecessors, the Hawker Hart and the Hawker Hind, was that it could carry twice the bomb load, which was still only 1,000lbs. Performance and defence armament were lacking, and these crucial areas would mean that the Battle was totally outclassed by German opposition at the start of the Second World War.

207 Squadron became the first of the two to become fully equipped with twelve brand new Fairy Battle Mk.Is. The last of their trusty Wellesleys left Cottesmore at the end of May 1938. Similarly, 35 Squadron had a full complement of Battles by

Cottesmore's C-Type hangars provide the backdrop to this line up of 207 Squadron Fairey Battles in 1939.

93

August and both units spent the summer months getting familiar with their new aircraft.

A sign that war was not that far away came in September 1938, when the 'Munich Crisis' prompted the RAF to step up to a war footing. Cottesmore prepared to mobilize its Battle squadrons and plans were in place to form a new squadron at the airfield. The situation was temporarily diffused when the Prime Minster Neville Chamberlain returned from Germany, waving his piece of white paper and declaring 'Peace in our time'.

The RAF could not have been convinced by Chamberlain's comment and continued to train harder each day, practising low-level flying and bombing sorties. Both squadrons received more Battles, bringing the total to sixteen aircraft on each unit, with many in reserve. As the political situation continued to break down, all buildings on the station were painted in camouflage in the spring of 1939. Nets were draped over the hangars, roads near the station were camouflaged, and dummy hedgerows were painted across the airfield, to give the impression from the air of a collection of fields.

Both squadrons were up to 24 Battles apiece by the summer and, after more regional air exercises, were prepared for a move to a more southerly airfield. On 24th August, 35 and 207 Squadrons left Cottesmore for Cranfield in Bedfordshire. Luckily for both units they were not amongst the many Battle squadrons

A 35 Squadron Battle K9471 after its undercarriage collapsed as a result of a heavy landing in April 1939. Within months the RAF's Battle squadrons departed for France, where against superior German forces the Battles were shot from the sky.

who left for France at the start of the war. They both remained in the country and became crew training units. Their fellow Battle units suffered terrible losses against the Luftwaffe.

Cottesmore was not quiet for long, 185 Squadron arrived from Thornaby in Yorkshire on 25th August. The squadron had been recently equipped with the Handley Page Hampden and was immediately designated as a training squadron and so would never take the Hampden into combat. They were followed a few days later by 106 Squadron from Evanton in Highland, an airfield where they were on detachment, their home base being at Thornaby. Also flying the Hampden, 106 Squadron had first received in May 1939 an aircraft that would become a very common sight in the skies around Cottesmore.

The Handley Page Hampden was a twin engined medium bomber that, together with the Wellington and Whitley, carried the brunt of all early Bomber Command operations. First flown on 21st June 1936, its unusual fuselage and slender twin-finned tail earned it the nickname the 'Flying Panhandle'. As a pre-war bomber, its performance was excellent, with a top speed of over 250 mph and an impressive payload of up to 4,000lbs. It was highly manoeuvrable, but Bomber Command's decision to send the Hampdens on unescorted day raids was a disastrous one and losses were high. Its defensive armament was weak and had many blind spots, but the Hampden struggled on, continuing to fly with Bomber Command until 1942. The Hampden was powered by a pair of Bristol Pegasus air cooled, radial engines.

A 185 Squadron Hampden on a training sortie from Cottesmore in early 1940 displaying the rare 'ZM' code, which was used only for a few months by the squadron before it was disbanded into 14 OTU.

Another variant was also produced by Handley Page, powered by Napier Dagger in-line engines, these engines were never as reliable as the Pegasus. The Dagger-powered aircraft, named the Hereford, only saw service with training units and several were stationed at Cottesmore.

With the outbreak of war on 3rd September 1939, Cottesmore was transferred to 5 Group Bomber Command based at St Vincent's in Grantham. At the same time, 5 Group Pool Squadron was formed from 185 Squadron and these Pools would eventually turn into the new Operation Training Units (OTUs), that were essential for the preparation of crews for the front line squadrons.

106 Squadron was not destined to stay at Cottesmore for very long. It left for Finningley in Yorkshire on 6th October and went on to have a very distinguished career, playing an important part in the strategic bomber offensive against Germany. However, 207 Squadron returned on detachment at the beginning of December, due to Cranfield's grass airfield being in such poor condition. An indication of Cottesmore's impending training status occurred on 20th December, when the station and 185 Squadron was transferred to 6 Group, which had temporarily become an Operational Training Group.

New Year's Day 1940 saw the first wartime fatality occur at Cottesmore. Pilot Officer E A C Hill was carrying out circuits when he stalled his Hampden, L4205, after overshooting the runway. Hill was the only occupant of the Hampden, which crashed into the ground on the very edge of the airfield, killing the pilot instantly. The weather was the main enemy during the first few weeks of 1940. Heavy snowfalls of a severity that had not been seen in the area for over 50 years brought Cottesmore and the surrounding area to a standstill. The airfield was closed until 22nd February. March brought more pleasant conditions, with 207 Squadron achieving over 1,300 hours, a record for the unit.

Another change of titles and units occurred in April 1940. 207 Squadron left on the 5th for Benson in Oxfordshire and was absorbed into 12 OTU. The most significant change to affect Cottesmore was the formation of 14 OTU from 185 Squadron on 8th April. The role of the OTU was to train night bomber crews and the aircraft on strength were initially 39 Hampdens and

Herefords along with 39 Avro Ansons. The last were employed for navigational training and for general duties work.

As Cottesmore was a very tempting target for the Luftwaffe, it was allocated a decoy or 'Q' site dummy airfield. The object of the exercise was to simulate a full-size airfield complete with dummy aircraft and lighting. Cottesmore's decoy was established in March 1940, a few miles north-east of the airfield, at Swayfield in Lincolnshire, and was littered with dummy Fairey Battles. The decoy proved its worth for the first time on 26th June, when it was bombed with several High Explosive (HE) bombs and over 100 incendiaries. One aircraft was not fooled by the decoy and dropped seven HE bombs across the technical site at Cottesmore, causing some structural damage, but no casualties. The decoy successfully distracted the German aircraft on two more occasions before the end of June. It was bombed heavily on both raids. More raids followed, and Cottesmore was hit again on 6th September, when a single raider dropped several incendiaries. Fortunately, the only disruption caused was to a meeting in the Sergeant's Mess – those involved in it went from sitting around the table to crouching under it! The Luftwaffe soon got wise to the brightly lit decoys and turned the tables by using them as a navigational aid to helpto locate their main targets.

The serviceability of the aircraft on the OTU was a constant headache for the ground crew who could toil all night only for a student pilot to wreck all their work the following day. During October, for example, out of 32 Hampdens available, only 17 were serviceable and the Herefords, with their fragile Dagger engines, were even worse, with only three airworthy examples out of 16 on strength.

Regardless of the difficulties with serviceability, many training sorties per day were still possible, and Cottesmore's circuit was often over-crowded with returning aircraft. With this in mind, the opening of Woolfox Lodge, a few miles to the south-east, during December 1940, came as quite a relief. On the 14th, several Hampdens and Ansons began using Woolfox Lodge for night flying training, taking some of the strain away from Cottesmore.

As will be mentioned many times in this book, training stations can be very dangerous places and Cottesmore had the

The Handley Page Hereford was powered by Napier Dagger engines and the unreliability of these engines was a constant headache for the ground crew who struggled to keep them flying. (Via author.)

unenviable label of being the most accident prone in Leicestershire and Rutland. By June 1940, the OTU had earned itself the dubious distinction of being the first OTU in Bomber Command to have lost ten aircraft. The figures did not improve and, by the end of 1940, the OTU had lost 23 aircraft in a host of different accidents, ranging from those which occured when taxiing to total write-offs, with many valuable aircrew being lost before making it to the squadrons. One of the main reasons for the high loss rate was that the Hampden could not be converted into a trainer. The cockpit design was almost fighter-like, which meant a new pilot was literally on his own, with the instructor watching from the ground. Many airmen have commented that flying on an OTU is a lot more dangerous than operational flying!

Cottesmore, and its aircraft, were involved in two major exercises during January and February 1941. The first was an anti-invasion exercise that involved 18 Hampdens and 18 Ansons. The other was a realistic gas attack on the station. Bristol Blenheims, acting as the enemy, sprayed real gas over the airfield

An He.III, mainstay of the Luftwaffe bombing fleet

to test the defences of the airfield. The whole exercise was filmed and reproduced as a training exercise and many of the machine gun posts scored hits on the attacking aircraft using camera guns.

A more realistic display was performed by the Luftwaffe on the evening of 9th April, when a single German aircraft dropped several incendiaries on the station, one of them crashing through the roof of 'A' hangar; little damage was caused. Two days later, a larger force of approximately ten to fifteen enemy aircraft bombed the airfield but, once again, the force could not press home their attack and Cottesmore survived to fight another day. The next day, 12th April, two more German aircraft dropped HE bombs on the Swayfield decoy, much to the annoyance of a gun post on the decoy, which opened fire but was not able to claim any hits. This decoy airfield was attacked twice more during May but, as the threat of invasion faded, many were closed down, including Swayfield, which was abandoned by the end of June 1942. The Luftwaffe turned its attentions to Woolfox Lodge at the end of April.

The phasing out of the Hereford from the OTU came as welcome news to the ground crews and aircrews alike. The last aircraft had departed Cottesmore by the end of July 1941. This made little difference to the accident rate though as hardly a Hereford sortie had been flown since the beginning of the year.

An unusual incident took place when a Hampden unexpectedly landed at Cottesmore after making no radio call. The crew leapt out of the aircraft and immediately set fire to the Hampden in front of a crowd of stunned spectators! The extremely embarrassed airmen had become lost and thought that they had landed in enemy-occupied Holland, much to the annoyance of their commanding officer. A similarly bizarre incident, which was almost a mirror image, allegedly occurred at Cottesmore a few weeks later. This time, an unidentified aircraft landed, once again without a radio call, late one summer's evening and taxied up to the tower. With its engines still running, a crew member exited the strange aircraft and approached an airman who was stood outside the tower. The stunned airman was rooted to the spot when the crewman spoke a language he had not heard before. The crewman looked equally surprised and ran hell-for-leather back to his aircraft. In no time at all, he was back in the aircraft and they were on their way, bouncing across Cottesmore's grass before becoming airborne. The aircraft turned out to be a Luftwaffe Heinkel He. 111 and the crew were as lost as their English counterparts had been a few weeks earlier!

Many of the instructors who served on the OTU had completed full operational tours and were already highly decorated. Flight Sergeant J Hannah was a wireless instructor who earned himself the Victoria Cross (VC) while serving with 83 Squadron. At the age of eighteen, Hannah was the wireless operator of a Hampden. On 15th September 1940, his aircraft was set on fire by flak while bombing invasion barges in Antwerp harbour. He had the opportunity to bail out, but chose to stay with the Hampden and fight the flames. His actions saved the life of the Canadian pilot, who managed to return the aircraft to its home base at Scampton. Hannah was the youngest airmen to win the VC and, after being involved in two serious accidents while flying with the 14 OTU, was invalided out the RAF only to succumb to tuberculosis at the age of 25, in 1947.

A second VC winner was Flight Lieutenant R A B Learoyd, who was a pilot instructor on the OTU. On 12th August 1940, Learoyd was leading a formation of nine Hampdens from 49 and 83 Squadrons in a low-level attack on the Dortmund-Ems canal.

Flak defences brought down one 49 Squadron Hampden and badly damaged Learoyd's aircraft, but he pressed home his attack at only 150ft, destroying an aqueduct. Learoyd managed to bring back his badly damaged aircraft to Scampton and earned himself the first VC awarded to an airman of Bomber Command.

Another future VC holder also served as a pilot instructor at Cottesmore. South African Flight Lieutenant J D Nettleton had already completed one tour of operations and, having served with 14 OTU, was posted and promoted to 44 (Rhodesia) Squadron, which was newly equipped with Lancasters at Waddington. Nettleton was the leader of a section of twelve Lancasters that took part in the daring or disastrous daylight raid on the MAN diesel engine factory at Augsburg. Most of the journey to and from the target was flown at an incredibly low level and, after Nettleton successfully bombed the target, he shepherded the surviving Lancasters home to Waddington. Only five aircraft made it home, but eight did manage to bomb the target; thankfully, this kind of daylight raid was very rarely employed.

The beginning of August 1941 brought a change of satellite airfield for 14 OTU. Woolfox Lodge was transferred to North Luffenham's control and Cottesmore gained a new satellite at Saltby a few miles north. New types of aircraft were also received by the OTU, including the Airspeed Oxford twin-engined trainer, which was introduced in an attempt to cut down on crew and aircraft losses. Later in the year, a pair of Westland Lysanders brought greater flexibility to OTU operations. They were employed in target towing duties which were carried out at Holbeach range on the edge of the Wash in Lincolnshire. Practice bombing ranges at Grimsthorpe, near Bourne, and Whittlesey Wash, near Peterborough, were also available to the OTU.

The year 1941 closed with no improvement in the accident rate, as another 30 aircraft had been lost, most as a result of pilot error; 1942 began much the same as the previous year, with heavy snowfalls, and Cottesmore was in such a state that 'A' Flight moved to Saltby for a few weeks while conditions improved. At the end of February, 'A' Flight returned and Cottesmore continued with its training programme.

Cottesmore was situated in a good position to receive aircraft that were in trouble and it served this purpose just after midnight on 20th May 1941. A 102 Squadron Handley Page Halifax II, W1099, had left its Yorkshire base at Dalton a few hours earlier, heading for Vichy, France. The Halifax suffered an engine failure and attempted to return to base, but the pilot, Flight Sergeant C R Barr RCAF, decided to make an emergency landing at Cottesmore instead. While on approach to the airfield, another engine failed and the Halifax crash-landed and quickly caught fire. All six crew managed to scramble to safety and Barr now held the unenviable distinction of writing off the first 102 Squadron Halifax.

Rumours were circulating around the station that a big operation was being planned and that the OTU might play a part in it. Both the instructors and trainees were keen to take part in anything that wasn't training and, at the end of May 1942, they got their wish. The unit was ordered to prepare 27 Hampdens for a flight of over 1,000 miles with a full bomb load. This was quite a tall order for the Maintenance Wing on station, with just over 40 Hampdens on strength; the ground personnel would have to excel themselves to achieve this figure. By 28th May, the maintenance personnel had not only achieved the required amount of serviceable aircraft but had exceeded it; 30 aircraft were ready for action with three in reserve. The selected crews were ordered to attend a briefing on 30th May, where they discovered that they would take part in the biggest raid of the war so far. Operation *Millennium* was Arthur Harris' brainchild and would involve over 1,000 bomber aircraft, made up of every type flying with both the Bomber Command squadrons and the OTUs.

The first of 30 Hampdens started to take off from Cottesmore at 22:43 hours on 30th May, their target being Cologne. Only one aircraft returned early and 27 reported successfully bombing the target but the German night fighters were ready for the aircraft returning over Holland. Pilot Officer T E P Ramsey and his crew were caught unawares when Lt Manfred Meurer shot them down near Diepenveen, north of Deventer in Holland. Ramsey managed to bail out and became a POW; the rest of his crew were not so lucky.

Flight Lieutenant W L Cameron RCAF had also received the attentions of the German night fighters; his Hampden was badly damaged and he had to make the entire return flight on one engine. Cameron elected to make an emergency landing at Horsham St Faith, north of Norwich. On approaching the runway, Cameron realised he was coming in too fast and decided to go around again, however, at 500ft, the Hampden's other engine failed and the powerless bomber crashed into Overbury Road, Hellesdon, on the western side of Norwich. Cameron and another crewman were killed, with the other two seriously injured; in their memory, a plaque was placed near the crash site on 30th May 1996.

The OTU lost a third Hampden that night when Squadron Leader D B Falconer DFC was nearly home over Cambridgeshire. His Hampden was emerging from a rain cloud when it was suddenly confronted by a Halifax of 78 Squadron on its way home to Croft in Yorkshire. With no time to take avoiding action, the two aircraft collided and both crashed near March. Falconer managed to bail out of his crippled Hampden but his three crewmen had no chance of escape; two of the Halifax crew were also killed and three were seriously injured.

A second '1,000 bomber raid' was planned for the following evening and, once again, the ground personnel managed to ready another 27 Hampdens in a short time. The target was Essen and, this time, 25 aircraft managed to bomb the Ruhr city, despite a thin layer of cloud. All returned home safely to Cottesmore, the only casualty being an airmen who was fatally injured when his Hampden was struck from above by a falling 4lb incendiary.

The third and final big raid that the OTU took part in was staged for the night of 25/26th June 1942 and another 24 Hampdens were made available for this final *Millennium* attack. The target was Bremen and, on arrival, the crews found the city covered in solid cloud and almost impossible to identify. Despite this, 19 aircraft claimed to have bombed the city, with the remainder suffering various mechanical failings which caused at least one to dump its bomb load in the North Sea. One aircraft did not return. Hampden P5312 had already aborted the first two raids and fate struck the aircraft and its crew for a third time. The aircraft came down near Borkum, killing Flight Lieutenant Count T E Salazar DFC and two of his crew instantly. Sergeant H S Cusden, one of the gunners, survived the crash only to die of his injuries in captivity a few days later.

During the summer, the OTU received word that their

Hampdens were to be replaced by the Vickers Wellington but, in the meantime, the unit was to continue to provide aircraft for training and more operations.

The next contribution to the Bomber Command offensive came on the night of 31st July/1st August 1942, when Dusseldorf was attacked. Thirty Hampdens joined a 630-strong force, which included over 100 Lancasters for the first time. It was not to be a good night for the OTU; before the main force had reached the target, four of the Hampdens had returned to base. One of the returning aircraft was minus its navigator, who had bailed out over the North Sea, thinking that his Hampden was going down.

Flak was heavy over the city and night fighters were also very active. They were responsible for the loss of four OTU Hampdens that night. The first of these was flown by Pilot Officer D J Curtin, who was an American student pilot on his very first operational raid. Curtin's Hampden was initially struck by flak over the target and then by two attacks by night fighters. Curtin managed to shake them off but not before all of his crew were wounded. With the aircraft badly damaged, Curtin managed to limp the Hampden off course, to the safety of Devon. He crash landed in a field at Loddiswell, sixteen miles south-west of Torquay. Three other Hampdens were also shot down that night, all victims of German night fighters; two came down in Germany; a third crashed at Leffinge, just to the south of Ostend airport. Airmen lost that night included New Zealanders, Australians and Canadians; by this stage of the war, the population of the OTU had a strong Commonwealth feel.

Just when the ground defences were beginning to relax at Cottesmore, the Luftwaffe paid another brief visit to the airfield. A Dornier Do 217E flew low over the airfield, dropped four bombs and strafed several buildings with machine gun fire. Several gun positions around the airfield fired at the Dornier, which must have convinced the German bomber that it was not wise to return for a second attack.

OTU participation continued through September, when three more raids on the Ruhr were planned. Serviceability and reliability were becoming the Hampden's enemy in addition to the German defences, and consequently the number of aircraft able to take part was becoming smaller. Twenty aircraft took off for Dusseldorf on 10/11th September, but several had to return early with a variety of mechanical failings. A single all-Canadian crew was lost, apparently struck by flak, killing the crew of four instantly. Seventeen Hampdens left Cottesmore for Bremen on 13/14th and, once again, an all-Canadian crew was lost on the return leg over Holland. Sergeant Beames RCAF crash landed his Hampden, AD845, into a field near to the airfield and this aircraft became the last Hampden to be written off under operational circumstances in Bomber Command. A few nights later, on the 16/17th, twelve Hampdens contributed to a raid on Essen, all returning safely to Cottesmore. This signalled the last Hampden raid for 14 OTU.

In between the flurry of operational activity, the station still managed to play host to Exercise *Liberator*. The 60th Troop Carrier Group (TCG), based at Aldermaston in Berkshire and flying Douglas C-47 Skytrains, was building up in preparation for the opening of the 'second front' in North Africa. As part of its training programme for Operation *Torch*, the 60th TCG dropped an entire battalion of the 82nd Airborne Division onto Cottesmore. The exercise was intended as a test of the airfield's defences and to give the airborne troops experience of dropping onto a defended airfield. A post-exercise assessment concluded that the defenders would have repulsed the attack – not exactly the outcome the 82nd would have hoped for. This was not the last time that Cottesmore was to receive the airborne paratroopers.

From early 1943 onwards, 14 OTU replaced their tired Hampdens with the Vickers Wellington. In some respects the unit's accident rate did not improve, as demonstrated by this Wellington Mk.Ic, which came down in Exton Park, near Cottesmore on 2nd December 1942. (P.H.T. Green Collection.)

The first Wellingtons arrived at Cottesmore in mid-September and were virtually all tired Mk.Ics. Many had already seen a lot of action with Bomber Command squadrons and other OTUs, but their introduction did marginally improve the unit's accident rate. With the arrival of the Wellington, the OTU's Airspeed Oxfords became surplus to requirements (as the Wellington could carry an instructor next to the pupil) and all but one had departed from the airfield by 10th October.

The first incident to involve a Wellington occurred one night late in the month when Sergeant Ryan was taxiing his aircraft ready for take-off. The bomber burst a tyre and Ryan chose the non-recommended method of trying to investigate how much damage had been caused. He climbed out of the Wellington, with the engines still running and, in the darkness, was struck on the head by one of the blades. Unbelievably, the lucky Sergeant was transported to Rauceby hospital near Sleaford in Lincolnshire and, after an operation, survived.

The long association with 14 OTU and the Hampden came to an end at the beginning of November 1942 when the aircraft was removed from the training programme. This was not before Sergeant M G K East RCAF managed to write off the last Hampden in Bomber Command service on 8th November. East and his all-Canadian crew were returning from a high-level, night-time cross-country exercise when the Hampden L4100 undershot the runway and crashed about a mile to east of the airfield. All of the crew survived with injuries, but L4100 was a write-off. Up until this accident, the aircraft had had a trouble free existence since entering service in July 1941 and had managed to achieve 876 flying hours – well above average for a Hampden.

Re-equipment of the OTU came swiftly and, by the end of November, the unit could boast 45 Wellingtons on strength along with eight Avro Ansons, two Westland Lysanders and a single Boulton Paul Defiant, the last complementing the Lysanders as Target Tugs. Before the year was out, though, eight of the Wellingtons had been written off in a variety of accidents, but this was still an improvement over the old Hampdens.

In January 1943, Cottesmore received another new station commander, Group Captain S Graham MC, the sixth since the opening of the station. The station commander featured prominently in an accident which occurred on a misty afternoon on 31st March 1943. Flight Sergeant Humphrey RAAF was returning from a practice bombing sortie in his Wellington Mk.Ic, AD628, when he landed too far down one of the short runways and headed straight for the control tower. Humphrey managed to swing the Wellington away from the tower, only to crash into another Wellington which was parked in front of 'C' hangar. AD628 continued out of control, before coming to rest next door to the hangar and setting alight offices that ran along the side of the building that contained several Wellingtons undergoing maintenance. Group Captain Graham was quickly on the scene, organising fire and rescue parties to extricate the three injured crew who were trapped in AD628. While this was going on, a 250lb bomb that was still aboard the burning aircraft exploded within a few feet of Graham and the rescue team, throwing everyone off their feet but, miraculously, it did not seriously injure anyone. Graham was taken to the sick quarters for treatment of minor injuries but, on his arrival, he insisted on directing more seriously injured personnel and quickly returned to the scene, directing fire fighters until the blaze was under control. Although two airmen on board Humphrey's Wellington were killed, the accident was handled with professionalism and bravery by many airmen and local fire fighters, who managed to save the hangar and the aircraft within it. Group Captain Graham was later awarded the George Cross for his gallantry and inspiring leadership under difficult circumstances.

The sole remaining Airspeed Oxford on the OTU was tragically lost a few days later when it was involved in a mid-air collision near Melton Mowbray. Sergeant A A Moors and Sergeant J A Lemmerick, both of the RCAF, were on a training exercise when they collided with a Lancaster Mk.I of 1654 HCU from Wigsley in Nottinghamshire. Both aircraft plummeted to the ground near Burton Lazars and, although the scene was quickly attended by emergency services from the nearby airfield at Melton Mowbray, nothing could be done for either crew.

24 Bomber Command airfields were selected in the spring and summer of 1943 to house Airspeed Horsa gliders in preparation for a potential invasion of Europe, which was still very much in the planning stages. Bomber airfields were the most popular choice for the open storage of the RAF's first troop-transport

glider, owing to the size of the Horsa. At 67ft long and with a span of 88ft it was comparable in size to the Wellington, and by 10th June, 27 were stored around the edge of the airfield. All of the Horsas were delivered by Whitley and Albemarle tugs, which cast off the gliders over the airfield.

The OTU's long stay at Cottesmore was approaching the end and, in late July 1943, the unit received a signal from HQ 92 Group that they were to move to Market Harborough and the satellite airfield of Husbands Bosworth in Northamptonshire. The bulk of the unit left on 1st August and some of the stragglers that had been undergoing maintenance departed Cottesmore for the last time on 28th August.

Cottesmore was placed under Care and Maintenance, with a detachment of 2 Heavy Glider Maintenance Unit (HGMU), which was formed on 16th August at Snailwell in Cambridgeshire, to store, maintain, repair and modify all of the heavy gliders attached to the glider tug squadrons within 38 Wing. The same day, No. 34 Heavy Glider Maintenance Section (HGMS) assumed responsibility for all of the gliders that were still on the airfield and oversaw the arrival of Wimpeys, the civil engineering company. Wimpeys had been given the contract to turn Cottesmore's grass airfield into a three runway 'A' class bomber station.

It would be several months before this was completed but it did not halt the brief transfer of the station to 5 Group Bomber Command on 1st September 1943. 5 Group was always given first refusal when a station within their area became available but, at this stage of the war, the Group had no squadrons needing Cottesmore as a home. Within a few days, though, Cottesmore was offered to the USAAF, and by 22nd September personnel of the Air Support Division Substitution Unit (ASDSU) or, in plain speech, an opening up party with combined RAF and USAAF personnel, had arrived. The station was then officially transferred and took on a new role as Army Air Force Station 489, which would form the hub of a collection of airfields allocated to the US 9th Air Force (AF), known as the Northern Carrier Group.

For the next few months leading to the completion of the airfield's new runways, Cottesmore became a transit point for many American units arriving from the North African and Italian theatres. The first to arrive was the HQ of the 9th Troop

Carrier Command (TCC), which was destined to stay at Cottesmore until 1st of December, when it moved to St Vincent's in Grantham. A few days later, the HQs of the 50th Troop Carrier Wing (TCW) and the 434th Troop Carrier Group (TCG) passed through before departing respectively for Bottesford and Fulbeck in Lincolnshire.

The Americans settled in at Cottesmore with little difficulty and took no time in transforming the station into their own little America. Their easy-going attitude made them popular with servicemen and civilians alike, but they lacked the discipline that senior RAF officers were accustomed to. This caused friction on many occasions as the RAF were still in charge of Cottesmore and the station commander had to order lights out for three nights in a row in an attempt to curb the high spirited Americans.

A water shortage did not help the situation and this remained an issue into the New Year, but the Americans made the best of it and knuckled down to the task ahead. The Horsas that were still stored on the airfield were now maintained by the Americans and eventually they would all be transferred to the 9th AF. Maintenance of the Horsas and vehicles provided by the RAF kept the American personnel busy until the arrival of their aircraft from Sicily a few weeks later.

Christmas was celebrated in style with many parties, and all ranks of the RAF were invited. The generosity of the Americans came through when they invited a group of physically disabled children from London as part of the seasonal activities.

In February 1944, Cottesmore's new runways were complete and the airfield was now more purposefully equipped with a 2,000 yard main tarmac runway and two shorter runways of 1,600 and 1,500 yards respectively. A connecting perimeter track was also built, which had 54 concrete and tarmac aircraft dispersals attached to it. Cottesmore was now ready to receive the 316th TCG, which flew in its first 26 aircraft on 15th February, under the command of Lieutenant Colonel Burton R Fleet. Like all TCGs, the group was made up of four squadrons, numbered 36th, 37th, 44th and 45th Troop Carrier Squadron (TCS). The 316th was equipped with the Douglas C-47A Skytrain and C-53A Skytrooper, the latter differing in that it was effectively a converted DC-3 airliner. The C-47 had more powerful engines, a strengthened floor and large rear door, which enabled it to carry

109

freight as well as paratroopers; the C-53 was restricted to the latter.

When the 316th TCG arrived, the American personnel strength swelled rapidly to over 3,700, a problem that was aggravated by the arrival of the 52nd TCW, which was also to be based at Cottesmore. Tented accommodation started to spring up all over the station, and many local properties were requisitioned, including Exton Hall, which was taken over by the 52nd TCW under the command of Brigadier General Harold L. Clark. The Wing was activated on 30th May 1942 and had already served for nine months with the US 12th Air Force in the Mediterranean area. As well as the 316th, the Wing had the 313th, 314th, 315th and 61st TCGs under its control. They were based at Folkingham in Lincolnshire, Saltby and Spanhoe in Northamptonshire, and Barkston Heath, also in Lincolnshire, and formed the bulk of what was to be known as the Northern Carrier Group.

In early February, a new unit was formed at RAF Cottesmore. The 9th Air Force Troop Carrier Command pathfinder School, under the command of 33-year-old Colonel Joel Crouch, was a very specialised outfit. The main role of the school was to provide pathfinder training to aircrews of the 9th Troop Carrier Command. They would also train and deliver British and Polish Airborne forces in this role. The main task, though, was to train and work closely with 82nd and 101st Airborne Division Pathfinders whom they would potentially be dropping into France. These parachutists would be the advance party of an airborne assault and would set up portable radio signal devices to guide in the main force to the drop zones. The unit also trained aircrews in the use of their special radar aids. Initially equipped with only seven C-47s, of which five were fitted with SCR-717 and two with 'GEE', it would grow to be made up of four squadrons, 1st, 2nd, 3rd and 4th Pathfinder Squadrons (PF Sqn). The unit would become one of the most significant ever formed within the 9th Air Force, although this has been played down to such an extent that it has almost disappeared in the history of the Second World War.

Cottesmore was a very busy place. The resident 316th TCG had over 70 aircraft and this resulted in the Pathfinder School looking for a new home, preferably not too far away. North Witham, a few miles to the north-east, was the obvious choice and the school's C-47s departed on 22nd March 1944 for the short flight over the border into Lincolnshire.

For the groups based at the Northern Carrier Group bases, emphasis was placed on paratroop operations, as the TCGs were too far north to tow gliders all the way to northern France. This kind of operation came easily to the 316th TCG as they had taken part in many such paratroop drops during their tour in the Mediterranean. The Group trained with the Leicestershire based 82nd Airborne and were up to scratch with this unit by the end of March. Although not tasked, the Group still practised glider towing from Cottesmore and were fully trained in this operation in case they were called upon to carry it out.

The officer commanding the 316th TCG, Lieutenant Colonel Burton R Fleet who was tragically killed in a mid-air collision near March in Cambridgeshire, during Exercise Eagle on 12th May 1944. (316th TCG Unit History.)

111

A full pre-invasion dress rehearsal was carried out on 11/12th May 1944 and was named Exercise *Eagle*. All three wings of the 9th Air Force TCC took part in the exercise, with the 52nd TCW providing 369 aircraft. The exercise was described as being 'as near to the real thing as it gets'. The aircraft from the 52nd TCW were ordered to assemble over March in Cambridgeshire and proceed south-west to various drop zones in the Devizes area in Wiltshire. The operation was going well for the 316th, with all of the 82nd Airborne paratroops delivered to their correct drop zones at the right time, and the Group cruised back to the same Cambridgeshire assembly area ready for the return to their respective bases. It was during this stage of the exercise that disaster struck as the lead planes of the 36th and 44th TCS collided whilst circling over March. Both aircraft came down between the Fenland villages of Benwick and Doddington and all on board were killed. Amongst the dead were the pilots of the two aircraft – Lieutenant Colonel Burton L Fleet (who was also the 316th TCG Commander) and Lieutenant Joe Sharber – plus the Group Chaplain, Captain Floyd N Richert, who had gone along for the ride. Losing two aircraft in a single exercise would come as a shock to any Group, but to lose its commander, chaplain and several crew as well was tough to bear. The next day, the difficult task of taking command of the 316th befell Colonel Harvey A. Berger, only weeks before the unit was to take part in one of the greatest airborne operations in history.

In late May 1944, hundreds of soldiers from the 82nd Airborne Division began to arrive on station in preparation for the D-Day invasion. The individual units that would fly from Cottesmore were the 2nd and 3rd Battalions of the 505th Parachute Infantry Brigade (PIR) with several artillerymen of the 456th Parachute Field Artillery Battalion (PFAB). All were accommodated inside Cottesmore's big 'C' Type hangars and security was stepped up on station, with all resident personnel confined to the station. After several false alarms regarding whether they were to go or not, the green light was finally given on the evening of 5th June, when 1,276 troops filed across the airfield to board the C-47s and C-53s that were waiting for them. 72 aircraft were involved in the operation from the 316th TCG and the first C-47 left Cottesmore at approximately 22:00 hours, heading for the Wing assembly point east of Birmingham. Their objective, along with 48 aircraft from the 315th TCG at Spanhoe, was Drop Zone (DZ) 'O', which was a collection of fields to the north-west of Ste Mère Église in Normandy.

The massed formation followed a chain of lights and beacons which were positioned at 30 mile intervals all the way to the DZ. Navigational aids were placed on ships in the channel to make the journey as straightforward as possible for the troop carrier aircraft. An hour earlier, the Pathfinder School aircraft had dropped their troops and they were busy setting up beacons at the DZs to guide the main force in. An unexpected cloud bank appeared near many of the DZs, causing several drops to be made much higher than planned. Not to be deterred, though, the 316th managed to deliver the majority of its 82nd Airborne paratroopers to the right location and its part in the operation was later assessed as one of the most accurate. All but two wounded paratroopers had dropped, one crew member was killed and at least twelve aircraft had been damaged by small arms fire. On the return to Cottesmore at 04:00 hours, the 316th TCG was still in the same tight formation which had left Rutland only a few hours before. For the Group, this initial operation was a total success.

The following day, a resupply mission was launched, called *Freeport*, in support of the 82nd Airborne troops, who had become temporarily bogged down in the Ste Mère Église area.

A Douglas C-47, nicknamed Michael, of the 44th TCS soaks up the sun at Cottesmore. (D Wills.)

Two hundred and eight aircraft took part in the mission, which involved TCGs from the 52nd TCW, including 52 aircraft from Cottesmore. The day did not start well for the 316th; two C-47s of the 36th TCS collided while taxiing into position ready for take-off. Both aircraft were seriously damaged; the nose of one C-47 was almost sliced off, killing the pilot instantly. After a delayed departure, the remaining 50 aircraft began to leave Cottesmore at 03:30 hours on a second journey to Normandy.

Compared with the previous day's success, the operation was a near disaster, as many aircraft lost contact with the main formation after encountering thick cloud in the assembly area. Many aircraft then became lost on the way to the DZs, even though the same navigational aids were in place. On their arrival over France, the German defences were more prepared for their arrival and several aircraft were shot down. One hundred and fifty aircraft managed to drop their supplies in or around the DZ, although a certain amount did fall into enemy hands. Many of the 316th TCG's aircraft suffered flak and small arms damage and that included the C-47 being flown by Colonel Berger. Luckily, none was shot down. At least two aircraft returned to Cottesmore on one engine, and the expected tight formation return to airfield did not happen; instead damaged C-47s limped home in dribs and drabs. Several more resupply missions were flown from Cottesmore, but with the rapid advance of the Allied forces through France, the Group prepared for new challenges.

For the next few months, several airborne operations were planned for the 316th, but the speed of the Allied advance cancelled all of them. The TCG continued to fly supply missions into France and returned to a routine of training and exercises at Cottesmore, with more emphasis on glider towing, which would feature more strongly in the near future.

Considering how many aircraft were using Cottesmore at this time, air accidents were relatively infrequent. But a spate during June and July 1944 highlighted what a dangerous place an airfield could be. Most TCGs had a collection of liaison type aircraft at their disposal and the 316th was no exception, a few Piper L-4B Grasshoppers being used by the Group. On 14th June, Lieutenant Frederic I Barlow landed heavily in an L-4B, 43-724. The aircraft was wrecked but Barlow escaped with minor injuries. On 30th June, the crew of a visiting Douglas A-20, 43-

10194, of the 416th Bombardment Group, based at Wethersfield in Essex, were not so lucky. The pilot, Lieutenant Scott B Ritchie Junior, and his crew were killed instantly when their twin engined light bomber crashed after take-off, one mile north of the airfield.

An Armstrong Whitworth Albemarle ST.1, P1601 glider tug from the Operational and Refresher Training Unit (ORTU), based at Hampstead Norris in Berkshire, experienced engine problems when in the vicinity of Cottesmore on 28th July 1944. The Albemarle was towing an Airspeed Horsa at the time and, wisely, chose to release the heavy glider over the airfield before attempting an emergency landing. On approach to the main runway, both engines of the Albemarle failed and the aircraft crash landed just short of the runway. All escaped injury and the Albemarle was considered for repair, but was struck off charge later in the year.

The 316th TCG had to wait until September 1944 before they were involved in another major airborne operation. *Market* was the airborne assault of Holland, specifically designed to capture the important bridges at Nijmegen, Arnhem and Grave in the Netherlands. Operation *Market Garden* was a bold plan designed to use the three divisions of the 1st Allied Airborne Army to take the bridges which lay in the path of General Montgomery's advancing forces.

Once again, Cottesmore's aircraft would carry troops of the 82nd Airborne, who had by now established a permanent detachment in one of the airfield's 'C' Type hangars. On the morning of 17th September, soldiers of the 1st Battalion, 505th PIR and its divisional HQ prepared to leave Cottesmore for DZ 'N', which was south of the town of Groesbeek. The first of 45 aircraft began to leave the airfield at 10:35, and within fifteen minutes they were all on their way. That same morning troops of the 1st Battalion, 504th PIR also departed Cottesmore, this time in 32 aircraft. Their task was to drop the paratroopers at a DZ near to the village of Overasselt.

This first *Market* mission was a total success, the 316th lost only one aircraft when it had to ditch in the sea on its way home. The crew were picked up by an air sea rescue launch a few hours later. The following day, aircraft of the 52nd TCW were called upon to take part in another *Market* operation and, this time, each aircraft would be towing a Waco CG-42 assault glider. Eighty-two aircraft were made available by the 316th, and the cargo this time was the 319th and 456th Field Artillery Battalions (FAB), complete with 38 jeeps and 575 mm Howitzers, 384 troops and nearly 44,000lbs of vital equipment. Fog and low cloud at Cottesmore delayed the departure of this impressive fleet of aircraft but, once airborne, the force found their relevant DZs with little difficulty. The main DZ was also near Groesbeek so it was a familiar sight but, despite this, several gliders were launched either early or too late. The latter was a particularly tragic error as the gliders came down in enemy held territory and 45 men of the 319th FAB were either killed or captured. All 82 aircraft returned safely to Cottesmore, but many had received flak damage as the German forces had significantly strengthened their positions since the previous day's operation.

Poor weather prevented any further missions to Holland until 23rd September, when 89 C-47s and their gliders were assembled at Cottesmore. Soldiers of the 325th Glider Infantry Regiment (GIR), two batteries of the 80th Airborne Anti-Aircraft Battalion, the 508th Command Vehicles and divisional reconnaissance platoon were all delivered to a DZ near Overasselt between 16:24 and 16:59 hours. All of the gliders were released at the correct moment and, out of the 2,900 troops that were dropped, only ten were unfit to fight. Two of the 316th TCG's C-47s failed to return, both victims of the intense flak barrage that the German defenders managed to put up; numerous others returned to Cottesmore with damage.

During ground fighting in the Grave area, Allied forces managed to capture a grass fighter strip at Oud Keent, west of Grave. Its potential as a forward air-head was quickly realised and plans were made to land a British air supply unit called an Airborne Forward Delivery Airfield Group (AFDAG) and place several anti-aircraft batteries around the airfield. The 216 aircraft of the 52nd TCW, including 72 from Cottesmore, were quickly rallied into action and, on 26th September, flew 105 men of the AFDAG, several war correspondents and nearly 150 tons of equipment into the grass airfield. The mission was a success. However, it tempted disaster, as over 40 German fighters were fast approaching. With over 150 C-47s on the ground at the time, it was thanks to excellent Allied fighter cover that the day was saved and 32 enemy aircraft were shot down.

During December 1944 and January 1945, two new American aircraft made an appearance at Cottesmore. The first was a conversion of the Consolidated B-24 Liberator in fuel transporters. The C-109 was a tanker conversion of the B-24E (and later B-24D), able to carry 2,415 imperial gallons of fuel in metal tanks in the fuselage. Two were assigned to the 316th TCG and several crews were trained to fly the C-109, but very little use was made of the tankers and they were all eventually transferred to the 349th TCG, based at Barkston Heath in Lincolnshire.

The other new arrival was the underrated Curtiss C-46 Commando twin engined transporter. More common in the Pacific theatre, the Commando was capable of carrying more paratroops and greater loads than the C-47 but arrived too late in the war to make any significant impact on the 9th Air Force TCGs. Only two C-46Ds arrived at Cottesmore to equip the 44th TCS; this later variant had an additional door on the starboard side of the fuselage to make it easier to load.

Orders were received in February 1945 by the 52nd TCW HQ at Exton Hall to move out and occupy an airfield at Amiens in

A Curtiss C-46 Commando of the 316th TCG parked in front of Cottesmore's hangars, with the original wartime control tower in the background. (L Drake Collection.)

France. The 52nd Wing moved on 5th March. With the HQ's move came a torrent of rumours that the 316th TCG would be moving as well, and it was hoped that a return to the USA was in order, as the Group had been overseas for almost three and half years.

Fears that the Luftwaffe would find Cottesmore and many other Troop Carrier airfields too much of a temptation were realised on the night of 3rd/4th March 1945. Even though the war was drawing to a close, the Luftwaffe still managed to carry out Operation *Gisela* and cause destruction and chaos to both aircraft and airfields. At 01:00 hours the station air raid 'Red' was sounded and, less than half an hour later, seventeen anti-personnel bombs were dropped across the airfield by an unidentified twin-engined German intruder. Luckily no one was injured, but a pair of C-47s and a Waco glider were damaged and superficial damage was caused to part of the perimeter track. The night was more costly for Bomber Command and, in particular, 1651 Conversion Unit (CU), which was based at nearby Woolfox Lodge. At 01:15 hours the first of two Avro Lancaster Mk.IIIs was shot down – ND378, with Flight Sergeant A Howard at the controls, was brought down near Woolfox Lodge, and only the rear gunner survived. Twenty minutes later, JB899 was desperately trying to shake off the attentions of the same night fighter, but succumbed to its fire over Cottesmore. The Lancaster plunged into the ground only 500 yards away from the airfield's control tower. It was totally destroyed and its pilot, Flight Lieutenant D J Baum, and his crew stood no chance.

Before the 316th TCG could even be considered for return to the US, the Group was to take part in the final major airborne operation of the war. *Varsity* was the Allied assault across the Rhine, which, at this point in the war, was the last major obstacle before Berlin. The three groups of the 52nd Wing that still remained in England, the 61st, 315th and 316th TCGs, were given the job of delivering paratroops of the British 6th Airborne Division. To make the journey shorter, the Groups were allocated three forward operating bases in Essex at Boreham, Chipping Ongar and Wethersfield. The 316th was given the latter and 80 left Cottesmore for its temporary home on the night of 20/21st March 1945. Operation *Varsity* began on the morning of 24th March and 40 aircraft of the 316th joined the 61st TCG aircraft in

Despite suffering serious flak damage during its part in Operation Varsity, this C-47 of the 37th TCS still managed to make it home to Cottesmore. (L Drake Collection.)

a lead group, carrying the 3rd Parachute Brigade into action. They were followed by 40 more 316th aircraft which, along with the 315th TCG, were carrying the 5th Parachute Brigade. The destination for the two formations was near the Diersfordter Wald, north-west of Wesel. The flight into the DZ was straightforward and unopposed, but once the British paratroops were dropped and the first formation turned for home, the German flak defences opened up. The second formation was hit worst of all – ten aircraft were shot down into enemy territory and another seven had to force-land behind Allied lines. Over 70 aircraft were damaged in the second Group; the 316th alone suffered, with initial reports of twelve aircraft missing, but personnel losses were limited to a dozen aircrew. The original *Varsity* plan dictated that the 316th aircraft would land at a French airfield, but the airfield chosen was not ready in time to accommodate the Group. The majority of the Group's aircraft returned direct to Cottesmore, and by 13:00 hours the survivors were all on the ground. *Varsity* was a success as far as delivering the 6th Airborne was concerned, but this final wartime mission for the 316th TCG was a costly one.

The dream of returning home became reality for personnel of the 316th when it was announced in mid-April that the Group was to leave Cottesmore. With the exception of a few C-47s, all of the Group's equipment was dispersed to other TCGs, including the 349th TCG, which collected all of the remaining gliders with their C-46 Commandos. The last aircraft left Cottesmore, bound for Pope Field in North Carolina, on 14th May, and all the remaining American personnel had left by 11th June 1945.

Station 489 became RAF Cottesmore again on 1st July 1945, when the airfield was transferred back to the RAF and became part of 7 (Training) Group, Bomber Command. At the end of July, Bottesford's station commander, Group Captain J H T Simpson, inspected the airfield in preparation for the move of 1668 Heavy Conversion Unit (HCU). Cottesmore was found to be in order, but it was not until 1st September that an advance party from the HCU arrived in preparation for the new arrivals. Between 15th and 17th September, the HCU's Avro Lancaster Mk.Is and Mk.IIIs, a pair of Spitfire Mk.Vs and two Beaufighter Mk.VIs were all resident at Cottesmore. The training continued much the same as it had at Bottesford, but on a greatly reduced scale, as the demand for bomber crews was diminishing.

On 21st December 1945, the station was transferred to 91 Group Bomber Command, but this made no difference to the HCU's activities. Like so many other post-war RAF units, 1668 HCU's days were numbered and it began to shrink in size in February 1946 as, one by one, its Lancasters were resigned to the scrap heap. On 7th March 1946, the unit was disbanded, but even during its short time at Cottesmore it had managed to train 57 crews and fly for 4,285 hours.

For the next eight years, all of Cottesmore's flying activities centered around the training role and it was now the turn of 16 Operational Training Unit (OTU), which moved in from Upper Heyford in Oxfordshire on the 1st March 1946. The role of the OTU was changed in March 1947, when all bombing training was stopped and its role moved from operational to crew training. Renamed 204 Advanced Flying School (AFS) on 15th March, and now equipped with Mosquito T.3s and FB.6s and the odd Tiger Moth and Auster, the AFS remained at Cottesmore until 10th March 1948, when it moved to Driffield in Yorkshire. The AFS was replaced by another training unit, which was first formed at Peterborough in December 1935; 7 Flying Training School (FTS) moved from Kirton in Lindsey in Lincolnshire on 16th April 1948.

7 FTS was equipped with the venerable Tiger Moth and the North American Harvard T.2bs, and its main task was to train pilots for the Royal Navy, but it also ran RAF pilot refresher and instrument rating courses.

Congestion at Cottesmore was becoming a problem in the early 1950s and, to alleviate this, three other airfields were made available for the FTS. Relief Landing Grounds were used at Wittering in Northamptonshire, Woolfox Lodge in Rutland, and Spitalgate near Grantham, which was shared with the RAF College aircraft from Cranwell in Lincolnshire. With the Korean war at an end, the demand for FTSs was diminishing and 7 FTS officially disbanded at Cottesmore on 14th April 1954. During their six years at the airfield, 7 FTS performed up to 2,500 sorties per month and hundreds of pilots gained their wings. The school was re-formed at Valley in Anglesey on 1st June 1954, and was renamed 202 AFS. The unit brought in a new age of pilot training by re-equipping with de Havilland Vampire T.11.

After the departure of the FTS, the airfield became part of 3 Group, Bomber Command and was introduced to the jet age when it received four English Electric Canberra squadrons: 15, 44, 57 and 149 Squadrons were all equipped with the B.2 version of this excellent twin-engined jet bomber. 149 Squadron's stay was brief. It departed for Ahlhorn in West Germany on 24th August 1954 and became the first Canberra unit to join the 2nd Allied Tactical Air Force. It was also during 1954 that Cottesmore was selected as one of the new V-Bomber bases and all trace of the wartime layout disappeared beneath a single 3,000 yard runway, which was the requirement for the new heavy jet bombers.

Included in the alterations were new taxiways and dispersal points, all capable of supporting aircraft of over 220,000lbs in weight – over three and half times that of a fully loaded Avro Lancaster! The airfield was re-opened in March 1958 under the command of the wartime fighter ace, Group Captain J E 'Johnnie' Johnson DSO, DFC. The first V-Bombers to arrive were Vickers Valiant B.1s of 90 and 199 Squadrons from Honington, which were attached to the station while the runway surfacing at their home airfield was completed. It was a good initial test of the airfield's new facilities, and paved the way for a more permanent resident, which arrived on 9th April.

Cottesmore's status as one of the RAF's premier stations was reflected in the number of VIP visits that occurred there. Princess Margaret and the Duchess of Kent presented standards to both squadrons in 1958 and 1961. The Prime Minister, Harold Macmillan, the Shah of Persia and King Hussein of Jordan all visited the Rutland airfield; King Hussein was treated to a 70-minute flight in a 10 Squadron Victor.

During 1961, the new improved Victor B.2 was being prepared for service with the RAF, and Cottesmore was chosen as the venue for the flying trials of the new aircraft. The first trained crews left Cottesmore on 26th January 1962, bound for Wittering, to begin the re-formation of 139 Squadron, another Victor V-Bomber unit.

'C' Flight of the OCU was renamed the Victor Training Flight and moved on 31st March 1964 to Wittering, a station which was fast becoming the centre for Victor V-Bomber operations. With this in mind, Cottesmore's role was once again changing and, on 1st March, 10 Squadron was disbanded as a bomber squadron and was re-formed within Transport Command on 1st July 1966, flying the Vickers VC-10; it still operates the tanker version today. The disbandment of 15 Squadron followed on 31st October, but the disappearance of the Victor did not remove Cottesmore from the V-Force operations.

On 2nd November 1964, Avro Vulcan B.2s of 9, 12 and 35 Squadrons all arrived from Coningsby in Lincolnshire and the Cottesmore Wing was formed. Like the Victors before them, the role of the Wing was to maintain both their nuclear and conventional capabilities and continue training for this role. Many overseas deployments, exercises and goodwill visits were carried out by the Wing aircraft.

Changes in the Government's defence policy affected both Cottesmore and the RAF as a whole during the late 1960s. The United Kingdom's nuclear deterrent was transferred to the Royal Navy and this caused a dramatic reduction in the V-Force squadrons. As a result, 12 Squadron became the first victim of the policy change at Cottesmore, and was disbanded on the 31st December 1967. The following year, a shake-up of the RAF as

122

whole resulted in the amalgamation of Bomber Command and Fighter Command, to become Strike Command, on 30th April 1968. Cottesmore was now under the control of 1 (Bomber) Group and, in a move to add security to NATO's southern flank, the remaining Vulcan squadrons at Cottesmore would relocate to warmer climes at Akrotiri in Cyprus. The first of 9 and 35 Squadrons' aircraft began to leave Cottesmore in January 1969, but the last four Vulcans did not leave the Rutland airfield until 19th March.

Within a few weeks, the role of the station changed yet again, and in April 1969 three squadrons arrived from Watton in Norfolk – 98 and 360 Squadrons, flying Canberras, and 115 Squadron, flying Bitteswell-built Armstrong Whitworth Argosy E.1s. These squadrons were joined by 231 OCU from Bassingbourne in Cambridgeshire (also flying Canberras) on 19th May and, once again, Cottesmore was covered in aircraft.

A radical defence review in 1975 resulted in the closure of twelve RAF airfields, and this affected operations at Cottesmore as well. 360 Squadron moved to Wyton, Cambridgeshire in August 1975; next, the OCU and 115 Squadron moved in February 1976 to Marham in Norfolk and Brize Norton in Oxfordshire respectively. The same month, 98 Squadron was disbanded, and all its aircraft were transferred to 100 Squadron at Marham.

The airfield was placed under care and maintenance for the next two years, and extensive work was carried out in preparation for its new role as the Tri-National Tornado Testing Establishment (TTTE). Opened on 1st July 1978, the TTTE received its first Panavia Tornados on 1st July 1980. Cottesmore would now train all crews, pilots and navigators who would fly the British, German and Italian Tornadoes. The TTTE became Cottesmore's longest serving unit but, sadly, under pressure from three countries' economic strategies, the unit flew its last sortie on 19th March 1999.

With the withdrawal of the Harrier force from Germany and the subsequent closure of its Gutersloh home, both 3 and 4 Squadrons took up residence at Cottesmore. BAe Harrier GR.7s of 4 Squadron arrived first on 13th April, followed by 3 Squadron's Harriers on the 11th May 1999. Cottesmore obviously suited the operation of the versatile jump-jet, and the announcement on 1st April 2000 that a new 'Joint Force Harrier' was to be formed strengthened its position. More Harriers arrived on 28th July when, after spending 31 years at Wittering, 1 Squadron joined the force at Cottesmore. At this stage, planning was conducted to move 800 and 801 Naval Air Squadrons equipped with the Sea Harrier, to Cottesmore. Unfortunately, on 28th February 2002, the Secretary of State for Defence announced that these aircraft would no longer be moving to Cottesmore although the Royal Navy personnel would. The intention is to start disbanding the Sea Harrier squadrons in 2004, ultimately enabling both RAF and RN personnel to operate an all Harrier GR.9 fleet by 2007. Cottesmore has now become one of the busiest airfields in the country, and the Harrier, like the Tornado before it, will remain a familiar sight over Rutland until at least 2012, when the proposed multi-role Joint Strike Fighter will replace it.

8

DESFORD

National Grid Reference SK478020; 6½ miles SW of Leicester

Anyone visiting the former airfield at Desford today will be bitterly disappointed with what lies before them. The vision of a pristine large grass airfield surrounded by equally attractive buildings has unfortunately disappeared forever. Instead the modern-day visitor will be presented with two factory complexes, totalling over 1 million square feet, owned by the successful American company Caterpillar. Only sharp-eyed individuals will notice that a few hangars still survive, although even they are incorporated into part of the factory.

Desford can trace its routes back to the First World War, when an emergency landing ground for 38 (Home Defence) Squadron was established south of Desford village in 1916. Several landing grounds of this nature were built around the Midlands in an attempt to deal with Zeppelin attacks. It was named Peckleton after the village about a mile and a half to the south, even though it was actually closer to Desford. It was little used by the squadron's Be.2s and Be.12s and, after being briefly upgraded to a night landing ground, it was closed and returned to farmland at the end of 1918.

Over ten years elapsed before any further interest in the old landing ground was shown. The Leicestershire Aero Club (LAC) was formed in 1929 and its members were scouring the area for suitable flying fields to operate from. After encountering many obstacles in their quest, they inspected the Peckleton site and an agreement was quickly reached with the landowner. On 21st

125

May 1929, nearly twenty acres of land was made available, followed by a further fourteen acres a few weeks later.

Enthusiast club members immediately set to work, turning the fields into a proper flying ground. Buildings were also acquired for use as a clubhouse and small hangar. By the end of August, more land had been acquired and the clubhouse and hangar facilities were expanded. In early September, work had progressed to such an extent that the field was fit to receive its first aircraft, a de Havilland DH.60M Moth G-AAIF, donated by the LAC's president, Lindsay Everard. A few days later, 'Desford Field' was officially opened, on 14th September, with a two day air show, or 'Leicestershire's First Great Air Pageant', as it was known at the time. The weekend was a great success, with over 30,000 people and many aircraft attending, including three Armstrong Whitworth Siskins from 3 Flying Training School at Grantham, Lincolnshire.

The club continued, going from strength to strength and with membership and aircraft based at Desford on the increase. Bigger and more adventurous displays were organised for the following year. A four day event over the Easter holiday in April 1930 was unfortunately disrupted by poor weather. The reputation of the club and the facilities put it in a good position to be included in the King's Cup air race on 5th July. The airfield was used as a turning point in the annual 750 mile race, and the general public could pay to watch as 62 aircraft out of 88 starters passed over Desford.

Desford was not shy of visits from dignitaries at this time either; the Prince of Wales flew in on 6th June 1932 on his way to opening the Leicestershire Agricultural Show. Sir Alan Cobham made the first of several visits to Desford in 1932 as well, bringing his entourage of display aircraft with which he toured the country.

Back in 1928, the LAC looked at an airfield at Braunstone on the western edge of Leicester, and at that time it was their preferred choice of site, but council complications prevented its use. The airfield was to become a municipal airport for Leicester and the LAC would manage the airfield for the city council. The LAC was due to move to Braunstone in the summer of 1934, but problems with the landing ground postponed the move until the following year.

The LAC was able to use Braunstone's facilities from November 1934, but they did not leave Desford until March 1935. Desford was now temporarily empty, with only model aircraft flying taking place. This was soon stopped, as Desford's role was about to change. The RAF were going through a period of change and expansion which required the training of more pilots. Thirteen civilian flying training units were set up throughout the country to train pilots for the RAF and an aircraft instrument maker called Reid and Sigrist (R&S), based in New Malden, Surrey, was awarded a contract to set up one of the schools.

Reid and Sigrist were well established in the design and manufacture of aviation instrumentation but, even though they had been awarded a contract to set up a flying school, they had no home airfield to operate from. A hasty search of the country by R&S's managing director, Squadron Leader George Reid, ended in a meeting with the owner of land at the airfield at Desford in August 1935. The Cart family had farmed the land since 1884 and John Cart, the farmer, was used to negotiating with individuals wanting to rent his land for aviation use. On this occasion, though, George Reid made Mr Cart an offer he could not refuse and purchased the existing aerodrome, along with Mr Cart's farm.

In early September, local contractors poured onto the site and set to work lifting hedges and trees and levelling the land to accommodate a new runway of nearly 1,000 yards in length. In a very short time, several new buildings appeared, including a large new hangar, lecture rooms, a first aid room, a parachute store and a bayed building for the use of emergency vehicles. Centrally heated bungalows were built to accommodate students and a large administration block was constructed, which contained more lecture rooms, offices and a photographic laboratory. To top it all, a modern clubhouse was built as a centrepiece of the new buildings. It contained a large lounge and dining room, complete with a control tower on top of the building. In only a few weeks, Desford was ready for a new unit, complete with new aircraft.

One of thirteen new Civil Flying Training Schools (CFTSs) was formed at Desford on 25th November 1935. The CFTS was, however, quickly renamed 7 Elementary and Reserve Flying Training School (E&RFTS) to accommodate service pilots from

Desford's old clubhouse, seen here in the 1950s. Built in 1935 it was positioned on the northern side of the airfield, at the junction of Desford and Peckleton Lanes.

the RAF Volunteer Reserve. This was not officially formed until April 1937, and the scheme enabled men between the ages of 18 and 25 to enrol as airman pilots with the rank of sergeant.

The aircraft flown by individual schools differed throughout the country, many schools choosing to fly the Hawker Hart, Hind or Miles Magister, but R&S made a wise choice by picking the de Havilland DH.82A Tiger Moth. The Tiger Moth is undoubtedly one of the world's most famous training aircraft, and it remained in RAF service for over 15 years. A development of the DH.60 Gipsy Moth, the first Tiger took to the air on 26th October 1931. Designed as a fully aerobatic trainer, the little biplane was an instant success with many civilian owners and operators. The Tiger Moth Mk.Is were powered by a 120 hp Gipsy Major engine but later on the main production version, the Tiger Mk.II, had a 130 hp Gipsy Major fitted. The following year, 1932, the first of many were ordered by the RAF. Production had reached over 1,000 by the outbreak of the Second World War. The majority of Tigers ordered before the Second World War served on E&RFTSs, equipping 44 out 52 schools by 1939.

This de Havilland DH.82A Tiger Moth II, R4922 served with 7 Elementary Flying Training School at Desford and was a common sight around the airfield until 1951. (P.H.T. Green Collection.)

The E&RFTS had its official opening ceremony at Desford on 13th December 1935 and it was attended by many local dignitaries. Viscount Swinton of Masham, who was the Minister of State for Air, had the honour of opening the new school and praised Reid and Sigrist for their speed and efficiency in getting the school established. By the end of the year, over twenty brand new bright yellow Tigers had been delivered and the first intake of many student pilots were being taught the basics of flying.

During the late 1930s, the RAF was increasing in size and this led to a close look at aircrew roles on the more complex aircraft that were now entering service. The old aircrew job of observer was under scrutiny and it was decided that this role had to be more flexible. Observers would now be trained in the multitask jobs of navigation, bomb aiming and gunnery and new schools were set up to accommodate the new training syllabus. 3 Civil Air Navigation School (CANS) was formed at Desford from 7 E&RFTS during August 1938. It was redesignated 3 Air Observer and Navigation School (AONS) the following year and mainly flew the Avro Anson.

The influx of personnel and students that came with the arrival of another unit meant that more building work was undertaken at Desford. At the north side of the airfield more accommodation bungalows were built, along with another hangar that had a new control tower on top. On the south side of the airfield, next to

Pre-war photograph of Desford taken from the airmen's crew room, showing student pilots relaxing between lessons.

Peckleton Common, another large hangar complex was built with more lecture rooms.

With the outbreak of the Second World War on 3rd September 1939, a few changes occurred at Desford. 7 E&RFTS had 'Reserve' dropped from its title and became 7 EFTS and all of the Tiger Moths, which numbered over 120 by now, were repainted with camouflage on their upper surfaces. The population on station continued to increase and temporary accommodation was built on the north and south sides of the airfield. The aircraft were now dispersed around the airfield in four separate flights so that there were no more neat rows of aircraft to tempt a German raider. A temporary landing ground was built at Kirkby Mallory and was allocated for use by Desford's Tigers, who would often use it to disperse the ever increasing population of aircraft.

Boulton Paul Defiant Mk.I N1673 visited Desford's CRO on at least three occasions between 1941 and 1943. (Via author.)

As at all training stations with many aircraft in the air at any one time, flying accidents were commonplace at Desford. In the first six months of 1940, sixteen Tigers were involved in various airborne misadventures; luckily, only a few airmen were hospitalised as a result.

On 11th July 1940, the Civilian Repair Organisation (CRO) was formed to relieve the pressure on the RAF units responsible for aircraft repair work and the manufacturers themselves. Many civilian companies were tasked throughout the country and R&S had the foresight to construct facilities at Desford to cope with such work well before the CRO was officially formed. A large hangar was built on the north side of Desford Lane, on the perimeter of the airfield, and a T2 hangar and several Blister type hangars were also constructed on the south side of Peckleton Common later on during the war. The first repair contract was completed by early 1940, when the first of many Boulton Paul Defiants arrived for repair. Many were flown in, while others were in such a poor state that they arrived by road on RAF 'Queen Mary' transporters. Later on, R&S won a contract to convert Defiants into target tugs and, by the end of the war, over 700 of all Defiants built had passed through Desford's CRO.

R&S, in conjunction with Air Service Training at Hamble in Hampshire, had also planned to carry out repairs on the Bell P-39 Airacobra. But, after an initial assessment by the RAF, the American fighter was found unsuitable for their requirements. Another American type was to become a common sight at Desford, though. The North American B-25 Mitchell first entered service with the RAF in September 1942, equipping 98 and 180 Squadrons at West Raynham in Norfolk. Over 800 of these twin-engined medium bombers were built for the RAF and R&S received its first aircraft from Boscombe Down in Wiltshire on 9th April 1943. Work carried out on these aircraft was mainly battle damage repair and by the war's end over 140 Mitchell Mk.Is and Mk.IIs had passed through the CRO at Desford. The last aircraft departed the airfield on 16th November 1945 and the CRO, sadly for the many civilian workers employed there, closed down.

A hangar originally occupied by 3 AONS on the south side of the airfield was visited by officials from Vickers Armstrong in late 1940. The aircraft manufacturer was based at Castle Bromwich, where there was increasing concern about German

Another aircraft handled by the CRO at Desford was the North American Mitchell. This particular aircraft is a Mk.III, HD375, and it passed through Desford in late 1944. (Via author.)

attacks on the factory. The solution was to disperse their operation throughout the Midlands and, in February 1941, Vickers Armstrong moved part of their Spitfire production to Desford. An additional Bellman hangar was constructed and the two hangars became No. 8 Factory, within a dispersal scheme. Component parts were brought into Desford and newly built Spitfires left the assembly shops after a few weeks. Spitfire Mk.IIas, followed by Mk.Vs and Mk.Ixes, were built at Desford, all main components being supplied by the Castle Bromwich works. On completion, every Spitfire was air tested by a test pilot from Castle Bromwich and on many occasions this was conducted by Alex Henshaw, who was in charge of the sixteen man test pilot team. Henshaw was already a legend as a result of his pre-war racing efforts which had won him a King's Cup Air Race in 1938. He tested many aircraft for the Castle Bromwich works including the Hawker Hurricane and Avro Lancaster, one of which he rolled with a full crew on board as witnesses!

An exact figure for the quantity of Spitfires assembled by No. 8 Factory workers at Desford is not known, but an estimate of nearly 1,000 aircraft would be a conservative one.

The RS.1 'Snargasher' was a three-seater that Reid and Sigrist designed to serve as an advanced trainer for the teaching of navigation, bombing, wireless telephony or gunnery. (Via author.)

R&S launched itself into building an aircraft of its own in early 1938. Known unimaginatively as the RS.1 Trainer, the aircraft was brought to Desford for final assembly and flight tests. The RS.1 was an attractive twin engined, three-seater monoplane that was intended as a mass production trainer for the RAF. Unfortunately, the RAF showed little interest in the RS.1, which R&S workers named 'Snargasher'. The aircraft was utilised by 7 EFTS in 1941 in a training experiment which was a veiled attempt to raise service interest in the type. Although used for several months by the flying school, with good results, the RAF was already settled with the Anson and the Oxford for its multi-engine training.

Desford was visited on many occasions by aircraft that were lost or in difficulties, and nearly all were caught out by the lack of space that Desford offered. A Bristol Blenheim IV overshot its landing run and hit a gun emplacement on 8th July 1941. A Douglas Havoc from Wittering in Northamptonshire did the same in November 1941, followed on 21st February 1942 by a Handley Page Hampden that also ran out of runway. None of these incidents was classed as serious, but care had to taken with larger aircraft.

Tiger Moth accidents varied from heavy landings to fatal mid-air collisions, the latter being less common. With so many Tigers on 7 EFTS's strength, an area in one of Desford's hangars was allocated to the repair and servicing of the aircraft. At one point during the war, more than 70 people were employed on a production line keeping the Tigers in the air, many of them women who, after training, became very skilful fabric repairers.

During late 1942, both 7 EFTS aircraft and personnel from Desford were involved in a variety of local exercises. A two-week Army Co-operation exercise was held in September and included the use of Tiger Moths as enemy aircraft, simulating dive bombing on the units involved. This was followed on 10th October by Operation *Partridge*, which was a ground exercise to test the airfield defences at Desford. Aircraft were involved in the final exercise of the year, when 7 EFTS's Tigers again simulated enemy aircraft bombing and machine gunning troop concentration. This time, the Leicester Home Guard were on the receiving end.

In hindsight, it is almost comical to think of some of the mishaps that Desford's Tigers experienced. There were two incidents of Tigers striking hangars in 1942. LAC Jamieson stalled on to the roof of the north hangar, while LAC Denton had a memorable first solo when he did the same onto the roof of the south hangar a few weeks later. Tigers landed on top of each other, tipped over on starting and taxied into bowsers, buildings and windsocks, often without injury to the student pilot. While student pilots struggled to land Tigers at Desford, the pilot of a 106 Squadron Lancaster was presented with the problem of diverting from his large home base of Syerston at night into the small grass airfield at Desford. Ordered to divert because weather had closed the Nottinghamshire bomber station, the pilot of W4367, a Lancaster Mk.I, touched down on the damp grass and almost made it into the airfield without mishap. In the darkness, the pilot did not see a pair of parked Tigers and clipped one and then wrote off the other. Despite this, the pilot skillfully brought the big bomber to a halt within the boundary of the airfield, and the Lancaster only suffered minor damage to its tail and propellers. Quickly repaired, the Lancaster rejoined 106 Squadron only to be lost along with 33 other bombers on a disastrous raid to Gelsenkirchen on 25/26th June 1943.

Emergency services from the station had been called when a pair of USAAF Republic P-47 Thunderbolts collided near the airfield earlier in the year. But, up until the 10th October 1943, no American aircraft had attempted an emergency landing at Desford. Boeing B-17F Flying Fortress *Yankee Girl* was returning from a raid on rail and canal targets near Munster, when the aircraft became lost on return to its home base at Grafton Underwood in Northamptonshire. The Fortress was from the 547th Bombardment Squadron, part of the 384th Bombardment Group, and piloted by 2nd Lieutenant William E Kopf. It was more by luck than judgment that Kopf and his nine-man crew found themselves over Desford, by now very short of fuel. Kopf was used to landing such an aircraft on a runway twice the size but, faced with no choice, the B-17 landed at 17:30, carrying far too much speed. The American bomber sped across the airfield and crashed into No. 8 Factory's Bellman hangar, injuring only two of the crew. The aircraft was later dismantled on site, being damaged beyond repair.

Training continued unabated throughout 1944 with many Tigers and the odd visiting aircraft 'making a mess of it' on Desford's grass runway. One of the year's victims was the resident RS.1 Snargasher, which continued to be used as a liaison aircraft, and was also still flown by a few privileged student pilots. Unfortunately, during the summer of 1944, a Canadian student pilot made a heavy landing in the Snargasher, the undercarriage collapsed and this caused a lot of damage. R&S considered repairing their first aircraft, but the damage was so severe that all of the components except the fuselage were scrapped. The remains were tucked away in the corner of a hangar and lingered on until 1953, when the RS.1 Snargasher was cleared out and burnt.

With the end of the Second World War, the workload and demand for new pilots dramatically decreased. 7 EFTS had made a major contribution to the war effort, with several thousand pilots gaining their wings through the efforts of the R&S school. The CRO's repair of Defiants and Mitchells and No. 8 Factory's Spitfire production had also made their own mark, never to be forgotten by all who worked there. The painful process of making a loyal workforce redundant began in late 1945, with all at Desford affected.

R&S attempted a recovery in the summer of 1945 when it unveiled its second design, the RS.3, which was named after its home airfield, 'Desford'. The RS.3 was similar to the RS.1, but had much slimmer lines and a two-seat tandem accommodation; once again, the aircraft was intended as a multi-engined basic trainer like its predecessor. The RS.3 Desford flew for the first time on 9th July 1945, instantly displaying excellent flying characteristics and receiving flattering reviews in all the aviation literature of the time.

The fully aerobatic RS.3 attracted a lot of attention, much of it from overseas, with many displays being put on for visitors from Argentina, Egypt and Spain. But, even though the aircraft was offered for sale in a variety of different guises, including crop spraying, not a single order was received. The RS.3 then spent the next few years languishing at the back of a hangar until the Air Council bought the aircraft in May 1949.

The RS.3 was to be involved in ground-breaking prone pilot experiments and this would involve redesigning the front of the aircraft to accommodate a pilot. The original rear cockpit now contained a conventionally seated pilot, but the RS.3's front cockpit was removed, and the nose extended to include a full set

The RS.4 Desford, later known as the Bobsleigh, was Reid and Sigrist's final design. Although G-AGOS went on to complete a varied and full flying career, no orders were forthcoming for more aircraft. The RS.4 survives today in storage at the Snibston Discovery Park, near Coalville. (Author.)

of controls and sufficient room for the prone pilot. The RS.3 was officially redesignated RS.4 and renamed Bobsleigh, gaining the military serial VZ728. The RS.4 Bobsleigh flew for the first time on 13th June 1951 and spent much of its time carrying out tests at the Royal Aircraft Establishment at Farnborough in Hampshire. Sold by the Air Ministry in 1955, the Bobsleigh passed through many owners before it returned to Leicestershire in 1991. Unfortunately, at present, the RS.4 Bobsleigh is in storage at Snibston Discovery Park, patiently waiting to be restored and displayed for the general public to enjoy.

7 EFTS continued to reduce in size throughout 1946 and by the end of May 1947 had only five officers, fifteen other ranks and three training officers remaining as permanent staff. R&S, like many other companies at the time, purchased a few ex-service aircraft with the intention of converting them for civilian use. With so many surplus aircraft around, the venture met with little success and work for the R&S aircraft involved only pleasure flights.

On 9th May 1947, control of the airfield moved to 64 Group, Reserve Command and an upsurge of activity followed. The EFTS was renamed 7 Reserve Flying School (RFS) and the aircraft and training remained the same as in wartime days. Tiger Moths remained at Desford until 1951, when they were replaced by Percival Prentices. The departure of the Tigers brought to an end a sixteen-year association with the biplane trainer; the Prentice could never replace the magic of the Moth.

Events overseas, including the Berlin blockade and then the Korean war, resulted in the activation of several new units. 1969 Air Observation Post (AOP) was formed as part of 664 (AOP) Squadron, which was based at Hucknall in Nottinghamshire. They were equipped with the Rearsby-built Auster AOP.6s and T.7, employing their aircraft in the role of spotter and observing the results of artillery fire. 1969 AOP's stay at Desford was short, the unit returning to the HQ airfield at Hucknall in January 1953.

Demand for fully trained National Service pilots resulted in the formation of a new unit at Desford in January 1952. 5 Basic Flying Training School (BFTS) flew the de Havilland DHC-1

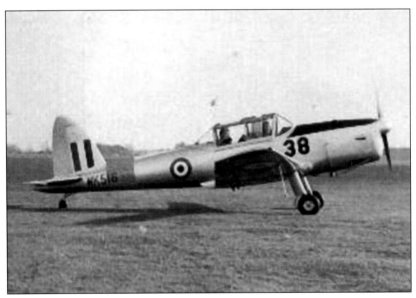

A de Havilland Canada Chipmunk T.10 WK516 taxies along the grass at Desford after another training flight with 5 Basic Flying Training School.

Chipmunk T.10, a more worthy replacement of its older brother, the Tiger Moth. The Chipmunk was a two-seat tandem, low wing trainer and would remain in RAF service even longer than the Tigers. In the short time that 5 BFTS was active at Desford, it had the misfortune to lose four aircraft in accidents. The final accident unfortunately was a fatal mid-air collision between Chipmunk WK506, piloted by Pilot Officer K W Mitchell, and another 5 BFTS Chipmunk, WG478. Mitchell's aircraft struck a glancing blow from above, behind and to the left of the aircraft, but suffered critical damage when the propeller of the other aircraft cut through the rear fuselage. Mitchell's Chipmunk was sliced into two parts and he had no chance or time to escape the crippled aircraft before it crashed near Kirby Muxloe.

The end of aircraft operations at Desford was swift: a parliamentary statement in December 1952 announced that National Service pilots were to be reduced and training schools operated by civilian contractors were to close. This was a double blow for Desford and R&S. Both 7 RFS and 5 BFTS would be affected. 5 BFTS was disbanded on 30th June 1953, followed by 7 RFS on 31st July 1953. R&S decided to sell the airfield, as no more government contracts existed, and the airfield officially closed in early August 1953.

9

LEICESTER EAST

National Grid Reference SK656015 4 miles SE of Leicester

In 1932, a regional planning report for Leicestershire proposed that a municipal airport could be built on the eastern side of the city, near the village of Stoughton. The site lost out to Braunstone, located on the western side of the city, which was opened in July 1935 as Leicester's new airport.

The eastern area therefore remained as farmland until a visit by Air Ministry officials in 1942, followed by the sale of nearly 500 acres of land by the Co-operative Wholesale Society. The airfield was to be located south-east of Leicester, between Stoughton and Little Stretton, and was officially known as Leicester East. Stoughton was thought to have caused confusion with the Cambridgeshire airfield of Little Staughton, and the 'East' label was added to single it out from Desford and Braunstone, which were both known as Leicester airfields.

The base had three concrete runways, one of 2,000 yards and two of 1,400 yards, plus four T2 type hangars and accommodation for a total of 1,917 personnel.

By September 1943, the airfield was approaching completion and was originally intended to house two squadrons within Bomber Command, but, by the 7th of the month, this order was changed. Leicester East was to house a three-quarter strength (approximately 40 aircraft) Operational Training Unit (OTU) within 93 Group. The first servicemen began to arrive on 8th October 1943 from HQ Bomber Command, under the control of Squadron Leader J B Connolly. The station needed to be prepared for the arrival of the OTU by 15th October, leaving very little time for Connolly and his men. Their efforts to receive the new unit were, in the end, unnecessary, as the day before it was due to arrive a signal from Bomber Command HQ stated that no OTU would be arriving and the station was to be reduced to a Care and Maintenance footing.

The confusion continued throughout November, when another signal was received stating that Leicester East was to provide temporary accommodation for a 9th Air Force Troop Carrier Group (TCG). By 14th November, these orders had been changed and the original decision to receive two heavy bomber squadrons was to be carried out. The two units were to be from 3 Group Bomber Command but would be at the airfield for only a short while, pending their transfer to 38 Group, which was in control of all RAF airborne forces.

No sooner had this signal been received than the first of the two bomber squadrons prepared to move from its Cambridgeshire base. 196 Squadron was formed as a bomber unit at Driffield in Yorkshire on 7th November 1942. The

Rare photograph of a 196 Squadron Short Stirling Mk.III parked at a dispersal in late 1943 at Leicester East. LK403 'ZO-W' was transferred to 1665 CU, stationed at Tilstock in Shropshire, and was written off there in a landing accident on 27th March 1944. (R.C. Sturtivant.)

squadron's first aircraft was the Vickers Wellington X, with which it flew its first Bomber Command operations in early 1943, from Leconfield in Yorkshire. From July 1943, it started to replace the Wellington with the Short Stirling Mk.III and moved to Witchford, near Ely in Cambridgeshire, to become that station's first resident unit. The squadron flew its first Stirling bombing operations in August 1943, but these were be short lived as the squadron was earmarked for a transfer to airborne support duties. The officer commanding 196 Squadron was Wing Commander N Alexander and he led the advance party that arrived at Leicester East on 16th November.

Two days later, the squadron's equipment and personnel began to arrive by air, road and rail, and Leicester East began to feel like an RAF station at last. This feeling was endorsed by the arrival of Leicester East's first station commander on 19th November, Group Captain R E de T Vintras.

The sudden activity on station increased with the arrival of the second bomber unit's advance party, 620 Squadron from Chedburgh in Suffolk, on 20th November. 620 Squadron was a new squadron, formed at Chedburgh on 17th June 1943, and was equipped with the Stirling Mk.I and Mk.III. By this stage of the Second World War, the RAF's first four engine bomber was slowly being withdrawn from front-line operations. The Stirling had been serving Bomber Command since its arrival in late 1940 on 7 Squadron at Oakington, Cambridgeshire. The move of both 196 and 620 Squadron reflected the new role that the Stirling would perform until the end of the war.

Under the command of Wing Commander D H Lee, all of 620 Squadron's personnel and equipment were in place by 23rd November. Both squadrons were officially transferred from 3 Group to 38 Group on 1st December and began training from Leicester East in preparation for their new roles. The first few days involved long-range cross-country exercises but the crews did not have to wait very long for a chance to practise towing a glider. The first of many Airspeed Horsa heavy gliders was delivered from Netheravon in Wiltshire on 13th December 1943. Wing Commander Lee volunteered himself for the first tow on 19th December and remained airborne with the Horsa for 30 minutes before he released it over the airfield.

As expected, 196 Squadron's stay at Leicester East was to be short. The unit departed on 7th January 1944 to Tarrant Rushton in Dorset, a better positioned airfield from which to launch their part in the forthcoming Normandy invasion. Two days before 196 Squadron left, an Air Ministry decision was made to re-activate 190 Squadron, which had disbanded a few days earlier, on 31st December. The unit had first formed in the First World War as a night training unit and had not survived the post-war cuts that hit the RAF. Re-formed on the 1st March 1943 at Sullom Voe on Shetland, with Consolidated Catalina flying boats, the unit briefly performed anti-submarine patrols over the North Atlantic before being disbanded for a second time. The squadron was re-formed at Leicester East and conveniently filled the space left by the departed 196 Squadron. The new squadron would be equipped with the brand new Stirling Mk.IV, which differed from earlier marks, and was tailored to the requirements of the airborne forces' squadrons.

From late 1943 onwards, Short Brothers of Belfast focused all of its efforts on converting earlier Mk.IIIs into Mk.IVs as well as on producing new aircraft. The Mk.IV differed from previous builds in a number of ways, the most obvious of which was the removal of the nose and dorsal gun turrets, leaving only 'tail end Charlie' for self-defence. The shape of the nose was changed by the fitting of a transparent perspex fairing and a 6ft by 4ft hatch was fitted into the floor of the rear fuselage to allow for clean access by paratroopers. For glider towing, a horseshoe-shaped metal towing bridle was fitted aft and below the tailplane, with three points for connecting two ropes and a provision to link into the tug's intercom by means of an audio lead and plug.

190 Squadron had its first new Mk.IVs delivered by Air Auxiliary Transport (ATA) on 20th January, much to the annoyance of the resident 620 Squadron, which had to wait until 2nd February before its first Stirling Mk.IV arrived. By the end of January, the squadron had received virtually all of its aircraft, and squadron personnel had swelled to over 700, including Wing Commander Harrison, the new squadron commanding officer.

During February 1944, 620 Squadron carried out several sorties for the Special Operations Executive (SOE). This entailed the delivery of agents and the dropping of various supplies to resistance groups in France. All of these particular sorties were flown from Hurn on the south coast in Hampshire, all but one aircraft making it home: Squadron Leader Fyson and his crew was reported missing on 5th February 1944.

With the build up of American airborne forces in the local area, the 82nd Airborne Division requested the use of gliders to practise unloading drills. On 1st March, three Horsa gliders, with USAAF markings, were delivered, and these were complemented by a pair of American Waco CG-13As later in the month. The RAF continued to exercise with their own gliders, practising mass take-offs and cast-offs over the airfield. A combined group from both resident squadrons carried out a fourteen aircraft mass take-off on 6th March. All went well until, on release, one of the Horsas landed outside the airfield boundary and struck a tree, fortunately without injury to the glider's crew.

A sign of both squadrons' departures came on 12th March 1944, when Group Captain Wheeler, who was the Station Commander of Fairford in Gloucestershire, arrived by novel transport in a Gloster Gladiator. Six days later, 620 Squadron moved, followed a few days later on 25th March by 190 Squadron. The squadron had spent most of its flying time while at Leicester East, collecting their own Horsas from Marham in Norfolk and, like 620 Squadron, departed for their new home towing the Horsas with them.

With both units gone, the airfield was once again temporarily placed on a Care and Maintenance footing and became the responsibility of Wymeswold. This did not deter flying at Leicester East. A total of 88 visiting aircraft passed through the airfield in March. Several of the visitors were American aircraft and a number of the visits were by Consolidated B-24 Liberators that were collecting special stores for the Middle East. A unique unit also made use of the airfield for two weeks at the end of April. 93 Group Screened Pilots School was detached from Church Broughton in Derbyshire and flew the Vickers Wellington Mk.III and Mk.X. The unit was formed to reduce the fatal accident rate that bomber OTUs were experiencing at that time. Screened OTU instructors in the unit were those who had completed one or more operational tours and were therefore 'screened' for a period from further operations.

At the end of April 1944, Leicester East was transferred to 46 Group, Transport Command and was prepared for the formation of a new unit. 107 (Transport) OTU was formed at

On a misty morning at Leicester East, a 107 OTU course parade stands at attention with a Douglas Dakota Mk.III in the background. (PRO 28/440.)

Leicester East on 3rd May 1944, under the command of Wing Commander Howie DSO. The objective of the OTU was to train transport and glider-tug crews, and its main equipment was the American twin engined Douglas Dakota C.III, along with several Airspeed Horsas and Oxfords. The first six weeks of training commenced on 13th May and was made up of eighteen crews. The courses were very intensive, and included many additional lessons and lectures in airborne operations, navigation, night vision and signals as well as the art of paratroop and supply dropping.

By the end of May, Dakotas delivered to the OTU numbered fourteen and flying training was well under way, with long cross-country flights and container dropping exercises already being accomplished. The weather did, however, seriously disrupt flying training in the early part of June, to such an extent that it warranted a special mention in the OTU's Operational Record Book: *'Still raining, beginning to wonder if Summer is really arriving.'*

Undeterred by the English weather, the first course successfully completed their training on 24th June. Fourteen of

One for the album, not all OTU courses were lucky enough to have a group photograph taken. This is No.1 course, captured for posterity, who completed their six week training programme in late June 1944. (PRO 28/440).

the crews were posted to Dakota Squadrons and four crews stayed at 107 OTU and continued as instructors. This was the pattern for many of the early courses and it was a convenient way of building up the OTU's core instructor experience. The quantity of aircraft had increased to 34 Dakotas, fifteen Horsas and eleven Oxfords by the end of June, and this increased the capability of the unit to take part in bigger exercises.

The first of two exercises during July took place on the night of the 6th and involved a night navigation exercise followed by a mass cast off of gliders over the airfield. All went well until one of the Horsas, RJ158, was accidentally released early because of a tow rope failure. Luckily, the weather was clear with a full moon and the pilot skillfully made an emergency landing near Illston Grange, about five miles from the airfield. The glider was undamaged and was later dismantled and returned to Leicester East by road.

Another exercise followed on 13th July, and this involved 370 members of the Parachute Regiment. Eighteen Dakotas took part; the exercise, crewed entirely by No.2 Course, provided the airmen with valuable experience of a mass parachute drop. The aircraft collected the paras from Melton Mowbray and at 11:30 hours dropped them onto the grass airfield at Netheravon in Wiltshire. The exercise was a complete success from the OTU's point of view, although one para broke his leg and another received a cut to his face. Both injuries were probably due to colliding or falling heavily. This exercise terminated No.2 Course and all involved were posted out two days later to various units.

A unique unit was formed from 107 OTU during July 1944, which employed a rather novel technique to remove gliders from small airstrips. The Special Pick-up Flight was equipped with five Dakotas and sixteen Hadrian gliders and experimented with snatching the gliders off the ground by flying the Dakota very low and picking up the tow rope. It was hoped that the system would be implemented to collect senior officers and possibly injured personnel from front line areas where no major airfield was accessible. In the end, the Allied advance was so swift that the method was never implemented, but this did not stop the Glider Pick-up Training Flight being formed from 107 OTU on 8th January 1945, at Zeals in Wiltshire.

Leicester East was the host to two unique events on 5th and 9th August 1944. The 82nd Airborne had returned from northern France after their successful participation in the Normandy landings. The 82nd was still based all around Leicester and 1,400 of them paraded in front of their Commanding Officer, General Matthew Ridgway. Many were presented with decorations and 107 OTU provided a fitting flypast for the occasion. Four days later, an even larger parade took place; this time the troops were reviewed by the Allied Forces Europe Commander, General Dwight D Eisenhower. After the parade, Eisenhower praised the 82nd Airborne for its actions in northern France but warned that the campaign in Europe was far from over.

Space at Leicester East was becoming very limited with the US Airborne forces making more use of the airfield. Leicester East, unlike many other airfields in Leicestershire, did not have a satellite airfield to which it could disperse its aircraft. Several airfields were investigated in and around the county. Ringway (now Manchester International Airport) and the comparatively local airfield of Melton Mowbray were available for use from the beginning of August on into September. A detachment of 107 OTU used Ringway from August 1944 until 18th January 1945, while Melton Mowbray was used for only a few weeks in September, both airfields helping to ease the congestion at Leicester East.

General Dwight D Eisenhower (second left on the saluting base) watches as the 82nd Airborne Division parade past at Leicester East on 10th August 1944. (via D Wills).

The accident record at the airfield, considering the large number of aircraft movements, was very good until September. Dakota III KG547 and its student pilot were practising a glide approach; the pilot failed to round the aircraft out and literally flew the Dakota into the runway. The undercarriage failed and the aircraft slithered along the runway on its belly and was a write off, luckily without serious injury to the crew. Accidents like this were a very rare occurrence, owing a lot to the skill of the OTU's instructors and the relatively easy-to-handle Dakota.

The number of station personnel was at its peak in November 1944, but this did not stop another unit attaching itself to 107 OTU on the 9th of the month. The Air Ambulance School was formed within the Technical Training Command and entailed nursing orderlies attending a one week course in general air ambulance duties, including at least ten hours of familiarisation flying in the Dakota.

February 1945 was possibly the highest and the lowest point of the OTU's history, when the unit completed its 2,500th glider tow since its formation on 2nd February. This achievement was marred by the loss of Dakota III TS436, which crashed near Zeals. With Flight Lieutenant Mackay at the controls, the aircraft crashed into high ground with 21 crew and passengers, including sixteen aircrew. Tragically, all were killed except Mackay, who was seriously injured. This was 107 OTU's only fatal accident.

An RAF reshuffle resulted in a change of name for 107 OTU on 12th March 1945 to 1333 (Transport Support) Conversion Unit (CU). This had no effect on the CU's training programme, although the unit was now complemented by a newly formed Radar Flight operating Oxfords.

By spring 1945, the airfield and its buildings were beginning to look shabby. Even though the station had been open for less than two years, it had been used for thousands of aircraft movements. While work was carried out to repair runways and taxiways, the majority of 1333 CU's operations were carried out from Bruntingthorpe and Market Harborough.

Yet another re-organisation of units by the RAF was to have a more significant impact on Leicester East during October 1945. The CU was to move to Syerston in Nottinghamshire and shuttle flights began moving equipment on 20th October, followed by the main unit on the 25th. The Radar Flight departed for Snaith in Yorkshire a few days later, on 30th October, and, after nearly two years of almost continuous flying, Leicester East fell silent.

Placed on Care and Maintenance in November, the airfield was then transferred to 40 Group, Maintenance Command. 216 Maintenance Unit (MU) took over Leicester East as a sub-storage site on 15th November. 216 MU was a ground equipment depot and they quickly filled all of the airfield's hangars and buildings with surplus RAF equipment, ranging from knives and forks to aircraft engines and vehicles. 216 MU was replaced by 255 MU on 21st January 1946 and served as a Equipment Disposal Depot until 5th May 1948.

From this point, the RAF had no more use for Leicester East, and after a few months it was taken over by the Army as a camp and training area until 1949. Leicester East was not without aircraft for long. The sad news of Sir Lindsay Everard's death in late 1949 meant that the Leicester Aero Club's (LAC) home at Ratcliffe was being put up for sale. Although they had been offered first refusal, the LAC could not raise the necessary funds and so had to look for a new home. During 1950, the club spent many months looking for somewhere suitable. Leicester East was still in government hands, but this did not prevent the LAC negotiating a lease to use the airfield for storage of the club's aircraft, and to use a single hangar and the wartime control tower.

The chairman of the club, Wing Commander P Russell DFC, managed to gain permission for the club's aircraft to have their engines run and to be taxied for short distances around the airfield. This led to aircraft carrying out circuits there and, by 1951, the Air Ministry lease was re-negotiated and was promptly reduced to allow the club to divert its funds for the refurbishment of the control tower and hangar. The same year, the Air Ministry returned the land occupied by the airfield to its original pre-war owners, making the Co-operative Wholesale Society the club's new landlords.

The aircraft at Leicester during the 1950s included several ex-military de Havilland Tiger Moths, a Miles Messenger, and various marks of Auster. Local business began to show an interest in the airfield as well, and the club were training pilots for both civil and commercial flying.

Leicester Airport's excellent, fully restored, wartime control tower is the present home of the Leicestershire Aero Club. (Author.)

Enthusiastic members worked tirelessly on turning the control tower into clubhouse, bar and kitchen, with an air traffic control building on the roof, and it remains a superb example of utilisation of a wartime building today. A Festival Air Rally was held at Leicester in 1951, and this was followed in 1952 by a well attended Air Day. The LAC was going from strength to strength when the first of many hurdles reared its ugly head in 1954. The Government announced the drastic decision to shut down all civilian flying schools! Fortunately for Leicester, the flying school was not officially recognised and so escaped the attentions of an Aviation Authority visit.

The Queen and Prince Philip were to visit Leicester in 1958, and it was planned that they should fly into the old airfield. The royal visit benefited all using the airfield, as the Leicester City Council felt it was necessary to resurface the main runway, a huge expense that the club would never have managed.

During construction of Leicester East in 1942, a minor road had been torn up to make way for the new airfield. In late 1959, the Ministry of Transport decided to reinstate the road and, with very little thought for aviation activities, proposed that the new road be laid down the main runway. Understandably, from the LAC's point of view, this was unacceptable; even though three runways were in use, the road would severely restrict the airfields operations. The club managed to persuade the Ministry to use the old northern perimeter tract instead, but the LAC had to contribute £2,000 towards the cost of the diversion. The road went ahead, but the club suffered financially for many years after the building of the road, and club facilities suffered as a result.

Larger aircraft such as a de Havilland Heron, owned by Fox's Glacier Mints, and a de Havilland Dove, flown by the Pollard Ball and Roller Bearing Company, were now resident at the airfield. Privately owned aircraft were also on the increase, and the club was now operating Cessnas as well as the usual group of Austers that would always be resident at Leicester. Only one hangar remained on the airfield, positioned directly behind the control tower; the others had become derelict several years earlier and were dismantled. The sole hangar was always in need of attention, and the landlords delivered another body blow to the club when they announced that the LAC was in contravention of the lease, because of the condition of the hangar.

The modern day Leicester Airport makes use of all the original wartime runways, but not to their original length. In total the airport actually offers five different runways: three asphalt, which are the originals, and two shorter grass strips laid out in the centre. (Crown Copyright).

On top of this, the Co-operative Society were unhappy about the larger aircraft operating from Leicester and demanded that they stop flying from the airfield immediately. The Co-op wanted the club to spend £3,000 on refurbishing the hangar. Coupled with the loss of £2,000 per year incurred by stopping the larger aircraft operating, this amounted to a dire situation.

Unpaid bills had mounted up on the club aircraft as well. The engineer who looked after the LAC's Austers flew them to Tollerton near Nottingham and impounded them until the bills were cleared. With only one aircraft now available to the club which was capable of generating income, the LAC's position grew steadily worse.

The local press were now in on the act and, along with Leicester City Council and many local businessmen, campaigned to keep the airfield open. After a meeting with the Chamber of Commerce in November 1966, the Co-op proposed to stop all business and executive flying and close two of the runways. They said they were prepared to accept private flying, but anything else was a violation of the lease.

By April 1967, a bank loan was gained and all outstanding debts were paid. A shake-up at the club resulted in the employment of a full-time airport manger and secretary; a pair of full-time flying instructors and one part-time were taken on; and three new Cessna 150 aircraft were leased from VicAir Limited for training. During this rocky period, the club was being run by four local businessmen, in a self-proclaimed syndicate that claimed to own the club. This 'consortium' had already tried to sell the club illegally in 1966, and, when the club began to experience financial difficulties again in 1968, the group put the club up for sale in *The Times* newspaper. This was obviously illegal, and a change of organisation in the financial running of the club had to take place. Several members of the LAC took legal advice and, after involving Bill Ford, a local solicitor, managed to remove the group of businessmen and quickly change the constitution of the club. A council of management was then elected.

The effect on the LAC's financial position was dramatic. Between 1968 and 1969, the club's situation had improved from four aircraft rented to four owned, and a loss of over £1,200 was turned into a profit of over £3,000. Flying membership doubled and the flying school became approved by the Civil Aviation Authority, which turned it into a profitable business.

From the early 1970s, Leicester airfield hosted an annual air display, which contributed greatly to the club's bank account. Years of effort by club members resulted in the now well equipped airfield being officially renamed 'Leicester Airport' in

A single wartime T (Transportable) 2 hangar survives at Leicester, a new hangar stands alongside and more expansion plans may be in the offing. (Author.)

1974. Today, the facilities at Leicester are superb and they continue to grow, with a second hangar having been constructed and a third in the planning stage. After decades of struggle, the Leicestershire Aero Club lives on, and through thick and thin has survived into the 21st century, providing Leicestershire with an airport that it can be proud of.

10

LOUGHBOROUGH

National Grid Reference SK525215; NW of Loughborough

The Brush Electrical Engineering Company could trace its roots back to the late 1870s and Francis Brush, an American, the inventor of the Brush arc lamp and dynamo. Brush was first associated with Loughborough in 1889, when, after a merger with the Falcon Engine & Car Works Ltd, the company moved to the Leicestershire town from London.

Brush's association with aviation began in 1915 when Winston Churchill, the First Sea Lord of the Admiralty, announced that the Royal Naval Air Service (RNAS) was to be expanded. This led to the need for civilian factories and Brush was one of the many organizations with the necessary skills to produce aircraft for the RNAS and, later, the Royal Flying Corp (RFC). Between 1915 and April 1919, the company produced over 650 aircraft, including the Avro 504, Short Seaplane and Maurice Farman 'Longhorn'. All this led to the first of two airfields being built in Loughborough and Brush were fortunate that a suitable site was near to the factory. Loughborough Meadows was a large flat piece of land which was used by the company for test flying and delivery flights.

When aircraft production ended in 1919, the Loughborough Meadows airfield fell into disuse and was later used for many years as a racecourse and flying never returned.

The site for a second airfield at Loughborough was encouraged by the popularity of civil aviation in the late 1920s. An area of land at Bishop's Meadow, situated on the north-west side of the town next to the Grand Union Canal, north of the A6 (Derby road), was first viewed in 1929. A detailed study carried out by a representative of the Automobile Association Aviation Department and dated 6th May 1933 made many proposals and endorsed the suitability of the site. It was a further three years before the site was purchased, in May 1936, by Loughborough Corporation at a cost of £17,000. After the deal had been struck, the principal of Loughborough College approached the corporation enquiring about the possibility of leasing or buying a piece of the airfield to be used by the college's Department of Aeronautical Engineering.

The project progressed at an agonizingly slow pace; work did not begin until January 1939, almost ten years after the airfield had first been surveyed. A hangar, assembly and rigging shop were the first buildings to be constructed, all destined for use by Loughborough College. The Second World War had started by the time construction on the airfield itself began, the work finally being completed in early 1940.

Although the college made use of the hangars and buildings it had leased straight away, the landing ground remained unused. In mid-1940 the threat of invasion was high and all potential areas the enemy could use to land troops were blocked, in Loughborough's case the runway was obstructed with disused vehicles.

The airfield did not go unnoticed for long: the Ministry of Aircraft Production (MAP) requisitioned it in 1940 with the intention of using it as a repair base for RAF aircraft. Airwork was the company selected, as for this kind of work they were a leader at the time. The airfield was first inspected in early 1941 and work began to build more hangars and extend the size of the runways. The main runway was unusual: it totalled 3,330ft in length of which only 2,000ft was tarmac; the remainder of the runway and airfield was grass.

Airwork's contract was for the repair and modification of the American Douglas Boston and Havoc twin-engined bombers. The Boston was the bomber variant while the Havoc was the night fighter version. The majority of aircraft were brought in by road, dismantled and stored around the hangars, eventually taking their turn to be restored to airworthy condition. One of

Airwork were contracted to overhaul, refurbish and convert the Douglas Boston and Havoc. All the aircraft were flown by Airwork's own test pilot, Peter Clifford, and his spirited flying gained quite a reputation around Loughborough. (Via author.)

*Brush's Falcon Works in Loughborough was employed to repair Avro Lancaster wings,
with the main aircraft, which were quickly returned to the air.*

ιgs were all salvaged from crashed aircraft, then repaired, reassembled and reunited

Airwork's tasks was to convert the Boston and Havoc into the Turbinlite version, although most of this work was done at Burtonwood in Lancashire. This involved the fitting of a high-powered searchlight in the nose of the aircraft. The intention was that the Turbinlite would illuminate enemy aircraft for the benefit of accompanying night fighters to shoot down. The concept may have been good on paper, but it was a dismal failure in the air. After a year in service, the 32 aircraft converted to Turbinlites were withdrawn from operations, having achieved virtually no success against the enemy.

As in the First World War, the Brush Company was involved in the repair, and later the construction, of aircraft. The Brush works officially became part of the Civilian Repair Organisation (CRO) on 12th July 1941, but had by this time already been carrying out repair work for the Air Ministry. Between March 1941 and December 1943, the company repaired Handley Page Hampden fuselages, which were brought to the works by road, usually on RAF 'Queen Mary' transporters. Over 100 Hampdens were overhauled by Brush; all of them were re-assembled by Tollerton Aircraft Services at the Nottinghamshire airfield.

The Brush Company were also briefly involved in the production of the Armstrong Whitworth Albemarle, building nose sections before this work was transferred to MG Motors at Abingdon in Oxfordshire. This coincided with a dilemma facing the de Havilland Aircraft Company based at Hatfield in Hertfordshire. Their priority was the production of the Mosquito, and this left no room for Dominie, production, which was still in demand by the RAF. Fortunately, Brush had the workforce and the capacity to take on the Dominie and a new production line was set up by late 1942. The first aircraft left the production line in March 1943. All Dominies were towed, with wings removed, to Loughborough airfield for re-assembly and flight testing.

The Dominie was the military version of the famous de Havilland DH.89, Dragon Rapide, the aeroplane that had done so much to promote light commercial aviation in the 1930s. Chosen by the RAF for training and communications work, it was later used by the Fleet Air Arm (FAA), a service with which it served until the 1950s. Brush Co. was contracted to build 455 Dominies, but the contract was terminated after 335 had been

Three hundred and thirty-five de Havilland Dominies were built by Brush between 1943 and 1946. Every one was flown out of Loughborough airfield, the last TX319 leaving on 2nd July 1946. (Via author.)

built. The last aircraft left the Bishop's Meadow airfield in July 1946.

By the war's end, Airwork had carried out repairs and conversions on over 72 aircraft, and employed over 400 people in the process. They also became involved with the Dominie after the war, converting several aircraft into civilian Dragon Rapides.

Accidents were few and far between at Loughborough and thankfully none involved the loss of life. On 17th September 1945 a Miles Martinet I belly-landed in a field next to the landing area and the following year a Handley Page Halifax Mk.VI made a much more spectacular arrival. The Halifax was being delivered to Loughborough College on 4th July 1946 as an instructional airframe by a crew of 4 Ferry Pool based at Hawarden in Cheshire. Although ferry pilots were well used to landing large aircraft on small airfields, on this occasion, the Halifax overshot the runway, ripped off its undercarriage and crashed into a field beyond. The staff of the college stayed well clear of the wrecked bomber, worried that they may have to accept the bomber *in situ*! A few weeks later, the Halifax was removed by an RAF salvage crew who were unaware of that the bomber was destined for the college.

In 1947, the airfield was de-requisitioned and this brought forward a flurry of applications to obtain an operating licence. The Ministry of Civil Aviation approved a licence in 1949 but the anticipated arrival of large amounts of air traffic did not come to fruition. The occasional Olley Air Services charter flight did make use of Loughborough, but the most visits were by Tiger Moths from Nottingham University Air Squadron (UAS).

With so little aviation going on, much of the airfield was turned over to agriculture. The college's lease of the airfield ended in 1961, and what was hoped would become Leicestershire's second municipal airport closed to flying. The aeronautical section of Loughborough College cleared out the airfield's remaining hangar, and several Second World War airframes that had been used for training found new homes in museums around the country. Two of these aircraft went to the Shuttleworth Collection in Bedfordshire; Hawker Sea Hurricane Mk.IIb Z7015 and Supermarine Spitfire VIc AR501 were both restored to flying condition and are still flying.

11
MARKET HARBOROUGH

National Grid Reference SP712887; 2 miles NW of Market Harborough

Construction of Market Harborough airfield, situated between the villages of Foxton and Lubenham (which both, incidentally, claim it as their own), began in the spring of 1942. Like so many other airfields, it was built with operational bomber units in mind but even before it opened Market Harborough's role had changed.

J R Mowlem and Company were given the main contract to built a three runway 'A' Class airfield two miles north-west of the Leicestershire market town. The approaches to all of the runways were carefully planned to avoid the town and this resulted in the main runway being slightly shorter than usual, at 1,900 yards. Two other runways of 1,400 yards each were also built, and the connecting perimeter track had thirty dispersals attached to it which could handle the RAF's heavy bombers.

Several months before the airfield was complete, it received a visit from a group of representatives from 92 Group, Bomber Command. The purpose of their visit was to see if Market Harborough would be suitable for housing an Operational Training Unit (OTU). The results of their visit must have been positive, as the airfield became part of 92 Group on 7th August 1942. Work on the airfield continued unabated, and it was officially opened on 1st June 1943, although much more work was needed on technical and domestic buildings.

Cottesmore in Rutland was about to have its hard-punished

grass runways replaced by more durable concrete. This decision dictated that 14 OTU, which was based there, would have to move. The first of the Vickers Wellingtons were due to arrive at Market Haroborough in early July, but, as completed accommodation was still lacking, the move did not begin until 28th July. The initial move of the OTU was complete by 7th August, but several aircraft were still undergoing maintenance at Cottesmore and would be delayed for several weeks. The OTU also continued to use Cottesmore's satellite airfield at Saltby until 10th September, by which time all the aircraft on strength had settled at Market Harborough. Husbands Bosworth in Northamptonshire had been delegated as Market Harborough's satellite airfield and 'A' and 'B' Flights first moved there on 17th August.

The OTU settled back into the same training routine that it had been carrying out at its old base: circuits and bumps, cross countries, bombing exercises, both by day and by night, and the odd leaflet raid into France, which did break up the monotony for some of the instructors.

A 14 OTU Vickers Wellington Mk.Ic, parked at a dispersal at Market Harborough in late 1943. After spending over three years at Cottesmore, the OTU settled at Market Harborough until it was disbanded on 24th June 1945. (Via author.)

The nearest the station got to Bomber Command operations was in providing sanctuary for aircraft returning from operations. In the early hours of 6th September 1943, Pilot Officer J Allen and his 434 Squadron crew were returning from a raid over Mannheim. Their Halifax Mk.V had an engine failure and Allen decided to look for an alternative airfield rather than risk trying to make it home to Tholthorpe in Yorkshire. The all-Canadian crew landed safely at Market Harborough and returned to their Yorkshire home the next day. A similar incident occurred the following month when another Canadian crew made use of Market Harborough. Flight Sergeant S Wick had to divert from a fog-bound Leeming in his 429 Squadron Halifax Mk.II, and once again found Market Harborough very accommodating.

It was a relatively quiet start for the OTU at Market Harborough, the unit had already had a rough time operating the Hampden in the early war years and the safety record had not improved with the arrival of the Wellington. The twin engined bombers were all the early Mk.Ics and so were all past their best. The first accident to involve a 14 OTU Wellington happened on 25th September 1943, when X9871 crashed on take-off. The pilot, Sergeant S E Martin, was taking part in a night bombing exercise when he retracted the flaps of the bomber too quickly after take-off . The Wellington lost height and crashed into the ground but, luckily, all the crew escaped injury. X9871 never flew again. The crew of another Wellington Mk.Ic was not as lucky on 24th October when DV839 came down near Wittering in Northamptonshire. Flight Sergeant E G Reading RAAF and his crew of four took off from Market Harborough for a night cross-country exercise. Disaster struck a few hours later: in an attempt to establish their position, they descended through cloud, but their descent was too rapid and they crashed near to the fighter station. Three were killed outright and the fourth died of his injuries in the Stamford and Rutland General Infirmary. Amazingly, Sergeant Buckley, the Wireless Operator, walked away from the wreckage and was returned to Market Harborough that same day.

The year ended with the hope of a replacement for the death trap Wellington Mk.Ics, and the first Mk.X arrived in January 1944. The Mk.X was the most numerous of all Wellingtons

165

produced and, by the war's end, 3,803 had been built. It served with 29 RAF squadrons and countless training units and, because of this, the majority of Mk.Xs that arrived on the OTU were in equally as a poor a state as the aircraft they were meant to replace.

The first Mk.X to be lost had been on the OTU for only a few days when the engine gremlins struck. On 24th January, Flight Sergeant R W Meekings was climbing away from the airfield, when, at only 1,000 ft, the starboard engine failed. For a Wellington in the climb, 1,000 ft is not very high, and Meekings had no time to recover the aircraft before it crashed to the ground in a ball of flames at Braybrooke, two miles north-west of Desborough. Out of the six crew on board, three were killed instantly. Three managed to escape the burning bomber with injuries.

To give bomber crews the necessary training and experience of an enemy fighter attack, the Bomber (Defence) Training Flights (BDTF) were formed, which simulated the German fighter aircraft. 1683 BDTF was formed at Bruntingthorpe in June 1943 to serve 29 OTU, and operated the Curtiss Tomahawk, which was a rare machine in the hands of the RAF. It was decided to centralize the operations of the BDTF and the flight moved to Market Harborough on 3rd February 1944 and would not only serve 14 OTU aircraft but 29 OTU, 84 OTU at Desborough and 12 OTU at Chipping Warden, both in Northamptonshire. By April, the troublesome Tomahawks had been replaced by Hawker Hurricane FB Mk.IIcs, which took over their fighter affiliation role.

The arrangement at Husbands Bosworth was proving itself to be so efficient that the flights based there were removed from 14 OTU to form 85 OTU on 15th June. Husbands Bosworth was now no longer a satellite airfield, which reduced the OTU to a three-quarter status, but this meant that at least 40 Wellingtons were still on strength. The OTU still retained many of its support aircraft, which at that time included a Miles Master and Martinet, an Airspeed Oxford and the odd Tiger Moth, quite typical of any OTU.

While the losses from the OTU continued to mount, the majority involved damage to aircraft, rather than loss of life. But to suffer two fatal accidents on the same day was always a heavy

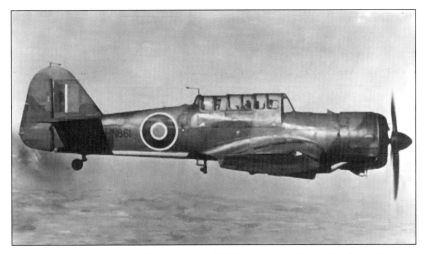

*Air gunnery was a crucial part of any OTU course, and to cater for this
14 OTU operated a number of purpose designed Miles Martinet target tugs.
(Via author.)*

cross to bear and never more so than on the afternoon of 13th July
1944. Flight Lieutenant A C Shilleto in Wellington Mk.X LN509
took off from Market Harborough at 15:15 hours for a routine air
test. He was to be accompanied by Flight Lieutenant W D
Browne DFC, also in a Wellington Mk.X. Fifteen minutes later,
Brown was closing in on Shilleto's aircraft so as to fly a tight
formation, but misjudged his closing speed and collided with the
Wellington. The two aircraft crashed at East Farndon, five miles
west north-west of Desborough. The only positive thing that can
be said of this accident is that both aircraft were carrying only a
wireless operator, and not full crews. Nonetheless, four
experienced airmen were killed. Shilleto had previously served
on 29 OTU and had been lucky to survive an accident in a Tiger
Moth in July 1942. He had also logged a total of nearly 1,500
flying hours, of which over 1,000 were on the Wellington. His
wireless operator, Warrant Officer J Everett, had won the DFM
whilst serving with Bottesford-based 207 Squadron in April 1942.

On 1st August 1944, the 1683 BDTF was disbanded and its
aircraft and operations were taken over by the OTU. Later in the
month, Market Harborough played host again to a group of
bombers returning from an attack on Brest, whose bases were

closed because of poor weather. The first aircraft to arrive was Flying Officer Sloski's Halifax Mk.III, of 429 Squadron, whose starboard inner engine had stopped on the outward journey. He was followed by Flight Lieutenant H Brawn, also of 429 Squadron, who was diverted to the Leicestershire base, as Leeming in Yorkshire was covered in a blanket of fog. Four more Halifax Mk.IIIs followed, all from 433 Squadron, and all for the same reason. Their home base of Skipton-on-Swale, also in Yorkshire, was closed because of the weather.

The training losses continued to mount throughout 1944 and by New Year 1945, another twelve Wellingtons had been lost in a variety of accidents. On 1st January 1945, in recognition of the unit's efforts in aircrew training, King George VI approved the award of an official badge for 14 OTU. In keeping with the unit's Rutland hunting roots, the badge depicted a hound's head with a hunting horn and riding whip, accompanied by the motto 'Keep up with the pack'.

The final aviation incident to occur at Market Harborough did not involve a Wellington as one would expect, but one of the unit's Hurricanes. On 10th May 1945, Flying Officer G M Buchanan RNZAF was taxiing his Hurricane Mk.Ic along a perimeter track when his brakes failed. He quickly chopped the throttle, but this did not stop the fighter from slicing into the back of a van. The van was being driven by LACW Huntsman and, luckily for her, the propeller missed her by only a few inches. She suffered only a few bruises and shock. The Hurricane would have been repaired and put back in the air in the earlier war years, but the end of the war was close and the aircraft became an instructional airframe instead.

14 OTU became the first bomber OTU to be disbanded, on 24th June 1945, and this was followed by a quick rundown of the airfield. Not including the unit's training operations at Cottesmore, the OTU had provided Bomber Command with 2,908 pilots, navigators, bomb-aimers, wireless operators and air gunners in their time at Market Harborough. Over 45,000 flying hours were achieved at the unfortunate cost of 61 aircrew lost on training sorties. The unit's disbandment was performed with clinical efficiency, and on 1st July the station was transferred to 91 Group, Bomber Command.

Bomber crew training was not on the agenda, though. The

Market Harborough photographed in August 1945. 14 OTU had disbanded only a few weeks earlier. The technical area on the left side of the photograph is the present day location of Gartree Prison and Gallow Field Road follows the line of the northern perimeter track. (Crown Copyright.)

Several wartime domestic buildings survive in the fields around the old airfield, in this case now catering for needs of a more equine nature. (Author.)

airfield became a short-term satellite for Leicester East, which was operating Dakotas of 1333 (Transport Support) Conversion Unit. The twin-engined transport aircraft used the airfield for only a few weeks, and Market Harborough was closed on the 18th August and placed under Care and Maintenance. Two days later, the airfield was taken over by 54 Group, Flying Training Command, but this did not result in a resurgence of flying activity as expected. 26 Aircrew Holding Unit became the new occupant instead, on 21st August, and was one of many holding units, tasked with finding the masses of ex-aircrew alternative trades, or processing them for de-mobilisation. In November the unit was disbanded and, in February 1946, a limited amount of flying returned to Market Harborough, when 273 Maintenance Unit (MU) used the airfield for 113 Storage Sub-site.

6 MU, based at Brize Norton in Oxfordshire, took over from 273 MU on 28th April 1947, by which time only Horsa gliders remained on the airfield. Still named 113 Storage Sub-site, the airfield was finally relinquished by the RAF on 5th October 1949 after the remaining gliders had all been re-housed at Brize Norton.

In the meantime, the Army had already taken over the station and by August 1948 the airfield had become known as 72 Brigade Vehicle Depot (BVD), Royal Army Ordnance Corps. From then on every available piece of runway, taxiway and dispersal was covered in surplus military vehicles, all pending disposal. When the last vehicles had been sold off, the requirement for the depot ended and the army vacated in February 1960.

The old airfield was now viewed as a possible location for a new prison and, despite local protests, the Home Secretary confirmed this on 30th January 1961. Work began on a 95 acre prison site in 1963, in the area which was originally the technical site of the airfield.

Many wartime buildings survive around the old airfield; some have even been turned into living accommodation. Generally, though, only a few strips of runway and perimeter track remain, the reminders of the heart of the station removed for the construction of the prison. Many developers have hung their noses over the airfield gate but today almost all of RAF Market Harborough has returned to agriculture.

12
MELTON MOWBRAY

National Grid Reference SK750158; 2 miles S of Melton Mowbray

Melton Mowbray had very strong connections with aviation for nearly 50 years, boasting three military and two civilian airfields, all huddled around the market town. Even before the First World War, a polo ground at Brentingby to the east of the town was used as a refuelling stop for the competitors of the *Daily Mail* Circuit of Britain air race of 1911. The excitement of the event brought the town and surrounding area to a complete standstill, with many schools closing and much work missed.

Three years later, the First World War began and a new threat presented itself to the East Midlands in the shape of the German Zeppelin airships. Whether the earlier aerial activities influenced the decision to use Brentingby as a night landing ground is not known, but by 1916 a 30 acre site was laid out between the village and Gravel Hole Spinney. The small airfield was intended for the use of 38 (Home Defence) Squadron, whose HQ was at Castle Bromwich in Warwickshire. Brentingby was little used, and by late 1916 a more suitable airfield site had been chosen near Scalford, north of Melton Mowbray. The new airfield was twice the size of Brentingby, and its location must have influenced the move of the 38 Squadron HQ to Melton Mowbray on 1st October 1916. The airfield was regularly used until May 1918, when 38 Squadron departed for its first tour in France. With the formation of 90 Squadron at Buckminster, responsibility for Scalford was taken over by this Lincolnshire airfield until the end of the First World War, when it was no longer required.

Both airfields lay dormant until the early 1930s, when Sir Alan Cobham used Scalford as part of his National Aviation Day Display, which was touring the country. This was a 'one off', and local civilian aviation favoured the smaller airfield at Brentingby, which was re-established on a Tempory Landing Ground Register under the Automobile Association. Once again, Brentingby was little used and yet another alternative was sought for an airfield around Melton.

The formation of the Leicestershire Flying Pou Club influenced the opening of Melton's last civilian airfield. The Pou de Ciel – 'Flying Flea' – was one of the world's first kit-built aircraft, available to the general public at a reasonable price. The club first attempted to fly their 'fleas' from the new airport at Braunstone, but were turned down. One of the club's committee members suggested looking at a suitable field south of Melton, off Sandy Lane, and after some negotiation the club members started to prepare the field in early 1936. A hangar was erected and at least one well attended air show was held there. The club grew very quickly during 1936 and with the arrival of more aircraft and the unceasing demand for pilot training the club started to look for an alternative site. Lindsay Everard came to the rescue of the club and made Rearsby available for the now re-named County Flying Club. By the end of the year, the hangar had been dismantled and moved to Rearsby and flying ceased at Sandy Lane.

The Second World War put great pressures on the Air Ministry to locate and survey innumerable airfield sites throughout the country. An elevated area to the south of Melton and north of Great Dalby was one of these locations. The building of the airfield was deeply unpopular with the locals, many houses and farm buildings were demolished and, additionally, a main road was removed, which caused great inconvenience throughout the war years.

Work began in late 1941 with the lifting of a large number of hedgerows and trees. The disappearance of the windbreak they provided made working conditions very grim, especially through the winter months. The airfield was allocated to 93 Group Bomber Command in September 1942, even though they had no plans or intentions of using Melton. With this in mind, the airfield was transferred to 44 Group Transport

Command on 1st August 1943 and eventually became the busiest airfield in Leicestershire.

Melton was 'christened' unexpectedly even before it officially opened. A Wellington of 29 OTU from Bruntingthorpe crash landed onto the airfield on 22nd July 1943 after its port engine failed, much to the dismay of workers on the main runway at the time. Pilot Officer Heath, an instructor, was at the controls and skillfully managed to put the crippled bomber onto the airfield without injury to his crew or the workers on the ground.

The airfield opened on 31st July, with Squadron Leader R J Sancaeu assuming temporary command until the arrival of Wing Commander B A Oakley on 3rd September. Oakley's arrival coincided with the formation of Melton's first unit, No. 4 Overseas Aircraft Preparation Unit (OAPU), under the command of Flight Lieutenant (later Squadron Leader) Ford on 1st September. As its name suggests, the unit's task was to prepare aircraft for service and for the transit flight to an overseas destination. At this stage of the war, the main overseas theatre of operations was the Middle East, and the majority of 4 OAPU's aircraft would make this journey.

In a move to centralize the training and preparation of crew to

More at home on a Coastal Command airfield, the Bristol Beaufort torpedo bomber was a common sight at Melton up until mid 1944. (Via author.)

ferry aircraft overseas, a pair of Ferry Training Units (FTU) moved to Melton during October. The first to arrive was 306 FTU from Maghaberry in County Antrim, Northern Ireland between 13th and 15th October 1943. 306 FTU was formed in December 1942 to train ferry crews to fly the Bristol Beaufort torpedo bomber, an aircraft more suited to Coastal Command stations. These were later complemented by the Bristol Beaufighter. In the middle of 306 FTU's move from Northern Ireland a second unit, 307 FTU from Finmere in Buckinghamshire, arrived on 14th October. They brought a host of different aircraft to Melton, including the Douglas Boston and Havoc, Beaufighter and Wellington Mk.XIIIs.

While the FTUs were getting settled in, the OAPU was ready for its first 'commitment' of aircraft, which arrived in the shape of three Wellingtons on 17th October 1943. A batch of Douglas Bostons arrived soon after, and a Boston BZ257 became the first aircraft to be despatched from the OAPU on 30th October.

Like all wartime stations, Melton was hastily brought into use well before the airfield was completely finished. Although Melton's three runways and perimeter track were complete, many dispersal points had yet to be linked to it. This meant that the aircraft delivered to the OAPU had to be taxied across grass before they reached solid concrete. The time of year aggravated this simple operation and the airfield steadily turned into a quagmire as rain, heavy frosts and snowfalls took their toll. The situation was further complicated by the lack of tractors available, which led many delivery pilots to try to taxi their aircraft to dispersal points where they became bogged down. This problem continued throughout November and December and the already overstretched personnel could have done without it.

Aircraft movements during December 1943 were probably comparable to East Midlands airport today and it was inevitable with so much activity that accidents would happen. The first serious incident involved a pair of Bostons of the OAPU and took place on 11th December, when Boston BZ386 overshot the runway and became bogged down. While the crew were extricating themselves from their stranded machine the aircraft was struck by another Boston, which had overshot the same runway. Both Bostons were written off, but luckily the crews of both aircraft escaped serious injury. A similar incident happened to another Boston a few days later, followed on 21st December by a classic example of 'It came off in my hand, chief'! The Boston was returning from a training sortie when, on arrival at Melton, the pilot attempted to lower the undercarriage, but the selector literally broke off in his hand! With no choice but to belly-land the Boston onto Melton's runway, the pilot made a textbook wheels-up landing with no injuries to the crew.

Within a few weeks, Melton had become the busiest airfield in the county and this trend continued with the arrival of another unit. 304 FTU arrived from Port Ellen in Strathclyde at the beginning of January 1944, bringing with it a variety of aircraft that included the Handley Page Halifax, Short Stirling and Douglas Dakota. 304 FTU was formed at its Scottish base in December 1942 to train ferry crews on the Beaufighter and the Boston, and had only recently started to incorporate larger aircraft into its training programme.

304 FTU's move was completed by 13th January, and two days later Melton experienced its first re-shuffle of units. Both 306 and 307 FTU were disbanded on 15th January and amalgamated into 304 FTU, making one large unit. The combination of units made little difference on the surface but it did improve control of aircraft and crew training. The next day, another new unit arrived from Lyneham in Wiltshire. No. 1 Ferry Crew Pool (FCP) was initially formed with 70 fully trained ferry pilots on strength, but this rapidly increased after only a few weeks at Melton. By the end of February, the FCP had over 160 fully trained aircrew able to operate nine types of aircraft.

Melton's exposed position offered no protection when the weather turned sour at the end of January. Six to twelve inches of snow fell on the airfield in a very short time on 27th January. All personnel on station were called upon to clear the runways and by 15:00 hours the main runway was cleared, followed by the two shorter runways an hour later. Their efforts were rewarded; Melton was the only airfield open in Leicestershire. This turned out to be very lucky for three USAAF B-17 Flying Fortresses which had to use the airfield as their own was closed due to poor weather.

January 1944 was a frustrating month for the OAPU, the unit lacking key personnel in a variety of ground trades, which limited the amount of aircraft they were capable of dispatching. Generally, the number of personnel on strength was quite high, even comparable to a two-squadron bomber station. At the end of January, 1,830 officers, S/NCOs and airmen, along with 295 WAAF officers and airwomen, were living and working at Melton.

Wing Commander Oakley's short tour at Melton came to an end at the beginning of February, when he was replaced by Wing Commander C F H Grace, who took over as station commander on the 9th.

The FCP's stay at Melton was also short; it was moved to Pershore in Worcestershire on 16th March, and was disbanded into No. 1 Ferry Unit the following day. The OAPU must have received the key personnel it was looking for by the end of March 1944. Aircraft despatched in January totalled only 44, and only 50 more were sent out in February. The total, however, in March was 105 aircraft and this was more like the number that the OAPU was designed to dispatch. Up until April, the OAPU's commitments were mainly Bostons and Wellingtons, but equipment began to arrive in April in preparation for receiving the Short Stirling. As this was a four engined aircraft, many of the OAPU's personnel had to attend additional courses in readiness, and one Stirling arrived from Hullavington in conjunction with the courses held. The Stirling Mk.V transport version would be the main mark handled by the OAPU and the first arrived on 23rd May 1944 with one Stirling that was placed on the unit's own strength.

The flexibility and workload of the OAPU increased in June when, on top of their usual dispatch commitments, they started to carry out inspections and servicing of all 304 FTU's aircraft, which by this time must have totalled over 100 on station. Ten Stirlings were dispatched every month and by July Beaufighter and Beaufort commitments were also occupying much of the unit's time.

An experimental amalgamation of 304 FTU and 4 OAPU began on 5th July 1944. The intention was for the units to operate as one. Called No. 4 APU, both units would still retain their individual identity during a trial period of only one month. The marriage of the two units worked very successfully and went well beyond the trial time limit. Aircraft still arrived at the OAPU

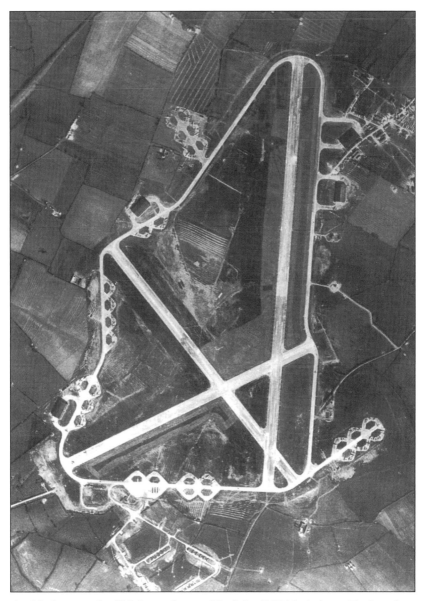

Aerial photograph of Melton taken on 22nd April 1944. At least 80 aircraft are present and this was a typical busy scene during the airfield's brief existence. (P.H.T. Green Collection.)

and when the preparation work was complete they were immediately handed over to 304 FTU, who would ferry the aircraft to the required location.

Douglas Dakota Mk.IIIs and Mk.IVs made use of Melton from the 9th September. The Dakotas were from 107 (T)OTU at Leicester East and used Melton for conversion training until the end of the month. September saw the first commitment of de Havilland Mosquito Mk.IVs arrive at the APU – initially only three, on 12th September, but this number had increased by the end of the year.

The engagement of 304 FTU and 4 OAPU became permanent from 9th October 1944. The arrangement had worked so well that both units were disbanded into 12 Ferry Unit (FU) and this situation would remain for the next year. The new unit now boasted several aircraft of its own and they included two Oxfords, three Beaufort Mk.IIs, three Beaufighter Mk.Xs, two Wellington Mk.Xs and two Ansons.

November's commitments were becoming more varied, with examples of the Beaufighter Mk.VI and Mk.X, Stirling Mk.IV, Hawker Hurricane Mk.IIc, Avro Anson Mk.XII and various marks of Mosquito, including the Mk.XIX and Mk.XXX. Mosquitoes received prior to this were the bomber variants, but these later marks were night fighters, and the MK.XXX was the ultimate wartime version. Flight Sergeant Higgins was flying a Mk.XXX on 30th November 1944 when the undercarriage failed to retract after take-off. Higgins quickly rejoined the circuit and, on final approach, the Mosquito stalled and crashed short of the runway, catching fire immediately. Unfortunately, Higgins' navigator, Pilot Officer Boudreau, was trapped in the fighter and died later that day from the burns that he received.

A ground breaking unit made temporary use of Melton for a few weeks from late 1944. 1341 Special Duties (SD) Flight was formed at Abingdon in Oxfordshire, flying the Armstrong Whitworth Whitley for signals and counter measures. 1342 (SD) Flight were using the Halifax when they arrived at Melton. Their aircraft were bristling with various antennae and always under guard. By 21st December, the crews had left for West Kirby transit camp and departed for Digri in India. Their aircraft were ferried out of Melton on 5th February 1945.

New Year 1945 began with poor weather and more emphasis

on dispatching single-engined fighter aircraft rather than the multi-engined types 12 FU were used to. The Supermarine Spitfire was the main fighter received; many of the 53 dispatched during January were Mk.Vbs destined for France. February was similar, with nearly 70 Spitfires being dispatched to various locations in Europe and, for the first time, naval fighters being prepared by the FU. Sixteen Grumman Hellcats were dispatched at the end of February. The Hellcat was a superb carrier-borne fighter that was proving itself in the Pacific fighting the Japanese. The Hellcat Mk.I first entered service with the Fleet Air Arm's 800 Squadron in 1943. The Royal Navy originally named it the Gannet, but this did not catch on. The majority of Royal Navy Hellcats served with the British Pacific Fleet and by the war's end nearly 1,200 aircraft had been delivered.

The following month, more interesting American aircraft passed through the FU's hands, including Vought Corsairs, North American Mustangs and Vultee Vengeances. The Corsair was a rival of the Hellcat, and actually entered carrier service with the Royal Navy before the United States Navy. The Vengeance was a rare machine in the country, let alone the county, and by this time was an obsolete aircraft that had been

Melton was certainly an airfield to catch sight of the unusual. Over 100 Grumman Hellcats destined for the Royal Navy in the Far East passed through 12 FU in early 1945. (Via author.)

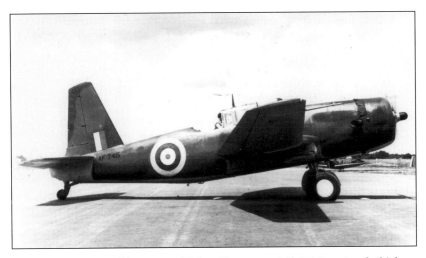

Only at Melton would you see a Vultee Vengeance Mk.IV, twenty of which passed through 12 FU during March 1945. (Via author.)

allocated to target tug duties. The Vengeance was unique when it entered service with the RAF in mid-1942. It was the only aircraft designed specifically as a dive bomber, in close support of Army operations, to enter the RAF.

There were two accidents involving the Vengeance at Melton in March 1945. On 23rd March a Mk.IV FD364 could only lower one undercarriage leg on approach and proceeded to perform an impeccable emergency landing. This was followed on the 27th by another Mk.IV, FD393, which undershot the runway, collapsing its undercarriage.

The end of the war in Europe brought an end to the single engined fighter commitments, but, with the war still raging in the Far East, multi-engined aircraft were still in demand. The majority of the single-engined ferry pilots began to leave Melton for Filton, near Bristol, and these were replaced by multi-engined crews, which brought no relief to the messing and accommodation situation. The new arrivals were to ferry aircraft to South East Asia Command but after they had spent a hectic few weeks at Melton preparing for this, the war against the Japanese came to an end.

Transport versions of the Handley Page Halifax and

Consolidated Liberator passed through the FU during the summer of 1945. They were followed by an influx of Canadian built Avro Lancaster Mk.Xs which had arrived too late for active service. Many of the Lancasters were simply prepared for the flight back to Canada and would serve with the RCAF, while others ended up at Colerne in Wiltshire and Aston Down in Gloucestershire, where they were scrapped.

Two more units were formed at Melton in September 1945; 1588 and 1589 (Heavy Freighter) Flights both flew the Stirling Mk.V. Both units were to serve in the Middle East in an effort to support other aircraft operating with 216 Group.

By September 1945 12 FU's workload was at an all-time low, and, with only 26 aircraft passing through the unit, the end was in sight for the FU. 44 Group's ferrying operations were rapidly shrinking and the decision to close 12 FU came as no surprise. HQ 44 Group decided it would place Melton on care and maintenance on 21st October. A final demand for additional spares overseas came as a short reprieve, but 12 FU was finally disbanded on 7th November 1945. 44 Group Transport Command gave up the airfield on 1st February 1946 and it was

Tucked away in the trees, off Sandy Lane to the east of the old airfield, is a good example of a domestic site. Originally used by airmen, then by Polish expatriates, these Nissen huts are slowly falling into decay. (J. Molyneux.)

*A modern day aerial photograph showing the remnants of Melton airfield.
The B6047 follows the line of a perimeter track and one of the old secondary
runways and then heads south to Great Dalby. The cold war Thor missile site
can still be seen clearly from the B6047 and is slightly right of centre in this
photograph. (Crown Copyright.)*

transferred to 22 Group Technical Training Command. Melton then became 14 Recruits Centre from 15th February, but this unit only remained until 27th September.

After a period of quiet, Melton's accommodation was prepared for Polish service personnel who chose to settle in Britain. 9 Resettlement Unit (Polish) was formed on the 5th October 1946, with the camp's first occupants arriving on the 26th November. On 4th June 1947, 6 RU(P) moved in from Nottinghamshire and was taken over by 9 RU(P). The unit remained at Melton until 10th June 1948, when it moved to Dunholme Lodge in Lincolnshire, to disband a few weeks later.

The airfield was now closed and farming quickly returned, but ten years later the RAF showed renewed interest in the old airfield for a totally different reason. Contractors began to arrive in late 1958 to start construction of a Thor missile site, which involved building launching pads and associated buildings in the centre of the airfield, surrounded by high security fencing.

Melton's new unit was 254 (Strategic Missile) Squadron, which re-formed at the former wartime airfield on 1st December 1959. 254 Squadron served as a fighter and coastal command squadron during the Second World War, flying Blenheims and Beaufighters, but was disbanded into 42 Squadron on 1st October 1946. On its re-formation at Melton, 254 Squadron was controlled by a central permanent RAF station, which, in this case, was North Luffenham. The Rutland airfield also controlled Thor sites at Folkingham in Lincolnshire and Harrington and Polebrook, both in Northamptonshire, collectively known as 151 Wing, Fighter Command.

The Thors did not stay for long; by the end of 1963, all of the United Kingdom's sites had been closed and disbanded. Melton's turn came on 23rd August 1963, and for the final time the old airfield fell into disuse. By 1966, the land had been sold off and the major part of it returned to agriculture.

Melton today still retains large sections of its runways and the B6047 between Melton Mowbray and Great Dalby now uses the eastern taxiway. Although very few buildings remain, a reminder of the cold war is present in the centre of the airfield in the form of the three Thor launch pads, still an intimidating sight many years on.

13

NORTH LUFFENHAM

National Grid Reference SK941098; 6 miles SW of Oakham

North Luffenham has enjoyed a varied role since it first opened in the early years of the Second World War. It has been used as a training, bomber, fighter and transport airfield as well as a strategic missile base. Removed from the RAF's inventory in 1998, it is still used by the military, but today the occupant is the Army and the airfield has been renamed St George's Barracks.

The site for an airfield between the villages Edith Weston, Ketton and North Luffenham was selected as early as 1939. The new airfield, named North Luffenham, was built to permanent specifications, and construction began in 1940. All of the main buildings were constructed by John Laing building contractors, and were built to wartime utility standards. This gave the airfield a permanent feel and the construction of brick-built accommodation and messes would make the airfield a reasonable posting for any airman sent there.

However, this was not the case when the airfield officially opened on 14th January 1941. Although the airfield and the majority of technical buildings had been completed, the accommodation had not. The officers' and sergeants' messes were far from finished, with only one wing of the sergeants' mess being habitable. This was further complicated by the weather; the winter of 1941 was one of the worst on record.

North Luffenham's first unit was formed there on 18th January. The airfield was under the control of 51 Group, Flying

Training Command and 17 Elementary Flying Training School
(EFTS) became the new unit. Sixty pupils arrived for training the
same day, but with no aircraft and the airfield covered in snow,
flying training did not start until the following week. The EFTS
flew Tiger Moths, delivered by Air Transport Auxiliary (ATA)
pilots a few days later. The weather had improved by the end of
January and the domestic accommodation was completed.

The EFTS quickly got down to the task of training new pilots
and the first had completed their course by the end of February.
By March, the EFTS had 40 Tiger Moths on strength, and were
flying circuits and bumps day in, day out. The unit's accident
rate was very good during their stay at North Luffenham. The
only recorded incident involved Tiger Moth II N9334 on 5th
March 1941. The aircraft crashed during a forced landing near
Rolleston in Leicestershire.

The EFTS was never destined to stay at North Luffenham for
very long. Two operational bomber squadrons, 61 and 144,
received signals on 21st June, informing them that they would be
moving to North Luffenham. The airfield was to be taken over by
5 Group Bomber Command on 17th July 1941. 17 EFTS left that
day for its new home at Peterborough and its Tiger Moths were
quickly replaced by Handley Page Hampden medium bombers.

The new squadrons had both moved in from Hemswell in
Lincolnshire. They had converted to the Hampden early in 1939
and had been in action from the start of the war. The Hampden,
along with the Whitley and Wellington, formed the backbone of
Bomber Command at the beginning of the Second World War.
The Hampden was first tendered as a design back in December
1933 and the prototype first flew from Radlett in Hertfordshire
on 21st June 1936. 5 Group received its first aircraft in August
1938 when 49 Squadron at Scampton became the first to convert
to the new bomber. The Hampden went on to equip 10
operational squadrons and a plethora of other units, before being
removed from bombing operations in September 1942.

Both squadrons flew their first operations from North
Luffenham on the night of 19th/20th July 1941. Both flew a
'gardening', or mining, operation, dropping the mines in the
mouths of the rivers Elbe and Weser. 61 Squadron took part in the
first large raid on Frankfurt a few nights later. Both squadrons
joined a second attack on Frankfurt on 22nd/23rd July, but the

raids caused little damage. All the crews did return to North Luffenham unscathed, though.

After mining and bombing German industrial targets since the start of the war, the focus for many Bomber Command squadrons became the threat of the German capital ships. *Scharnhorst, Gneisenau* and *Prinz Eugen* were all moored in Brest harbour. They had been causing chaos for Atlantic shipping and had become a priority target for Bomber Command. The first raid from North Luffenham against the ships happened in daylight on 24th July. This raid had been planned for some time and originally involved 150 aircraft. This was changed at the last minute because the *Scharnhorst* moved to the port of La Pallice and was attacked by a separate force of Halifaxes. The force dispatched was made up of 100 aircraft and included three RAF Flying Fortresses, which bombed at high level. Eighteen Hampdens, including six from 144 Squadron, were escorted by three squadrons of Spitfires that were fitted with long-range fuel tanks. The final part of the raid involved the main bombing force of 79 Wellingtons from 1 and 3 Groups. The Wellingtons were unescorted and as a result ten of them were shot down by enemy fighters. The weather was perfect over the target and the crews were easily able to identifying their objective. This also meant that the flak gunners and fighters could easily spot the Wellingtons. Two Hampdens were shot down, one of which was AE225. Flight Lieutenant R B Barr and crew were on board and were shot down by German fighters near Ploudalmezeau, 21 km north-west of Brest. Barr and another crewman became prisoners of war and three other crew members were killed. All of the five Hampdens that returned to North Luffenham had received flak damage.

Before 61 Squadron arrived at North Luffenham it had been given the unenviable task of operating the Avro Manchester. It was hoped that the whole squadron would have converted to the Manchester before moving to Rutland. Innumerable technical problems prevented this, and by August 1941 only a few were on strength. On the night of 14/15th August, Wing Commander G E Valentine, 61 Squadron's Commanding Officer, flew the first Manchester raid from North Luffenham. Valentine's aircraft was one of a force of 52 aircraft that successfully attacked railway sidings at Magdeburg. Two weeks later, Valentine was at the controls of a Manchester again, ready for a raid on Berlin's Schlesiger railway station. On this occasion, though, he was accompanied by North Luffenham's Station Commander, Group Captain J F T Barrett. The Manchester was flown all the way to Berlin at low-level and, while attempting to gain height over the target, was struck by flak. All on board were killed when the aircraft came down in the Schonefeld district of the city. As a result of this incident it was ruled that under no circumstances could senior officers such as station commanders and squadron commanders fly on operations, especially not together, without the permission of Group HQ.

September was a very rough month for 144 Squadron; out of six operations over Germany, ten aircraft were lost. In contrast, 61 Squadron had flown 37 Hampden sorties with no loss. While 61 Squadron's Hampden crews continued with the Bomber Command offensive, several crews had been receiving continuation training on the Manchester. By the end of the month, the unit was finally fully equipped with the Manchester and moved out to North Luffenham's satellite airfield at Woolfox Lodge, where it continued the Bomber offensive until re-equipped with the Avro Lancaster.

Throughout the remainder of 1941, the Hampdens of 144 Squadron continued operations against cities in Germany, as well as mine laying and shipping strikes. It was during one such patrol that a lone Hampden, piloted by Flight Lieutenant J F Craig RNZAF, scored a major success for the RAF. It was 3rd November and Craig was flying off the Frisian Islands when he came across a ten-ship convoy. He attacked at low level and scored several direct hits on the largest vessel in the convoy, leaving it on fire and apparently sinking. Craig and his crew did not realize that the ship they had attacked was carrying several enemy officers, who were keen to see their flak ships in action. Intelligence reports later revealed that one of the officers was Major General Felix Varda, who was commander of the Western anti-aircraft defence system. This success was a brief morale booster for 144 Squadron. Unfortunately, ten more Hampdens were lost before the year was out.

The winter of 1941/42 caused much disruption to Bomber operations throughout the East Midlands. This was reflected at North Luffenham by the arrival of a detachment of Hampdens

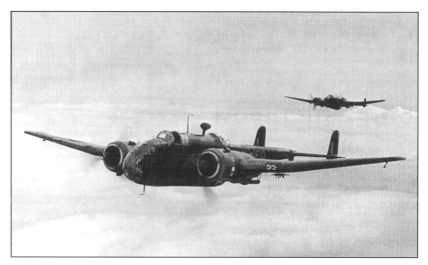

Handley Page Hampdens from 408 (Goose) Squadron, RCAF briefly operated from North Luffenham in early 1942. It would be nearly ten years before the Canadians returned. (PHT Green Collection.)

operated by 408 (Goose) Squadron, RCAF on 27th January 1942. Their home airfield, at Balderton in Nottinghamshire, had been declared unserviceable because of heavy snowfall and surface water. Originally formed at Lindholme, Yorkshire on 24th June 1941 as part of 5 Group Bomber Command, the Canadian unit flew the Hampden for over 1,200 sorties before converting to the Handley Page Halifax and, later, the Avro Lancaster Mk.II.

408 and 144 Squadrons flew a joint operation for the first time on 31st January / 1st February, another raid on the capital ships in Brest harbour. While all of the Canadians returned home safely, the luckless 144 Squadron crews suffered at the hands of the German flak defences. Two aircraft were brought down off the French coast, five crew were killed and three became POWs.

Bomber Command resources were stretched to the limit at this time. Raids into Germany, anti-shipping and mining sorties were all taking their toll. The Achilles' heel for the RAF was the constant distraction of the capital ships at anchor in Brest. This peaked when, during the night of 11/12th February, the ships made their move out of the French port. Although apparently under close observation, the ships managed to slipped away at night and the Channel Dash officially know as Operation *Fuller*, was launched. North Luffenham's contribution to the operation was eight Hampdens from 408 and nine from 144 Squadron. *Fuller* involved 244 aircraft in two waves; the first wave had a fighter escort, while the second, involving the North Luffenham squadrons, did not.

The weather conditions in the Channel were atrocious: almost solid cloud down to 700ft, with bouts of heavy rain. Three of 408 Squadron's Hampdens failed to locate the enemy convoy, and two located the ships but were prevented from attacking by the weather. The remaining three dropped their bombs on unidentified ships, but were unable to observe their results, due to the weather. 144 Squadron were struck again; two aircraft were lost, one of which was believed to have been the victim of fighters or flak from the convoy. A second Hampden crashed near Norwich with flak damage. Unfortunately, the pilot, Sergeant E J Nightingale DFM, died in hospital of his injuries later in the evening. Two aircraft also managed to attack the convoy but, once again, the weather prevented any results from being observed.

Operation *Fuller*, which the RAF had been preparing for so long, was, on the whole, a failure. Fifteen aircraft were missing, presumed lost, and two more crashed on return to England. The only long-term consolation was that both the *Scharnhorst* and *Gneisenau* suffered damage from mines as they sped through the Channel. There is a possibility that the mines were laid by aircraft from North Luffenham, as they had been operating in the incident area only days before.

The Canadian Hampdens of 408 Squadron departed from North Luffenham on 17th March 1942, when their home station at Balderton was declared fit for operations. The squadron had been lucky during their stay, losing only two aircraft, neither to enemy action.

The space created by the timely departure of 408 Squadron made room for a new unit to be formed. 61 Squadron Conversion Flight (CF) was formed on 27th March under the command of Squadron Leader Gascoigne-Cecil. The main squadron struggled on with the Manchester at Woolfox Lodge and needed new crews to replace their mounting losses. Conversion training would also have to take place on the Lancaster, which was earmarked for

61 Squadron. Initially they were equipped with two Manchesters and one Lancaster, but this increased to three Manchesters and two Lancasters before the unit departed to Syerston, Nottinghamshire on 5th May 1942 with the rest of the squadron from Woolfox Lodge.

Meanwhile, 144 Squadron carried on operating from North Luffenham with more raids deep into Germany. A change of scenery was in store for the long-suffering unit. A signal was received from HQ Bomber Command on 1st April stating that it was proposing to transfer North Luffenham and its satellite at Woolfox Lodge to 7 Group. This meant a training unit would replace 144 Squadron, which was told it would move to Swinderby on 18th April. The Hampdens flew their last sorties from North Luffenham on 15th/16th April 1942 without loss. The move to Swinderby was cancelled and the squadron was chosen as a torpedo bomber unit and moved to Leuchars, Fife on 21st April, joining Coastal Command. After completion of their training in the new role, they were moved to North Russia to help protect the Arctic convoys. Very little action took place, as the enemy warships never ventured out of their bases in northern Norway during the squadron's stay in Russia. Their aircraft were eventually handed over to the Russians and the squadron sailed home in a cruiser to start anti-submarine patrols and shipping strikes from Leuchars. In January 1943, the squadron converted to the capable Bristol Beaufighter and used this aircraft successfully against shipping until their disbandment on 25th May 1945. 144 Squadron did eventually return to North Luffenham, albeit in a completely different guise. They were re-formed on 1st December 1959 as No. 144 Intermediate-range Ballistic Missile Squadron with Douglas Thors, and this was finally disbanded on 23rd August 1963.

Also on 21st April 1942, the airfield changed hands from 5 to 7 Group and 29 Operational Training Unit (OTU) was formed. The new OTU was formed to train night bomber crews, and their main equipment was the Vickers Wellington. Twenty-seven Wellingtons were initially on strength, which was half the size of a normal OTU. They also had a pair of Westland Lysander Target Tugs and a few Avro Ansons

Just to add to the many changes that were occurring at North Luffenham, 7 Group Bomber Command was renumbered to

92 (OTU) Group. This was purely an administrative change, and had no effect on the role of 29 OTU. It was several weeks before the OTU settled in at North Luffenham, and it was not until 10th June that the first training course began.

It was not long before the OTU was involved in front line operations. Air Chief Marshall Harris had launched the first of many '1000 bomber' raids on Germany a few days earlier, on 30th/31st May. Harris had to call upon all aircraft available to him and that included OTU crews and aircraft. 29 OTU was first involved in the third of the huge raids against Bremen on the night of 25/26th June. Eight Wellingtons from the OTU contributed to the total force of 1,067 aircraft involved. Three of North Luffenham's aircraft returned early with engine problems, while the remaining five claimed to have successfully bombed the target. German air-raid officials, reporting from Bremen after the raid, claimed that only 80 RAF bombers had attacked. They also reported that a subsequent BBC broadcast claiming that over 1,000 bombers had been sent was a propaganda bluff! The Germans did, however, accurately claim that over 50 bombers had been shot down; this was the only statistic from either side that was near to the truth. Fifty-five aircraft had indeed been shot down that night and this was the last of the '1,000 bomber' raids for quite some time.

The OTU now settled into a training programme at North Luffenham and at the satellite at Woolfox Lodge. They were joined over the summer months of 1942 by twin-engined Airspeed Oxfords from Spitalgate near Grantham, Lincolnshire. The Oxfords were part of 12 Pilot Advanced Flying Unit (P)AFU and used North Luffenham as a Relief Landing Ground, mainly for night flying practice.

29 OTU did not take part in another major raid on Germany until the night of 31st July/1st August. Ten aircraft were detailed to attack Dusseldorf, along with 95 others from 92 (OTU) Group. The city was bombed accurately with over 900 tonnes of bombs. Seven of the OTU's Wellingtons managed to bomb the target and all ten aircraft returned safely to North Luffenham. The German officials who were keeping Düsseldorf's records at the time compiled them with great detail. Entries contain the usual casualty rate and bomb damage, and give details of a cow with an injured udder caused by a bomb splinter!

Eleven more aircraft successfully bombed Düsseldorf again on the night of 10th/11th September. Once again, all of the Wellingtons returned home and Düsseldorf was left to lick its wounds for the remainder of 1942. The final raid that 29 OTU flew from North Luffenham, was a return to Bremen on 13th/14th September. It was not on the same scale as the previous '1,000 Bomber', nonetheless 442 aircraft made up the first wave, which once again contained many OTU aircraft. Eight Wellingtons from North Luffenham were detailed, but only seven managed to bomb the target. Flying Officer J L Munro in Wellington Ic R1459 took off at 23:47, but three minutes later a textbook crash landing was carried out near Empingham, 6 miles east of Oakham in Rutland. The heavily laden bomber lost engine power immediately after take off; fortunately, none of the crew was injured.

The first indication that a move was on the cards for 29 OTU was received on 14th September. A signal from HQ Bomber Command stated that they intended to transfer the OTU to Bruntingthorpe. Movement began the following month when 'D' Flight, which had been operating from Woolfox Lodge, was moved back to North Luffenham. A few days later, on 20th October 1942, a detachment of men was dispatched to Bruntingthorpe to begin preparations for receiving the OTU's Wellingtons. 'A' Flight flew out of North Luffenham on 6th November for its new home, but this was a short-lived move, as they had returned to operate from Woolfox Lodge by the end of January 1943. Bruntingthorpe was in no fit state to operate aircraft and a great deal of work still needed to be carried out before the OTU as a whole could depart. In the meantime, training continued unabated and the strength of 29 OTU had risen to a full size OTU with 54 Wellingtons, one Boulton Paul Defiant and four Target Tugs on charge. It was another five months before Bruntingthorpe was ready, which gives an indication as to how premature the initial attempt to move was. 29 OTU finally started to move on 24th May, and all had made it safely to Bruntingthorpe by 3rd June 1943.

North Luffenham now went through a period of expansion and modification. The first indication of this had come about back in April with a visit by Air Commodore Darley, who was there to decide on the position of the new concrete runways. The airfield as a whole was officially handed over to civilian contractors George Wimpey & Co. Ltd on 15th June. The contractors were housed in the RAF barrack blocks and had full use of all the mess facilities. Work began immediately on building three new runways, the main one being 2,000 yards long, 36 hardstandings and a connecting perimeter track.

Like many other airfields in the region in late 1943, North Luffenham was allocated for use by the United States 9th Air Force. It was originally intended, like Woolfox Lodge, for housing Douglas C-47A aircraft arriving from the North African and Italian campaigns; a small contingent of American serviceman arrived in October, and North Luffenham was given the Army Air Force Station number 477, but the American forces used neither Woolfox Lodge nor North Luffenham.

The Ministry of Aircraft Production (MAP) was scouring the country for suitable sites for the construction, modification and storage of gliders. This was in preparation for the forthcoming invasion of Europe, as it was no secret that this would happen

The General Aircraft Hamilcar was the largest Allied glider built, bigger than a Lancaster bomber and capable of carrying a seven tonne tank. One hundred and twenty-one of the gliders were constructed at North Luffenham in the three T.2 hangars that still stand on the north side of the airfield.

sooner or later. North Luffenham was an ideal candidate for the assembly of the General Aircraft Hamilcar assault glider. Forty-five civilians from General Aircraft and 92 USAAF personnel arrived on 14th December 1943 to begin the preparations for receiving the gliders. The Americans did not stay long; originally intended for use by the USAAF, the Hamilcar was never used. The Hamilcar was the largest glider used by Allied forces during the Second World War. Slightly bigger than an Avro Lancaster, it could carry a seven-tonne tank and was the first British glider to carry a tank into action. The Hamilcar had a crew of two and its nose was hinged to enable vehicles to be driven straight into action on landing. Over 400 were built and a powered version was also developed for the Pacific theatre, but the Japanese surrendered before they saw action. The majority of the Hamilcars arrived at North Luffenham by road in kit form. Others were towed in by Handley Page Halifax glider tugs and released over the airfield. During their short stay at North Luffenham, the General Aircraft Glider Assembly & Modification Unit handled 121 Hamilcars, all of them in time for the forthcoming invasion of Europe, in which the majority of them took part.

The airfield was transferred to 23 Group, Flying Training Command early in 1944, with another new unit in mind. The Heavy Glider Conversion Unit (HGCU) arrived on 2nd March 1944 from Brize Norton, Oxfordshire. Formed on paper at Shrewton (which is not an airfield), Wiltshire on the 29th June 1942, to be equipped with Armstrong Whitworth Whitley tugs and Airspeed Horsa gliders, the HQ moved to Brize Norton two weeks later, where aircraft could be delivered. The HGCU arrived with 40 Whitley V, 36 Horsa and a variety of support aircraft that included Oxfords, an Anson, the odd Tiger Moth, and a Miles Magister.

The HGCU's main equipment, the Whitley V, was the most common mark of this pre-war bomber built. Designed in 1934, and first flown in 1936, the Whitley had ceased front-line operations with Bomber Command in 1943. The RAF had been looking for a replacement for the Whitley as a glider tug for over a year. The main candidate was another Armstrong Whitworth type, the Albemarle, also a pre-war design, that was intended as a reconnaissance and light bomber aircraft. It was, however,

The Heavy Glider Conversion Unit operated several Armstrong Whitworth Albemarles as glider tugs, but they were out-numbered by the more reliable Armstrong Whitworth Whitley Mk.VII.

relegated to glider towing and special transport duties, only once dropping bombs against the enemy. The HGCU had received its first Albemarles at Brize Norton in January 1943, but, deemed unsuitable, they had left by April. A single Albemarle, P1605, returned to the HGCU on 17th March 1944 and was evaluated at North Luffenham. On this occasion, the Albemarle passed all the necessary trials and was cleared for service with the unit. The first did not arrive on strength until July, and the hard working Whitleys were slowly replaced.

With D-Day rapidly approaching, the USAAF were looking at methods of getting their Waco CG-14A gliders off the ground quickly without building costly, time consuming landing strips. The solution was to snatch the glider from the ground using a low-flying Douglas C-47. Trials of this method were carried out successfully at North Luffenham on 30th May. How many of these snatches were actually carried out after D-Day is unclear, as it is possible that senior officers underestimated how quickly the allies were able to set up usable airfields.

Training intensified for the HGCU as the invasion of Europe drew closer. On 1st June 1944, the unit was involved in a large exercise at Hampstead Norris in Berkshire. Twenty-two Horsas were towed *en masse* and all were safely released over the Berkshire airfield. Six more carried out a night landing with

Gliders were a common sight throughout the county, and none more so than the Airspeed Horsas which were stored on many airfields. At North Luffenham they were used, rather than stored, firstly by the HGMU and then post war by 21 HGMU. (Via author.)

complete success. When D-Day finally arrived, on 6th June, many glider crews that were trained at North Luffenham took part. The total success of the glider operations on that day confirmed to many sceptics that this was the best method of getting troops into action quickly.

Training of glider crews continued unabated, as their role in any future operation during the war was vitally important. During June, 855 day and 296 night tows had been carried out, the majority without mishap. The satellite airfield of Woolfox Lodge became available from September 1944, as the resident 218 Squadron had converted to Lancasters and left for Methwold in Suffolk. This briefly expanded the capabilities of the HGCU, but a signal was received from HQ 23 Group saying that the unit was to return to Brize Norton. The proposed move date was 18th September, but this would have disrupted one of the courses, so a move date was set for 13th October.

Once again, North Luffenham sat empty awaiting a new unit and yet another change of Group. 7 Group had been re-formed and was now responsible for the organisation of heavy bomber conversion units. On 16th October, North Luffenham was transferred from 23 Group to be part of the reorganised 7 Group and new base system. The base system worked as a clutch of airfields (usually three), controlled administratively by one airfield. North Luffenham became the controlling airfield for 73 Base on 1st November 1944, with Woolfox Lodge and Spanhoe, Northamptonshire. The latter was still controlled by the US 9th Air Force at this time and remained so until the end of the war.

This did not affect the arrival of North Luffenham's new unit, 1653 Heavy Conversion Unit (HCU). Formed at Polebrook, Northamptonshire on 9th January 1942 to convert crews to fly the Consolidated Liberator for RAF Middle East operations, and disbanded and re-formed within three weeks at the end of 1943, it then changed its role and trained crews on Short Stirlings at Chedburgh in Suffolk. Before their move to North Luffenham, the HCU had 40 Stirling I and IIIs on strength. The Stirling at this time was coming to the end of its operational career with Bomber Command and was being replaced by the Lancaster. 1653 HCU started its move from Chedburgh on 16th November and all the aircraft had arrived by 27th November. All 40 crews that had been undergoing training were sent on leave while the HCU instructors converted to the Lancaster. North Luffenham was to house the Stirling only briefly, as 32 Lancaster I and IIIs quickly took their place. Once settled in, a menagerie of types including the Spitfire Vb, Hurricane IIc, Beaufighter VI and Mosquito night fighter XIX also supported the Lancasters.

At this stage in the war, there was no call for crews undergoing training on an HCU to take part in Bomber Command operations. But training was dangerous and, unfortunately, many crews never made it to front line squadrons. Seven Lancasters were lost in training accidents before the war's end, and, sadly, most were fatal.

73 Base's responsibilities were expanded on 1st April 1945, when two more airfields joined: Bottesford, operating with 1668 HCU's Lancaster Mk I & Mk.IIs, and Langar in Nottinghamshire with 1669 HCU's Lancasters and Halifaxes. Woolfox Lodge

remained in the base and had been operating 1651 HCU Lancasters since the end of October 1944.

On 8th May 1945, the war in Europe came to an end, and North Luffenham's personnel were all given a two-day stand down, a temporary respite, as now the HCU was training crews for the continuing war in the Far East. The Japanese surrendered in August and it was at this point that 1653 HCU and the RAF as a whole started to wind down.

Like many other stations around the country, North Luffenham opened its gates to celebrate Battle of Britain day on 15th September 1945. Nearly 13,000 people attended the show, which had ground and air displays. There were fly-pasts by the HCU's Lancasters, Spitfire aerobatics, a Hurricane dropping practice bombs and a Gloster Meteor jet performing some high-speed passes.

Virtually all of the Lancasters flown by the HCU had seen service with squadrons before being relegated to the training role. Many were getting tired and becoming more difficult to keep airworthy. By the end of 1945, the HCU had only eighteen

A tired Avro Lancaster Mk.III of 1653 HCU rests between sorties at North Luffenham in early 1945. Aircraft in the HCUs had all seen better days, often having served on several front-line squadrons and other HCUs. (Via author.)

aircraft on strength, and during February 1946 records state that only four were airworthy. Personnel dwindled rapidly at North Luffenham as well. There were many New Zealanders and Australians on station but by the beginning of March 1946 they had all gone home. The HCU struggled on through 1946, losing several more aircraft in flying accidents and through eventual scrapping. A new home was beckoning at Lindholme in Yorkshire and after two years at North Luffenham, 1653 HCU left for its new home on 28th October 1946.

When the HGCU returned to Brize Norton in October 1944, it was disbanded almost immediately and the bulk of the old unit was redesignated 21 HGCU. The remainder of the unit formed 22 and 23 HGCU, operating from Keevil, Wiltshire and Peplow, Salop, respectively. 21 HGCU remained at Brize Norton until it moved to Elsham Wolds in North Lincolnshire on 29th December 1945. Elsham Wolds had been a very busy bomber station during the war, and its general condition reflected this. All of the personnel were unhappy with their new posting as the living accommodation was far from ideal. Once again, an empty North Luffenham opened its gates to another new tenant, although not a totally unfamiliar one this time. 21 HGCU moved to North Luffenham on 5th December 1946. They were now operating Handley Page Halifax III and VIIs, Albermarles in quantity and the usual 30-plus Airspeed Horsas. With the arrival of this new unit, control of the station changed back to 23 Group, Flying Training Command.

By December 1947, the HGCU had been disbanded and in the same month the airfield was taken over by a pair of Transport Conversion Units (T)CU from Wymeswold, both operating the Douglas Dakota. Both 1333 and 1382 (T) CU lost their individual identities within weeks when they were disbanded and re-formed as 240 Operational Conversion Unit (OCU). The OCU continued to operate the Dakota, and while at North Luffenham used Avro Ansons, Vickers Valettas and de Havilland Devons as well. 240 OCU left North Luffenham for Dishforth in Yorkshire in March 1951 and was followed by 102 Flying Refresher School (FRS), operating Spitfire LF.16s and F.22s, but the school only stayed nine months before its personnel moved to Oakington in Cambridgeshire to become part of 206 Advanced Flying School.

The airfield then became the home to 1 Fighter Wing of the

Royal Canadian Air Force (RCAF), on 15th November 1951, as part of Canada's NATO commitment. The Wing at North Luffenham was made up of 410 (Cougar), 441 (Silver Fox) and 439 (Tiger) Squadron, all flying the Canadair Sabre Mk.2. This aircraft was the Canadian licence-built version of the North American F-86. The Sabre Mk.II also equipped several RAF squadrons. The RCAF began to leave North Luffenham towards the end of 1954. First to leave was 410 Squadron, which left for Baden-Solligen in West Germany on 14th November, followed by 441 Squadron, which departed on 21st December for Zweibrücken, also in West Germany. 439 Squadron was the last to leave, on 1st April 1955, when the unit re-located to Marville in France. On the same day, control of the airfield was returned to the RAF. During their stay, the three Canadian squadrons lost seventeen Sabres between them at the cost of six pilots' lives.

Training returned to North Luffenham in the guise of the All Weather Operational Conversion Unit (AWOCU), which, as the name suggests, trained crews to fly in all weathers, day or night. The AWOCU was disbanded on 31st December 1956 and re-formed within 238 OCU, which moved in from Colerne in Wiltshire the next day. On 13th March 1958, the OCU was disbanded, the occasion being marked by a formation farewell fly-past of nine Brigands.

During February 1958, the airfield, for the first and last time in

102 FRS was resident at North Luffenham for most of 1951 and here a pair of the school's Spitfire F.22s pose for the camera. (P.H.T. Green Collection.)

its history, became a fighter station. 111 Squadron moved out from North Weald in Essex while the airfield was having its runways resurfaced. The squadron flew Hawker Hunter F.6s and, at that time, made up the RAF's premier aerobatic team, the 'Black Arrows'. Within four months, the sleek, all-black painted fighters had returned to North Weald, bringing to an end seventeen years of military flying at North Luffenham.

14

NUNEATON

National Grid Reference SP375963; 4½ miles NNE of Nuneaton

Nuneaton made up part of the vast wartime jigsaw that saw fledgling airmen advance through their training to become tight knit crews. As important as any front-line bomber station, the airfield's wartime role has been hidden by the high speed tracks and test circuits that cover the airfield today.

Following a survey by Air Ministry officials in 1940, a site for a new airfield was selected between the Leicestershire villages of Fenny Drayton and Higham on the Hill that was locally known as Lindley. However, the Air Ministry chose to use the Warwickshire town name of Nuneaton, which was located four miles to the south. The bulk of the work to build the airfield went to Trollope and Colls of London, supported by a multitude of sub-contractors. Work began in March 1941, but was not in full swing until spring of 1942. Local disruption was minimal but, as usual, several farms were affected and in Nuneaton's case a parish church had to be modified as well. St Margaret's Church in the village of Stoke Golding was located directly under the approach to Nuneaton's main runway. By the time local officials realised this, it was too late to re-align the runway, so the only alternative was to trim the church down to size! After much discussion with the Bishop of Leicester, it was agreed that 60ft of the 120ft spire could be removed, on condition that the church was rebuilt after the war.

Nuneaton had three concrete runways, one 2,000 yards long and two of 1,400 yards, plus 27 hardstandings, one T2 hangar and accommodation for 1,461 personnel.

The new station opened on 7th February 1943, when a detachment of airmen arrived from Bitteswell, under the command of Squadron Leader L G Blomfield. Nuneaton became part of 93 Group Bomber Command and was to be used as a satellite for nearby Bramcote in Warwickshire. The resident unit at Bramcote was 18 OTU, which had been stationed there with its Wellingtons and Ansons since 7th November 1940. This set-up was to be short-lived, as 18 OTU was already preparing to move north, to Finningley in Yorkshire. Little evidence exists of any use made of Nuneaton by the OTU but, by 27th March 18 OTU had left Bramcote. Nuneaton was, however, still in an unfit state to receive aircraft and would remain so well into the summer.

On 5th April 1943, 105 (Transport) OTU was formed within 44 Group at Bramcote to train aircrews for transport squadrons. They were equipped with the Vickers Wellington, primarily a bomber aircraft that was converted to suit the task. Modifications included the fitting of dual controls and the removal of both the front and rear turrets, which were faired over. Nuneaton remained Bramcote's satellite and 105 (T) OTU started flying in their Wellingtons in early June. The aircraft at first were only

With its code letters obscured, this Wellington Mk.X is a good representative of the type of aircraft flown from Nuneaton. (Via author.)

dispersed on the airfield, with just minor maintenance tasks being carried out. After a visit from the Air Ministry Works Department on 26th July, the airfield was given the green light to commence flying training, which finally started on 18th August 1943.

One unit that did make immediate full use of Nuneaton was 1513 Beam Approach Training Flight, which arrived at Bramcote on 31st October 1942. Operating eight Airspeed Oxfords, the Flight's aircraft would often operate at night or in poor weather conditions. The unglamorous Oxford was one of the most common twin-engined aircraft in service with the RAF, but has received very little recognition. Designed in response to a 1936 Air Ministry specification, which called for a twin-engined trainer, the Oxford was based on the already successful civilian Envoy. The reputation of the Envoy influenced the Air Ministry to order 136 aircraft even before the Oxford's maiden flight on 19th June 1937. Five different marks followed and orders went through the roof as the demand for training aircraft increased at the beginning of the Second World War. The Oxford went on to serve in ten different air forces and 8,586 of them were produced, with the last leaving the production line in July 1945. The Oxford remained in service with the RAF at 10-Advanced Flying Training School, Pershore until 1954.

105 (T) OTU's safety record was not blighted until 4th December 1943, when a Wellington Ic, DV925, caught fire and crashed near Tilstock in Shropshire. Luckily, all on board managed to take to their parachutes and all lived to tell the tale. The first test of Nuneaton's emergency services did not come until the following year. On 14th January 1944, another Wellington Ic was taking off when an engine caught fire; after flying a very tight circuit the aircraft was crash-landed on the airfield. Although all on board escaped unhurt the Wellington was totally destroyed by fire, despite the efforts of the RAF fire tender.

With the invasion of Europe imminent, the county, along with many others, was inundated with American units and personnel. A few miles up the A5, the US 250th Field Artillery Battalion (FAB) was being housed in a temporary camp near Merevale, Atherstone, in Warwickshire. Part of their equipment was a pair of Piper L-4 Grasshoppers used for artillery spotting and close liaison duties. The L-4 was a two-seater light aircraft that could trace its roots back to 1930, when it first flew as the Cub. The US Army first showed an interest in the little plane back in 1941, resulting in 5,703 military Cub variants being produced. The first of the Battalion's L-4s arrived at Nuneaton on 11th March, with the second being delivered several weeks later, on 20th April 1944. During their brief stay at Nuneaton they participated in a local escape and evasion exercise, involving the RAF, Home Guard and local police. At the beginning of June, the 250th FAB moved to Derbyshire, which preceded their inevitable move to northern France.

The (T) OTU's Wellington Mk.Is were old and becoming more unreliable. Many of them had served on previous units, and retirement beckoned. From June 1944 onwards, the more reliable and more powerful Mk.Xs replaced the Mk.Is, although this did nothing to improve the safety record of the unit, which steadily deteriorated. As navigation exercises featured heavily in the training programme, many of 105 OTU's losses occurred far afield. Locally, the London, Midland and Scottish Railway Company feared that an aircraft would crash onto the railway line, as the main runway ran parallel to it and both short runways pointed straight at it. These fears were realised on 13th October 1944 when a Wellington Mk.X burst a tyre on take-off. The pilot quickly retracted the undercarriage to stop the bomber, but it was not enough to prevent it from coming to rest on the line. Luckily, it was the middle of the night; so no trains were running and no-one on the aircraft was injured.

From November 1944, 'A' and 'C' Navigation Flights were established at Nuneaton. Part of the new course involved participation in a shuttle service between Nuneaton and Nutt's Corner, County Antrim in Northern Ireland. The shuttles had a dual role, giving the crews experience of long-range navigation as well as delivering passengers and freight.

Nuneaton was not used to visits by aircraft from Bomber Command and the arrival of Lancaster DX-G of 57 Squadron at 3:30 in the morning on 7th March 1945 came as a surprise. Flying Officer Dimond and his crew were returning from an attack on the port of Sassnitz, on the Baltic coast, when the Lancaster's Loran navigation equipment failed. With the fuel load almost depleted, they found Nuneaton in the moonlight and elected to make a wheels-down landing on the grass next to the main runway. On touch down, the undercarriage collapsed and the aircraft crashed at the end of the runway. The crew escaped with only a few minor injuries, aided by the fact that their Lancaster did not catch fire.

In June 1945, both the station and 105 (T) OTU were transferred to 4 Group Transport Command. Whether the change in command had any effect on the OTU is debatable, but, coincidentally, dedicated transport aircraft finally began to arrive in the shape of the Douglas Dakota. Another reshuffling of the OTU meant that 'B' and 'D' Flights, which were at Bitteswell, moved to Nuneaton on 17th July. To make room, 'C' Flight left Nuneaton on 8th August for Crosby-on-Eden in Cumbria. This left 'B' and 'D' Flights carrying out conversion training on the Dakota and the resident 'A' Flight continuing with navigation training. To add to the confusion, two days later, on 10th August 1945, 105 (T) OTU was renamed 1381 (T) CU and for a while continued to operate the Wellington and Dakota side by side.

The Wellington had been phased out at Nuneaton by

Oblique photograph of Nuneaton taken in April 1944, looking north east with the A5 crossing the bottom left hand corner. Several of 1381 (T) CU's Wellingtons can be seen parked on the dispersals. (P.H.T. Green Collection.)

September, and the airfield's days as an active flying station were coming to an end. In November 1945, the (T) CU was ordered to move to a new home at Desborough in Northamptonshire. On 19th November, the remaining 35 Dakotas were prepared for the move but poor weather halted the short flight south until the next day. Less than ten days later, Nuneaton was placed under Care and Maintenance and remained so for many months before a new role for the site was decided upon.

Another RAF unit briefly made use of Nuneaton in December 1945; the Transport Command Air Crew Examining Unit was based at Bramcote. Nuneaton was still officially Bramcote's satellite, but there is little evidence to say·whether the unit's Oxford, Dakota or Avro Lancastrian made use of the airfield.

On 1st January 1946, the UK motor industry had its own research association for the first time in its history. The Motor Industry Research Association, or MIRA, was located in Brentford; lacking space, the MIRA laboratories could not be extended, and a vehicle proving ground would provide a better future for MIRA. Nuneaton was one of the options made available to MIRA, on lease from the Air Ministry. In the

The original control tower is still at 'Lindley', being put to good use by MIRA. (MIRA.)

meantime, other prospective sites were looked at, including the proposed new racetrack at Donington Park and 40 other disused airfields. Nuneaton was chosen and was first occupied by MIRA at the end of September 1947; it is now permanently know as Lindley. A rental figure of £2,000 was agreed with the Air Ministry, who eventually sold the whole site of 650 acres in 1963 for the very reasonable sum of £45,000.

The runways and perimeter tracks were all in good condition and testing of vehicles began in 1948. As soon as it was clear that Lindley was to be MIRA's long term home, it became possible to start planning and creating the new facilities for testing and research. The control tower and some of the other wartime buildings were taken over, road systems were marked out, white lines painted, traffic signs erected and the old airfield was transformed into a usable proving ground.

The one and only T2 hangar left on the airfield now houses two wind tunnels, one of which is big enough to take a double-decker bus!

Thanks to MIRA, the layout of the whole airfield still survives, only disrupted by the swirl of different test areas and circuits. The future for MIRA is a very bright one and long may it continue.

15

RATCLIFFE

National Grid Reference SK630160; NE of Leicester

The Air Transport Auxiliary (ATA) was the brainchild of Gerald d'Erlanger, Director of British Airways. It was 1938, and d'Erlanger had the foresight to realise that a war with Germany was inevitable. He knew that overseas routes would be suspended and that virtually all civilian aircraft would be impounded for the war effort. As a result, there would be a large surplus of commercial and private pilots with no planes to fly, and nowhere to go. Many of these pilots would join the RAF, but equally capable and experienced pilots would not be considered suitable for operational service in the RAF, owing to age and/or physical limitations.

D'Erlanger envisaged that the impending war would create a demand for pilots to take on tasks such as transporting mail, VIPs, supplies, medical officers, and ambulance cases. Wasting no time, he contacted the Under Secretary for Air, Harold Balfour, and the Director General of Civil Aviation, Sir Francis Shelmerdine. He proposed creating a pool of peacetime civil pilots. This proposal was accepted, and he was immediately given the task of organising it.

Thirty pilots were initially selected to form 1 Ferry Pilots Pool (FPP) at White Waltham in Berkshire. The RAF thought it could handle its own ferrying needs, but as the war progressed, their own pilots were needed in more operational roles, which in turn put pressure on the ATA to recruit more pilots. The Under

Secretary of State for Air proposed that the ATA open its ranks to women. There were many objections to women taking on this role, but fortunately old-fashioned opinions were overcome and the first of many women pilots entered the ATA in November 1939. One of these ground-breaking women aviators was Amy Johnson, tragically lost over the Thames estuary when flying for the ATA.

By the war's end, the ATA had established 22 Ferry Pools all over the British Isles. Some of these were all-women pools, such as at Hamble, Cosford and Hatfield. The ATA carried out an enormous amount of ferrying work. D'Erlanger once commented to a group of dignitaries: *'Every machine you see in the sky has been, or will be, flown at some period of its life by a pilot of the ATA.'*

ATA pilots delivered over 300,000 aircraft, of 51 different types, to practically every airfield in Great Britain. Men and women numbering 1,152 and 166, respectively, made up the service; of them, 149 men and women lost their lives. Thirty-six pilots, among them two women, received Certificates of Commendation from the British Government, not to mention the four women pilots who were awarded the MBE.

Situated next to Ratcliffe College, off the A46, the airfield is little changed from its days as a centre for aviation in Leicestershire. Sadly, the sound of light aircraft has long since gone. The airfield was built for Sir William Lindsay Everard, who was a true asset to aviation in the county. He was a key player in the family of Leicestershire brewers and was the president of both Leicestershire Aero Club, and the County Flying Club. Sir William was very influential within the Royal Aero Club, where he was chairman from 1936 to 1940. He also held the position of Racing Committee Chairman and, after the war, was vice-president, from 1946 to 1948.

Everard awarded the contract of building a 60-acre site in 1929 to James Hunter of Chester. Work began the following year and the airfield was complete enough to warrant an application to operate on 12th August 1930. The licence was received eight days later with restrictions which would allow them to fly Avro 504 type training and light aircraft only.

The airfield was officially opened on 6th September 1930 with a Gala weekend, which involved over 100 aircraft. In March 1931,

Ratcliffe pictured during the Second World War. The large hangar on the right was dismantled in 1948.

Everard offered Ratcliffe as an emergency landing ground for both RAF and civilian aircraft. An upgrade in its operating licence a few months later meant that the airfield was declared suitable for all types of aircraft.

Throughout the 1930s, Ratcliffe hosted a variety of events. These included international meetings, gliding displays, model aircraft, charity and public open days. The airfield was enlarged significantly between 1935 and the summer of 1936. The main runway was enlarged to 1,050 yards and the second runway was extended by 250 yards, giving it a total length of 800 yards. This enabled bigger aircraft, such as the Handley Page HP.42 airliner, to visit the small airfield. By 1937, over 50 aircraft were permanent residents.

A piece of aviation history was made at Ratcliffe in May 1939. Earlier that year, in February, a new company called Taylorcraft Aeroplanes (England) Ltd began to build aircraft at the Britannia Works in Thurmaston, north-east of Leicester. No facilities to test-fly its new product were available. Everard gave Taylorcraft permission to use Ratcliffe and on 24th April the new Taylorcraft Model C, minus its wings, was taken by road from the Britannia works to the airfield. The aircraft was then assembled and prepared for its first test flight. With G Winn-Eaton at the

The first British built Taylorcraft Model Plus C, G-AFNW, stands in front of Ratcliffe's hangars. First flown on 3rd May 1939, the aircraft was an instant success and was a major building block in the future of British General Aviation.

controls, G-AFNW took to the skies for the first time on 3rd May 1939. The aircraft was an immediate success and paved the way for the whole Taylorcraft and Auster production line.

Twenty-four Taylorcraft aircraft had been completed by the time the Second World War started on 3rd September 1939. The war's arrival brought an immediate ban on civil flying, bringing an end to all of Taylorcraft's activities at Thurmaston and Ratcliffe.

The airfield lay dormant, serving the local livestock rather than aviation. Its operating licence was removed in May 1940, but this was only a temporary situation. In August 1940, Ratcliffe received a visit from an official RAF contingent with a permit to inspect the airfield. A few days later, Captain Norman Edgar of the ATA arrived to view the airfield. This visit was later referred to by Sir Lindsay Everard as 'the battle of the light and dark blues'. The situation continued for several days, as each visiting group reported to their relevant headquarters.

The RAF intended to use both Ratcliffe and Rearsby for the

purpose of forming a glider training squadron. This never came about, as the Ministry of Aviation Production (MAP), which controlled the ATA, paid Everard the appropriate rent to use the airfield. 6 FPP was duly formed at Ratcliffe in November 1940 consisting of a mixed group of pilots, which included four women.

Situated in such a central position, 6 FPP was responsible for the movements of aircraft from and to many factories, Maintenance Units (MUs) and active squadrons. The factories included those at Castle Bromwich, Elmdon and Wolverhampton, which produced Spitfires, Lancasters, Stirlings, Defiants and Barracudas. Virtually every type of aircraft that the RAF operated was flown by 6 FPP pilots, and that included flying boats. Despite the fact that Ratcliffe could not have been further from the sea, the FPP was one of only three pools to be responsible for such types. Sunderlands were flown from the Short Brothers' factory at Rochester and Consolidated Catalinas were also dispersed around the country.

The FPP had to have several aircraft on strength to ferry their own pilots to the factories. Some of these taxi aircraft were small, single-engined aircraft that could hold only a few pilots at a time. Initially 6 FPP was equipped with Fairchild Argus, Percival Proctor and the de Havilland Dominie, but the Avro Anson was the most capable taxi aircraft. The Anson, affectionately known as 'Faithful Annie', was a twin-engine design originally intended as a light bomber. Never up to this task, it was relegated to training and communication duties and performed admirably for the ATA as well. It could hold eight pilots, but on many occasions would carry up to twelve.

During 6 FPP's stay at Ratcliffe, over 50,000 ferry flights originated from the airfield. Although the pool did have several accidents involving their pilots around the country, not a single one occurred at Ratcliffe. The most serious incident at Ratcliffe happened on 7th August 1944 to a Spitfire IX of 1 Ferry Pilot Pool. The aircraft was one of many that staged through Ratcliffe from other pools – unfortunately, it stalled after take-off and dived into the ground.

With the war at an end, the demand for the 6 FPP and the ATA was less. The pool organised an air display and show to mark its end on 6th October 1945. Over 30 different types of aircraft took part in the display, including Austers from nearby Rearsby and a

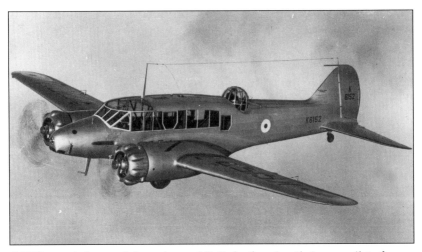

6 FFP operated several Avro Anson Mk.Is for ferrying their own pilots from airfield to airfield. Designed to carry eight, the FPP often managed to squeeze in twelve!

Handley Page Halifax. The Vickers-Supermarine test pilot Alex Henshaw performed aerobatics in a Spitfire, and a taste of the modern RAF was on show as well. A Gloster Meteor and de Havilland Vampire were put through their paces for the crowd; Geoffrey de Havilland flew the latter.

The unit continued operations for a few more weeks. The last flight was undertaken by a Fairchild Argus on 9th November 1945. This marked the end of five years of constant flying activity at Ratcliffe.

Sir Lindsay Everard subsequently made the airfield available again to local flying clubs and the Leicestershire Aero Club resumed its activities on 1st April 1947. A few months later, on 1st June, the club managed to arrange their first post-war 'At Home' day. With smaller displays than in the 1930s, it still managed to attract over 250 people (mainly members and their families), and twenty visiting aircraft. A Dakota from neighbouring Wymeswold made for an interesting visitor and a vibrant display was provided by a 605 Squadron Mosquito.

The club steadily flourished through the late 1940s, but this period was marred by the death of Sir Lindsay Everard on 11th May 1949. The club had not only lost its long serving president

Two birds with one stone! A Miles Monarch and a 1382 (T)CU Dakota from Wymeswold parked on the grass at Ratcliffe on 1st June 1947. (P.H.T. Green Collection.)

but its most generous patron as well. Another, more public display, was organised on 29th May 1949, which attracted over 10,000 people and a diverse collection of aircraft. 504 Squadron Spitfires from Wymeswold and Seafires from 1833 Squadron performed a very impressive fly-past. These were supported by an equally exciting display by Tiger Moths of 7 RFS from Desford.

On 21st June 1949, the club received notification from Captain Anthony Everard, Sir Lindsay's son, that the airfield had been put up for sale. The asking price was £15,000 and the club was offered the site first. Unfortunately, it was a figure that the club was unable to raise. With no hope of an extension to their lease, the Leicestershire Aero Club left Ratcliffe on 25th March 1950. A farewell party was held, at which 30 visiting aircraft, mainly Austers, were included. On 31st March 1950, after twenty years of aviation, the airfield closed for the final time.

Today, several buildings have survived that were erected during the Second World War. These buildings have been incorporated into a farm and the flying filed has returned to agriculture. The site of Ratcliffe has changed little since its closure over 50 years ago – a piece of important Leicestershire aviation history that until now has escaped an industrial or housing estate.

16

REARSBY

National Grid Reference SK650140; NE of Leicester

A decision by a local Leicestershire businessman to build light aircraft was to become a major influence on the British light aircraft industry. Alexander Lance Wykes was both a flying enthusiast and a member of the County Flying Club Ltd (CFC). Wykes also held the position of Managing Director for a textile machine manufacturer called Crowthers Ltd, based at the Britannia works, Melton Road, Thurmaston. The CFC had purchased a Taylorcraft Model A, and Wykes was so impressed with it that he travelled to America to gain a licence to build the aircraft in England. On 21st November 1938, Taylorcraft Aeroplanes (England) Ltd was formed and registered as a private company. Construction began during February 1939 in rented buildings at the rear of the Britannia works. The first aircraft, G-AFNW, was completed by 24th April, taken by road to nearby Ratcliffe and test flown a few weeks later; the aircraft was an instant success.

The plan for an airfield at Rearsby came about in 1936, when the Leicestershire Flying Pou Club replaced its Mignet Pou du Ciel, or 'Flying Flea' with a larger aircraft. A club flying display was organised at their flying ground at Sandy Lane near Melton Mowbray. One of the invited guests at this display was the influential Sir Lindsay Everard. He became the small flying club's president and immediately offered financial help to replace the 'Flying Flea' in the club. A Kronfeld Drone was purchased but it soon became apparent that the field at Sandy was inadequate for the operation of such an aircraft.

Everard came to the rescue and made land available to build a new aerodrome off Gadesby Lane at Rearsby. The land was prepared by a local firm called En-Tout-Cas Ltd of Syston in early 1937 and cost approximately £1,000 to complete. The newly formed County Flying Club moved in during the summer and, after construction of a hangar and clubhouse, began its operation. The airfield did not take on a permanent feel until the middle of 1938. Up until then, Rearsby had operated on a restricted Civil Aviation licence and had not met the necessary requirements to run a larger operation. Although the club had previously had all its faults pointed out to it, the CFC was slow to bring the airfield up to scratch. This meant that the airfield did not officially open until 23rd July 1938, when Air Commodore J A Chamier, the Secretary General of the Air League of the British Empire, performed the opening ceremony. The opening of a new clubhouse by the Lord Mayor of Leicester, Councillor F Acton, followed this. A flying display celebrated the opening, with over

The Taylorcraft Plus D Auster I was the first major order by the military of the Auster range. LB319 is pictured at Rearsby in June 1941, this particular aircraft became the prototype Auster Mk.III and spent its military flying career with the A&AEE at Boscombe Down in Wiltshire.

30 visiting aircraft, including that of Alex Henshaw, the winner of the 1938 Kings Cup Air Race.

Air Commodore Chamier took the opportunity to announce the formation of the Civil Air Guard (CAG). This was a government-sponsored scheme and it gave people the opportunity to learn to fly at a very reasonable rate. The response to the scheme was overwhelming, with over 80 applicants enrolling on the scheme in one day. The CAG scheme started in October 1938, and coincided with the issue of the first permanent licence. Comments by the inspectors which were relevant to their first visit included, 'This aerodrome now appears to be well maintained and controlled'.

Most of the flying carried out at Rearsby was by the CAG, although the resident club was steadily building its own fleet of Taylorcraft and, later, Piper J-4 Cubs. CAG trainees peaked at over 140 pupils in April 1939 and, with regular visits by 7 E&RFTS Tiger Moths from Desford, the airfield was a very busy place. This was to come to an abrupt end when war broke out in September 1939. Along with hundreds of other flying clubs and schools, Rearsby had to close. The CAG employees were dismissed and all the club aircraft were dismantled and placed in store.

The start of the Second World War affected the newly formed Taylorcraft Company as well. Production and orders were flowing in; 24 aircraft were built before the start of hostilities. Unfortunately all their order books were filled with civilian

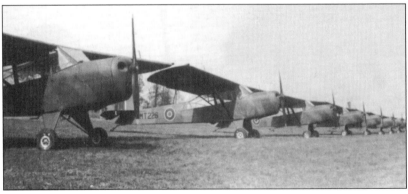

A total of 254 Auster Mk.IVs were built at Rearsby and this line up shows eight of them ready for delivery.

orders; so production had to cease and work was sought from military sources. Initially, Taylorcraft carried out small sub-contract work, but their situation improved in the early part of 1940. The Army had shown an interest in the Taylorcraft many months earlier and placed an initial order for eight Plus Ds for Air Observation trials. Simultaneously, the company won a contract to repair Tiger Moths at its Britannia Works.

The pressure on civilian companies increased alongside the demand for repair work on front-line aircraft. Taylorcraft unexpectedly received a request from the Ministry of Aviation Production (MAP) to repair Hawker Hurricane fighters. Taylorcraft accepted the work, even though their facilities were limited for such an aircraft. Several extra sites were taken over for the new task, including the airfield at Rearsby. Extra hangars and buildings were constructed and the runway was extended to cope with the demands of the Hurricane.

On 12th July 1941, Taylorcraft Aeroplanes (England) Ltd

View inside one of the main hangars at the Rearsby factory in 1948. (A.J. Jackson Collection.)

officially became a Civilian Repair Organisation (CRO). The first of over 400 Hawker Hurricanes left Rearsby in February 1941. The Hurricane was replaced on the repair line in 1943 by the Hawker Typhoon, the first of which left the airfield in May. The last of 339 repaired Tiger Moths left in March 1944, and a total of 281 Typhoons had been reinstated into RAF service by the war's end. Larger aircraft, like the Handley Page Harrow, were also handled, along with the occasional de Havilland Hornet Moth and Piper Cub.

Aviation accidents were few and far between at Rearsby, which is surprising considering the large number of wartime movements. The only incidents worthy of note involved an Airspeed Oxford that hit a hedge while trying to land at the airfield on 27th November 1940, and a Supermarine Spitfire Mk.V which was carrying out flight trails over Rearsby on 29th Dec 1942 when the engine failed. The Spitfire was written off after crash-landing on the airfield.

While the CRO was busy, Taylorcraft continued carrying out its smaller contracts, producing parts for various aircraft, which included the Albemarle, Audax, Hurricane, Oxford, Spitfire and Tiger Moth. It also continued to carry out its own aircraft development – the Army had been so impressed with the Taylorcraft Plus D that they placed an order for 101 Model D/1 Auster Is. By the end of the war, over 1500 Auster Mk.I to Mk.VIs had been built. Production was at a peak of 28 aircraft per week just before the D-Day landings in June 1944. As Rearsby's facilities could not cope single handedly with the Auster production ten different locations were used, which included three in Thurmaston and five in Syston. Sheet metal work was carried out in Mountsorrel and flight-testing and delivery happened at Rearsby.

With the war at an end the workload of both the CRO and Taylorcraft declined dramatically. The CRO did continue repair work on Kirby Cadet gliders until April 1946, when the organisation closed for good. Taylorcraft was renamed Auster Aircraft Ltd on 8th March 1946.

In late 1960 Auster and the Shoreham based company F G Miles Aircraft Limited were purchased by the Pressed Steel Company. The two companies then formed a subsidiary on 7th October 1960 that became known as British Executive and

*The simple design of the Auster range is evident in these tubular framed
fuselages ready for the next stage of construction at Rearsby in 1948.
(A.J. Jackson.)*

Auster Mk.IV MT225 at Rearsby. (Via R.C. Sturtivant.)

General Aviation Limited or Beagle. This later became Beagle Aircraft Limited, on 10th May 1962, and it was then planned that all company designs would be jointly built at Rearsby and Shoreham.

In 1965 the parent company was absorbed into the British Motor Corporation with the Government in an attempt gain further financial support and on 12th December 1966 it was announced that the Government had acquired the aircraft side of the company for £1 million but on 13th March 1970 the airfield's works were closed.

Briefly used by the Leicestershire Gliding Club, the entire site was then purchased by Rearsby Automotive Limited, part of the British Leyland company, manufacturing car components. Austers have returned to Rearsby on two occasions: the first was the 50th Anniversary of Taylorcraft on 10th September 1988; the other on 20th September 1997, when no less than 49 Austers of various marks returned to the airfield.

Today the buildings stand quiet, devoid of activity, awaiting a new tenant, and the landing strip is ploughed; but the possibility of another Auster gathering cannot be totally ruled out.

Looking south west, the old Auster factory at Rearsby is little changed from the air. (J. Molyneux.)

17

SALTBY

National Grid Reference SK868265; 8 miles NE of Melton Mowbray

Arthur Harris is a name synonymous with Bomber Command during the Second World War. During the First World War, however, he was a young officer tasked with travelling the area to look for suitable sites for Home Defence airfields. With the increase in German Zeppelin activity in late 1915 and early 1916, several new squadrons were formed for the protection of the industrial Midlands.

Harris chose a site near Buckminster, which lay to the north-east of the village and was quite literally just a few yards over the Leicestershire/Lincolnshire border. The airfield was first occupied by 'B' Flight of 38 Squadron, whose headquarters had been established in Melton Mowbray the previous September. Eight F.E.2bs operated from the airfield and responded to every Zeppelin raid without success right up until May 1918. 38 Squadron's role changed from that of defence to operational bombing and as a consequence they were moved to Dunkirk in northern France. Buckminster was then selected as an aircraft acceptance park but, with the war coming to an end, was used only for storage of aircraft. The airfield then became one of the many victims of post-war disarmament and was closed in late 1919.

Twenty years later, another European war started and, once again, the local area was surveyed for an airfield. All disused

First World War airfields were immediately viewed as suitable sites for expansion. Harlaxton, for example, over the border in Lincolnshire, was re-opened as a satellite for Spitalgate near Grantham. Buckminster, however, was restricted by its size, being only 125 acres. The Air Ministry needed a 700-acre site for an airfield that could operate the RAF's latest medium bombers.

One and a half miles north-west of the old Buckminster airfield, the ministry officials found a more suitable site. Construction of the new airfield, located between the villages of Skillington, Sproxton and Saltby, began in 1940. Completed by August 1941, Saltby was opened as a satellite airfield for Cottesmore, which was situated seven miles to the south. 14 Operational Training Unit (OTU) was the resident unit, and Cottesmore's satellite at that time was Woolfox Lodge. A reshuffle of responsibilities meant that Woolfox Lodge was to become North Luffenham's new satellite airfield and Saltby took on its new role.

Initially, the airfield's runways were all grass, and major building construction on the site was limited. However, this temporary situation did nothing to avert the attentions of the

Saltby became a satellite airfield of Cottesmore in August 1941 and 14 OTU's Handley Page Hampdens and Herefords quickly made use of it. A trio of Herefords fly a nice formation for the camera. (Via author.)

Luftwaffe throughout the summer of 1941. Although the airfield was attacked three times, no major damage was caused and the raids did little to disrupt the training programme. For those locals who could remember, a Zeppelin in March 1916 had caused more, albeit unintentional, damage near Sproxton. L-13 had found itself in difficulty and had had to jettison its bomb load, the main victim being an unfortunate cow!

Circuit training was the main occupation of the Hampdens of 14 OTU and this took place both day and night. The flying circuit around any airfield is a busy and sometimes hazardous place, and never more so, in this airfield's case, than on the night of 12th September 1941, when two Hampdens collided over the airfield. Sergeant A P Overall DFM was climbing away from Saltby when he crashed broadside into Flight Sergeant D H Bartlett's aircraft, which was in the circuit. Both aircraft crumpled to the ground and all eight aircrew were killed instantly. Before the year was out, three more OTU Hampdens crashed on or near the airfield.

Saltby's remote location did not help its situation during the winter of 1942. Heavy snowfall brought the whole area grinding to a halt, and to complicate matters further the airfield experienced complete power failure. This situation contributed to the loss of Hampden I P1316, which was undergoing a 40-hour inspection on Valentine's Day. The whole station had to use paraffin lamps for several days during February 1942 and one such heater lamp caused the Hampden to catch fire. The aircraft was destroyed in minutes. Snowfall at the parent station had been equally severe, if not worse, and 'A' Flight was detached to Saltby for two weeks until the weather improved sufficiently for them to return to Cottesmore.

Circuits, navigation exercises and bombing practice sorties continued throughout 1942 from Saltby. The Hampden had had its day and was being replaced by the Vickers Wellington. 14 OTU received its first Wellingtons in August, but was not fully re-equipped with the type until the end of 1942. The Hampden, though a popular aircraft to fly, had many accidents at Saltby. Eighteen were lost operating from the airfield. The arrival of Wellingtons brought with it a major reduction in the accident rate. Only three Wellingtons were lost operating from Saltby up until their departure between 28th July and 7th August 1943. The whole of 14 OTU moved to a new airfield at Market Harborough

The office of a Handley Page Hampden. Once mastered, the Hampden was a pleasant and popular aircraft to fly, but did not lend itself well to training. (Via author.)

and its satellite airfield of Husbands Bosworth in Northamptonshire.

Proposals for improving the airfield had been in place for quite some time and, with 14 OTU's departure, the opportunity arose to bring the airfield up to a Class 'A' bomber airfield. 5352 Airfield Construction Wing, detached from RAF Quy, the home of 5202 Plan Construction Squadron, located some 6½ miles from Cambridge, had already begun to move into Saltby, and Grantham-based Wimpey & Co. provided the civilian labour and materials for reconstruction of the airfield. Three new runways, a connecting perimeter track, and hardstandings transformed the grass airfield. A collection of three 'T2' and one 'B1' type hangars were built as well as new communal and domestic sites that could accommodate 994 RAF and 112 WAAF personnel.

While the commotion of rebuilding the airfield continued,

Saltby was one of 24 airfields selected to store Airspeed Horsa gliders. Thirty-two gliders were towed and released over the airfield by Whitley and Albermarle tugs and were stored on the airfield in readiness for the forthcoming invasion of Europe. All gliders were cared for by 2 Heavy Glider Maintenance Unit (HGMU), which was based at Snailwell in Cambridgeshire. One section of HGMU was responsible for looking after each airfield's gliders – in Saltby's case it was 32 Heavy Glider Maintenance Section (HGMS).

As work progressed, the airfield was transferred from 92 Group to 5 Group Bomber Command with the proposed idea of housing a bomber squadron at Saltby. An indication of its eventual use showed itself when several US engineers visited it at the end of August 1943. The USAAF took over the station from 5 Group, passing control to the US 9th Air Force Troop Carrier Command. Saltby became Army Air Force Station 538 on 18th December 1943.

At the end of January 1944, all military and civilian construction work had been completed, which was timely, as preparations were being made overseas for the arrival of the 314th Troop Carrier Group (TCG). First formed on 2nd March 1942 as the 314th Transport Group at Drew Field, Florida, by July of that year the unit was redesignated to a Troop Carrier Group. Then, after several moves around the United States, it settled at Lawson Field, Georgia on 24th February 1943. Since its activation, the Group had been training for overseas duty with the Douglas C-47A and the Douglas C-53. This duty finally came in May 1943, when the group was assigned to the Mediterranean theatre of operations, serving with the US 12th Air Force.

Within six weeks of arrival, the 314th TCG were involved in their first combat operations. In July 1943, they flew two night missions as part of the invasion of Sicily, Operation *Husky*. Initially dropping paratroops of the 82nd Airborne Division on 9th July, they followed up with the dropping of reinforcements on the 11th. The Group received their first Distinguished Unit Citation (DUC) for carrying out the second mission, despite the bad weather and a heavy attack by ground and naval forces. Major operations followed, and with the invasion of Italy in September 1943 the 314th TCG was again tasked with dropping paratroops and supplies, this time near Salerno.

The 314th TCG's job ended in the Mediterranean and a move to England beckoned as preparations gained momentum for a second front in northern Europe. The average TCG was made up of four Troop Carrier Squadrons (TCS). The 314th consisted of the 32nd, 50th, 61st and 62nd TCS. The first at Saltby was the 32nd TCS, which arrived on 20th February 1944, followed four days later by the 61st TCS. All the aircraft of the TCG had arrived by 6th March, and the personnel had completed their move from Sicily by the 20th. Still under the 52nd Troop Carrier Wing (TCW), which had moved locally to Cottesmore, the Group was now part of the US 9th Air Force, Northern Carrier Group. This Group contained nine other airfields – Bottesford in Leicestershire, Cottesmore and North Luffenham in Rutland, Langar and Balderton in Nottinghamshire, Spanhoe in Northamptonshire and Fulbeck, Barkston Heath, Folkingham and North Witham in Lincolnshire.

The 314th TCG was, by now, a veteran Group, so immediately

The 314th TCG spent over a year at Saltby and participated in both Operations Overlord *and* Market *from the airfield. The group's main equipment was the highly successful Douglas C-47 Skytrain; the example seen here is returning from a night training exercise. (Via author.)*

settled into a new training programme at Saltby. The Group was equipped with nearly 80 Douglas C-47s and C-53s. To avoid congestion, other airfields were used for the more mundane task of circuit training. The home of the 9th Air Force Pathfinder School, North Witham was the first airfield to fulfil this role, on 29th March. Many of the 314th's experienced crews would eventually be assigned to this specialist unit.

32 Glider Maintenance Section left the station on 15th March 1944. Their Horsa gliders had now been transferred to the 9th Air Force and were brought into immediate use by the 314th. The Horsa worked alongside the American Waco CG-4A glider, which was slightly the smaller of the two.

Another veteran unit that was familiar to the Group was the 82nd Airborne, who were deployed around the Leicester area. Exercises involving the 314th and the 82nd were staged weekly from the beginning of April 1944. The planned *Overlord* invasion had been set in stone from the beginning of the year and all of the units that were proposed to be involved were carrying out their own dress rehearsals. Exercises named *Dorothy* and *Tony*, involving 800 officers and men each, were staged at Saltby, and the group was a key player in the massive Exercise *Eagle* on 11th May. *Eagle* involved literally every troop carrier group and squadron that was to take part in the D-Day operation. The 314th TCG's part did not go that smoothly; Pathfinder troops dropped at the head of the formation had difficulty setting up the relevant markers and beacons for the following aircraft to locate. Faced with orbiting the drop zone a second time (an unappealing option over enemy territory), the majority of the group dropped their paratroopers successfully first time. Many lessons were learned from Exercise *Eagle*, and the 314th TCG hoped that the real thing would go a lot smoother.

While training continued, space at Saltby diminished owing to the arrival of even more American units, this time non-flying detachments. Anti-aircraft batteries of the 605th, the 546th and the 408th AAA arrived during May and early June with approximately 300 officers and men each. Station strength was also bolstered by the arrival of the 329th US Engineer Regiment. As a result, living accommodation was now at a premium.

Operation *Overlord* actually began on 5th June 1944. Pathfinder aircraft from their Lincolnshire base at North Witham spearheaded the invasion. Not long after their departure, 51 C-47s and nine C-53s of the 314th TCG prepared to leave Saltby. The Group was tasked with carrying the paratroopers of the 508th Parachute Infantry Regiment (PIR) commanded by Colonel Roy Lindquist, which included General James Gavin and the 2nd Battalion Regimental HQ. Over 1,000 troops, and nearly 43,000lbs of equipment were lifted out of the Leicestershire base, all heading for drop zones in northern France. The 314th TCG's drop zone (DZ) was coded 'N' and was located three miles south-east of Ste Mère-Église, near a confluence of the Douve and Mederet rivers. The 82nd Airborne Pathfinders had arrived at the DZ at 01:38 as part of Operation *Boston*, but, after encountering unexpected enemy troops, were unable to set up their markers and beacons in the correct place. The location of the DZ, coupled with poor weather conditions, meant that when the 314th arrived at 02:00, the paratroopers were scattered over a large area. Many were dropped into a swampy area and only managed to reassemble in small pockets of troops, but still were able to carry the fight to the German forces. All but one aircraft made it back to Saltby; eighteen aircraft had been badly damaged by enemy flak and small arms fire. The 314th suffered only one fatal casualty on the whole mission, when a pilot was killed by small arms fire. His co-pilot took charge, and brought the C-47 home safely. The only aircraft lost had bravely returned over the DZ for a third time when it succumbed to enemy fire, crash-landing in flames. The crew all survived and made it rapidly to the safety of the Allied lines.

The following day, the 314th TCG returned to Normandy as part of Operation *Freeport*. This was a resupply mission in support of the 82nd Airborne Division. With reassurance from the Meteorological Office that the weather was good over Normandy, 52 aircraft left Saltby in unfavourable conditions. Thirteen aircraft aborted the mission before reaching France, while another aircraft was damaged by anti-aircraft fire from an Allied ship. On the approach to the French coast, the remainder of the Group encountered such poor weather that the rest of the journey was flown on instruments. Unbeknown to them, the Germans had recaptured their designated DZ, so, frustratingly, most of the equipment dropped fell into German hands. The Germans had also strengthened their anti-aircraft defences in the

Although the photograph was taken at Prestwick, this is a C-47 of the 61st TCS – the large code 'Q9' gives away the aircraft's identity. (A. Pearcy.)

area and the relatively slow flying C-47s were becoming easier targets. The day had not gone well for the Group, three aircraft were missing and 30 had suffered flak and small arms damage. In addition several crew members were wounded. The 314th TCG's efforts had not gone unnoticed – they were awarded a second DUC for their actions during Operation *Freeport*.

While Saltby's RAF and USAAF emergency services were dealing with their own aircraft limping home to base, the dangerous world of training added its burden late in the day on 7th June. A 1654 Heavy Conversion Unit Short Stirling III from Wigsley in Nottinghamshire dived into the ground near the airfield. The crew of LK594 stood no chance; the aircraft had gone out of control while descending through cloud – another example of the difficulties of training pilots with limited flying hours and experience to fly on instruments.

The 314th TCG continued to visit Normandy, to fly cargo into the many forward airstrips that the Allied troops had constructed. Training continued in preparation for more paratroop drops into northern France, but the advance was so rapid that this was not required.

A bold plan to bring the war to a swifter conclusion was the next major mission for the 314th TCG. Operation *Market* was the airborne contribution to the capture of Arnhem in the Netherlands and the all-important taking of the bridges that crossed the Rhine. The Group was tasked with delivering the 2nd, 3rd, 11th and 156th Parachute Battalions of the British 1st Airborne Division. On 17th September 1944, the first of two groups left Saltby. 36 C-47s joined aircraft from the 61st TCG from Barkston Heath and headed for DZ 'X', north of Renkum and 6 miles west of Arnhem. Weather conditions were very good and the 314th TCG aircraft dropped 595 paratroops of the 2nd Battalion. Later that day, 33 C-47s and three C-53s also headed for the Renkum drop zone and successfully delivered another 520 paratroops, this time of the 3rd Battalion. Light flak was encountered by all the aircraft involved, but only three were damaged and all returned safely to Saltby.

The following day, the 314th TCG did not have the same comfortable ride. Sixty-nine C-47s and three C-53s left Saltby carrying over 1,200 men of the 4th Parachute Brigade. The drop zone on this occasion was Ginkel Heath, west of Arnhem, and unfortunately the German defences were more prepared for their arrival. Light anti-aircraft was encountered much further away from the Arnhem area, and defences had been reinforced at Wageringen, 10 miles west of the Dutch town. One C-47 was brought down by small arms fire, and another three fell victim to the Wageringen flak defences. Even with these higher losses, the mission was classed as a success and accurate drops could still be carried out. Six of the returning C-47s had flak damage and two crew had been wounded.

Undeterred, the 314th TCG were in action over Arnhem again a few days later. This time, their precious cargo was the 1st Polish Parachute Brigade, commanded by Major-General Stanislaw Sosabowski. The frustrated Polish commander and his men had been fog-bound at Saltby and were eager to get into combat, even though Sosabowski had his doubts about the location of the drop zone and the bleak-looking situation as a whole. Eventually, the group, along with the 315th TCG at Spanhoe, managed to get their aircraft into the air, even though the conditions were unfavourable. The rapidly deteriorating situation for the British troops in and around Arnhem meant that the missions had to go ahead. The first wave of 27 aircraft left Saltby with 395 Polish paratroopers, 112 parapacks, eight motorcycles, six bicycles and five mortar trolleys. The second wave left an hour later with 33 aircraft carrying 396 paratroopers and 116 parapacks. The entire force made up a weight of 29,183lbs. The first wave encountered bad weather and became lost, with many turning for home. The second wave fared slightly better, but at least sixteen aircraft were damaged by anti-aircraft fire. Cloud over the drop zone prevented many aircraft from dropping their paratroopers and some aircraft circled around at 10,000ft looking for a window in the cloud where they could make the drop. The Poles were eventually dropped accurately south of Arnhem, but unfortunately the Polish troops were cut to pieces and played no significant part in the battle for Arnhem. Sosabowski's scepticism was realised. 314th TCG's part in Operation *Market* came to a conclusion on 26th September, when desperately needed troops and supplies were flown into a tempory airstrip at Keent, 6 miles south-west of Nijmegen.

The group was now tasked with the safer job of general supply and casualty evacuation missions, the majority of these to forward airstrips in France. General routine returned to Saltby and the usual training exercises continued in preparation for more paratroop drops in Europe. On 7th October there was an indication that the future held a change of role for the airfield. Even though Saltby was still well and truly under American control, the airfield became part of 72 Base. Controlled by Bottesford, the base was part of 7 Group and, along with Langar in Nottinghamshire, was operating Heavy Conversion Units (HCU) at the time. 1657 HCU, based at Stradishall in Suffolk, was the unit earmarked to move into Saltby on 30th November 1944. This move never came about, as Saltby was not ready to receive the unit, which was equipped in part with Lancasters. 1657 HCU was then disbanded on 12th December.

Throughout the winter of 1944/45, the 314th TCG continued transporting troops into France in preparation for the final offensives of the war. The Ardennes, or 'Battle of the Bulge', over Christmas and New Year, took up most of the TCG resources, the C-47s travelling to the south of England to collect troops. This was the first indication that Saltby, like the other Northern Carrier Group airfields, was becoming too distant from the fighting.

One of many solutions for feeding the front with supplies was

233

a conversion of the Consolidated B-24 Liberators into fuel transporters. The C-109 was a tanker conversion of the B-24E (and later B-24D), able to carry 2,415 imperial gallons of fuel in metal tanks in the fuselage. The fuel could be extracted through a single socket in the side of the fuselage. One C-109 was assigned to the 32nd TCS and made several trips from Saltby into France. Its main limitation was the small number of forward airfields capable of handling an aircraft of such size and weight. The C-109s were used more effectively in the Far East, ferrying fuel 'over the Hump' from Burma to China in support of B-29 Superfortress missions against the Japanese.

The 314th TCG's stay at Saltby was coming to an end, and, with a view to the Group's forthcoming role in Operation *Varsity*, a base in France was made available. The 32nd and 61st Troop Carrier Squadrons were the first to leave at the end of February 1945, followed on 5th March by the 50th and 62nd TCS. Their new home was Poix in the Champagne-Ardenne area of France, 90 miles west of Paris. It was from here, on 24th March, that the 314th TCG towed 80 CG-4A gliders in their part in Operation *Varsity*, the airborne crossing of the Rhine.

All American personnel had departed from the airfield by 12th March and on that day an RAF contingent arrived in preparation for a new unit. 1665 HCU, stationed at Tilstock in Shropshire, was to be the new occupant. The HCU had operated Stirlings since their formation at Mepal, Cambridgeshire, in April 1943. They were still operating a later variant of the Stirling, the Handley Page Halifax, and the usual collection of support aircraft. Before the HCU's arrival the station, Saltby, changed its role once again. A strange decision was made on 20th March, which removed Saltby from 72 Base and placed it under Fighter Command's control, even though fighters never had been or would be stationed there!

This did not affect the arrival or operation of 1665 HCU, who brought their aircraft into Saltby on 25th March 1945. The Americans were obviously reluctant to leave. The same day, a Boeing B-17G Flying Fortress from the 401st Bomb Group at Deenethorpe crashed onto the airfield. The HCU began its flying training programme on 30th March and had the space to themselves until the beginning of May 1945.

Once again, airborne forces started to congregate on the

Along with the Handley Page Halifax, 1665 HCU operated the Short Stirling from Saltby during 1945. This particular aircraft is a Mk.III. (Via author.)

airfield, which was about to host another operation into Europe. On 5th May 1945, 38 Stirling IVs of 196 and 299 Squadrons started to arrive from their base at Shepherds Grove in Suffolk. Both squadrons had been involved in the Rhine crossing airborne operation and were now set to deliver more airborne troops into Europe. The passengers for this latest foray were the men of the 1st Airborne Division, and 33 of the visiting Stirlings delivered them to Copenhagen on 7th May. The remaining Stirlings returned to Shepherds Grove.

Another US 9th Air Force unit made use of Saltby during May 1945, albeit briefly. The 349th TCG had arrived in England only on 30th March and were stationed at Barkston Heath. No sooner had they started to settle in than they were moved to Roye/Amy airfield in Picardy, northern France, on 18th April. The 349th were then required to transport British airborne troops to Norway, which meant operating from an English base. On 14th and 15th May, 48 Curtiss C-46 Commando transport aircraft flew into Saltby, and, once again, the airfield was swarming with American servicemen.

The C-46A Commando was a highly serviceable transport aircraft whose success was totally eclipsed by the better-known Douglas C-47 and DC-3 family. The C-46 first flew as a 36-seat civilian airliner on 26th March 1940. The USAAF expressed an interest in the type and it first entered into military service in July 1942. At the time, they were the largest and heaviest twin-engine aircraft to serve with the USAAF, and proved to be a valuable asset, especially in the Pacific theatre. The Commando continued to serve the US military into the early years of the Vietnam War, and several remain airworthy today.

The 349th TCG were very active during their short stay at Saltby, transporting 1,163 troops of the 1st Airborne Division and delivering 1,700,000lbs of freight and supplies to Copenhagen, Oslo and Stavanger.

On the night of 29th May, the day before the 349th TCG were set to depart for their home base in France, one of the resident 1665 HCU Stirlings was about to take off on a navigation exercise. Flight Sergeant Nettleton was at the controls of Stirling IV PW386 when his aircraft suddenly swung off the runway. Several parked C-46s were struck by the out-of-control bomber, which, along with a C-46, burst into flames. A second C-46 had the rear half of the fuselage badly burnt before it could be taxied away. The Stirling crew made a remarkable escape; Nettleton, however, sustained multiple burns and cuts and was transferred to the RAF hospital at Rauceby in Lincolnshire. Unfortunately, an American airman who was sleeping in one of the C-46s was trapped in the aircraft and lost his life. The next day, the remaining 349th TCG aircraft returned to Roye/Amy airfield. It was a sad end to a very successful detachment.

On 1st June, control was transferred to 38 Group and Saltby became a Transport Command Unit, but 1665 HCU continued undeterred with its own activities. The same day 37 Douglas Dakotas landed with over 700 members of the 1st Battalion Parachute Regiment who were returning from Copenhagen. This was the only recorded occasion on which Transport Command aircraft made use of the airfield. The HCU was undisturbed until the end of July 1945, when a signal was received from HQ 38 Group giving instructions regarding a move for the HCU. An earlier inspection of the runways at Saltby may have influenced this decision; the continuous circuits of Stirling and Halifaxes had taken their toll. On 1st August, 1665 HCU departed for Marston Moor in Yorkshire, and Saltby fell silent as the airfield was reduced to a state of Care and Maintenance.

Responsibility for Saltby's upkeep was handed to Melton Mowbray on 24th August and then to Wymeswold on 21st October. Like many other non-flying stations in the area, Saltby was transferred for the final time to 40 Group, Maintenance Command. From 28th November 216, 255 and 256 Maintenance Units made use of the airfield until its closure in September 1955.

Over the next sixteen years, agriculture slowly re-occupied the site, but flying would return. In 1971, the Buckminster Gliding Club was formed. This brought aviation back to the old Second World War station. The Americans returned for one final time on 31st August 1980, when a Lockheed C-130E Hercules of the 62nd Tactical Airlift Squadron paid a goodwill visit to Saltby. The unit was based at Mildenhall in Suffolk and the visit was named Operation *Sentimental Journey*.

A proposal during the 1980s by the National Coal Board to start excavating a new mine near the airfield fortunately did not materialize. The board had planned that Saltby would become a dump for the colliery waste. Today, the Gliding Club is thriving and many regional gliding championships have been held there. The future looks good for the club and, hopefully, Saltby will remain one of the few places in Leicestershire where flying still continues.

18

WOOLFOX LODGE

National Grid Reference SK962132; 6 miles NW of Stamford on the A1

Woolfox Lodge is in a highly visible location in the east of Rutland. Many people will know of its existence next to the A1, but very few of them will know about the airfield's important contributions during the Second World War.

Positioned approximately 6 miles north-west of Stamford, the airfield was the second of Rutland's three active RAF airfields. It was initially allocated as a satellite for Cottesmore, which is 5 miles to the north-west. Construction began in mid-1940, with sand and gravel being supplied by local quarries and contractors. Stamford suffered during the months of construction. Virtually all of the vehicles travelled through the middle of the town, leaving trails of sand, gravel and water. The airfield was ready for use by December 1940, although it would be some time before the rest of the station was fully operational. Anti-aircraft defence was provided with the issue of six Lewis machine guns, which would prove useful in the future.

On 14th December 1940, 14 OTU (Operational Training Unit) from Cottesmore started to use the airfield for training in night flying. The unit flew Hampdens and Ansons, and the very nature of this type of training would result in numerous accidents.

The first of many incidents to occur on the station involved a 14 OTU Anson, R9609, which swung on take-off, resulting in the collapse of the undercarriage. This would set the tone for virtually the whole war at Woolfox; accidents of this type

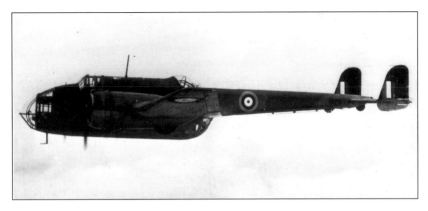

Woolfox Lodge was opened as a satellite for nearby Cottesmore in late 1940, and 14 OTU's Hampdens made use of the airfield until August 1941, when they moved to Saltby. (Via author.)

occurred with alarming regularity. One other such incident happened in spectacular style on the night of 22/23rd March 1941. A visiting Blenheim of 105 Squadron experienced brake failure on landing. The crew vacated the aircraft just in time, as a 14 OTU Hampden landed behind and failed to notice the stricken Blenheim. A collision was inevitable. Fortunately no-one was injured and both aircraft were repaired and put back into service.

The Luftwaffe discovered Woolfox's existence very quickly, probably because of its position in relation to Cottesmore and North Luffenham. The German Airforce visited Woolfox Lodge seven times between April and July 1941. None of the attacks was serious enough to disrupt training operations at the airfield, but all involved airfield defences. On 3rd June 1941, for example, a lone raider was seen circling the airfield. Before a warning could be given, an Anson on the flare path was subjected to machine gun fire. Fortunately, the Anson escaped damage. The airfield, however, received nine high explosive bombs from a second pass by the German aircraft. Two weeks later, an Anson was attacked again. But this time return fire was made by the turret gunner. On both occasions, the Lewis guns saw the enemy aircraft off. June 5th and 19th saw more enemy activity: more bombs were dropped and defensive guns replied, using 156 rounds on 5th June alone. The summer raids ended on 13th July, when a neat stick of 30 incendiary bombs was dropped across the centre of the airfield. As with the other raids, minimal damage was caused.

Activity at the airfield began to change when Saltby in Leicestershire – a new airfield – was made available for 14 OTU's activities. The unit vacated Woolfox at the end of July, and the airfield became a satellite of North Luffenham on 1st August. North Luffenham remained the parent unit on and off until the airfield's closure.

For the next couple of months, the airfield continued to be used for training by various locally based units. Operational units based at North Luffenham also used Woolfox. The first example of this was recorded on the night of 8th/9th August. Sixteen Hampdens of 61 Squadron took off from Woolfox to attack the Kiel shipyards. It was not a good night, little damage was inflicted on Kiel and three aircraft were lost, two over the target, the third crashing at Fosdyke, Lincolnshire after being engaged by an Allied convoy off Spurn Head.

61 Squadron was going through the unenviable task of re-equipping with the Avro Manchester. The Manchester was a troublesome aircraft and many pilots preferred the handling and reliability of the Hampden. The Manchester's main Achilles' heel was its power plants, which were powered by two Rolls-Royce Vultures. These engines were hopelessly underpowered for the task of lifting this type of heavy bomber and were constantly overheating and failing through mechanical breakdowns. Delivery of the aircraft was slow, with only a few, if any, on strength at all. The squadron had received its first Manchester on 8th March 1941. On 4th October 1941, more arrived, and 61 Squadron took on Woolfox as its permanent home.

The squadron was formed in the First World War as a home defence unit. It flew a variety of aircraft, which included the Sopwith Pup, Camel and the successful SE.5a. Re-formed as a bomber squadron in 1937, at Hemswell in Lincolnshire, it had already taken part in several notable operations since the start of hostilities. These included the first bombing raid on a German land target (Hornum, 19th/20th March 1940), the first big bombing raid on the German mainland (Münchengladbach, 11/12th May 1940) and the first bombing raid on Berlin (25/26th August 1940).

October and November 1941 were a working up period for the

squadron. During this time one Manchester was lost. Flying Officer Searby in L7520 had problems with the feathering mechanism after his port engine cut. The Manchester's inability to fly very far on one engine resulted in a forced landing near Roxton in Bedfordshire.

The first of many raids on Boulogne was launched by the squadron on 8th December 1941. This was designed as a gentle introduction to operations. 61 Squadron put up four aircraft. They were led by Wing Commander T C Weir, the squadron commanding officer, and were attached to 207 and 97 Squadrons, which were also flying Manchesters. Unfortunately, the 'A' Flight commander, Squadron Leader Riley, and crew were hit by a single flak shell. The aircraft crashed into the sea. There were no survivors.

Leading up to the Brest/Cherbourg raid on 9th/10th January

Wing Commander T C Weir RCAF DFC took over command of 61 Squadron on 5th September 1941 after Wing Commander G E Valentine was killed on operations from North Luffenham. Weir remained in command of the squadron until June 1942, nurturing the unit through their operations with the Avro Manchester.

241

1942, the squadron's record was not looking too good. The squadron had been attempting to re-equip with the Manchester as far back as March 1941. During this time, the unit had only managed 23 sorties, at a cost of five aircraft – three on operations and two in training. On this night, the squadron contributed six Manchesters. Their target was the docks at Cherbourg. The pace was picking up for the squadron, and from this night onwards, it would shoulder a major proportion of Manchester operations.

On the third consecutive operation, 61 Squadron lost a Manchester. Pilot Officer Matthews was on his first operation; also, this was one of two aircraft carrying passengers: two regional control officers (RCO) flew with the squadron that night to develop their experience into Bomber Command operations. The night did not start well. An aircraft had already crashed at Woolfox, so the Manchesters had to use North Luffenham instead. Matthews, along with his second pilot, Pilot Officer Wilson, managed to get their Manchester, R5789, to a few thousand feet when the starboard engine lost power and caught fire. The propeller was immediately feathered, and the fire extinguished. Their quick actions did nothing to resolve the fact that they had a full bomb and fuel load. An irreversible descent was the only option. As the aircraft was over the Wiltshire/Hampshire border the bomb load could not be jettisoned for fear of killing civilians. Matthews steadied the aircraft, allowing six of his crew to bale out. Wilson remained on board and together they attempted a blind forced landing. Luck was not on their side. After flaring for landing, the aircraft crashed into a belt of trees at Tidworth, near Wiltshire Cross. Both pilots were killed instantly and shortly afterwards the bomb load exploded. An investigation into the crash speculated that ice may have contributed to the engine failure. The RCO and remainder of the crew all escaped with minor injuries.

The rest of the attacking force fared better, but three were unable to locate Cherbourg and returned with their bombs. The remaining two descended below the cloud base and managed to attack, but no results were reported.

Wilhelmshaven, on 10th/11th January, followed by Hamburg shipyards, on the 14th, were both attacked by 61 Squadron. The latter raid involved a new tactic, which would be employed by Bomber Command for the rest of the war. Instead of taking off at irregular intervals and making their own way to the target by whatever route the captain and navigator favoured, the aircraft would take-off closely spaced and would fly the same route and speed. They would then join up with other units to form what came to be known as the 'bomber stream', concentrating the attack and allowing them to overwhelm flak and night fighter defences. The success of the Hamburg raid was restricted by poor visibility. Only 52 out of 96 aircraft involved claimed to have bombed.

The Hamburg raid resulted in the loss of L7495. Flying Officer Beard had been ordered to divert to Bottesford because of poor weather. After failing to raise the diversion station on the wireless/transmitter and being low on fuel, they were forced to abandon the aircraft near Grimoldy, 4 miles east of Louth.

The end of January saw no let up in operations: Bremen, Brest and Boulogne were all visited. The main focus of attention, though, was on three German capital ships in Brest harbour. The *Scharnhorst, Gneisenau* and *Prinz Eugen* were the pride of the German Navy and had been bottled up in Brest harbour for some time, impatient to cause as much havoc to Allied shipping as possible. These three heavy cruisers were built in the late 1930s in defiance of the Versailles naval agreement. They averaged 32,000 tonnes and each could travel at over 30 knots. Their armament comprised a formidable array of 8 and 9 inch main deck guns, and over 50 anti-aircraft guns apiece.

Over 300 raids had been directed at the ships, with little or no effect. As British intelligence were giving warnings of the imminent break out from port of the *Scharnhorst, Gneisenau* and *Prinz Eugen*, Bomber Command was making a maximum effort to disable the vessels. The importance of destroying the ships was brought to the fore by the Navy's involvment in briefings at Woolfox. A naval sub-lieutenant gave the crews pep talks about the official concern that the capital ships were about to break out and the havoc they would cause to Atlantic convoys.

On top of this there was concern that the ships may head for the Mediterranean, so the importance of crippling them could not be overemphasised.

The attack on Brest on 31st January 1942 involved nine aircraft from 61 Squadron. One of these had a unique role to play in weapon development. In L7472, Pilot Officer R D Fraser and his crew, plus squadron master bomber Flight Lieutenant Hannigan and the naval lieutenant who gave the pep talks, had been selected to introduce a new anti-shipping weapon to RAF service. A technical expert briefed Fraser and his crew separately on its operation and how it should be dropped for maximum effect. The weapon was described as 4,000lb armour piercing device with a double charge, designed to first blow a hole in the armoured deck of a battle cruiser and, secondly, to explode below. No records exist of such a device being used by the RAF, but the 5,000lb 'Capital Ship' was a similar device.

The 72 aircraft involved in the raid were directed to create a diversion so that Fraser could attack at about 2,000ft with the special weapon. For Fraser, this carefully planned operation fell apart at Woolfox. After a faultless test flight, L7472 developed engine trouble. This delayed the take-off and meant that they would have to attack without the cover of their colleagues.

Arriving over the target later than planned, and very much alone, every anti-aircraft gun around the harbour seemed to be targeting them. When the time came for Hannigan to descend to the bomb aimer's position, all was peaceful in the aircraft for several minutes. Fraser set the aircraft up for a gliding attack, when the flak started bursting closer and closer. Then, without warning, a searchlight locked onto them. Simultaneously, L7472 struck a barrage balloon cable inboard of the starboard engine. The aircraft immediately yawed to the right. Fraser, blinded by the light, counteracted the yaw; this was followed by the detonation of the cable cutter fitted into the leading edge of the wing on the Manchester. The flak continued while Hannigan tried to identify the ships. The target was spotted hard to port and heading adjustments were made before he called 'Bomb away'. Flak was continuous as the aircraft climbed away and so Fraser began to take evasive action; then the starboard engine burst into flames and cut out. Both the extinguisher and feathering mechanism failed to work, adding to their already desperate situation. On top of this, another balloon cable was hit in exactly the same position. This was even more serious than before, as their balloon cutter had been a 'once only' device, so they were stuck with it this time. By now, the flak had left them alone, but their situation was perilous. Despite all of this, Fraser still asked for a course for home even though the aircraft was already losing height. The balloon cable finally shook itself loose but by this time they were down to 300ft. Sergeant Marshall, the second pilot, decided to take his chance and bailed out. After the aircraft had skimmed houses, the port engine finally gave up and Fraser performed a copybook dead-stick landing on the water. Unfortunately, the front gunner, Sergeant McLean, drowned, but six survivors scrambled into their dinghy. After spending the rest of the night moored to their submerged aircraft, they came ashore the following morning into the waiting hands of the Luftwaffe.

Pilot Officer Fraser's brave attack on one of the capital ships was to no avail. No significant damage was ever reported. The device he dropped that night would be developed, and, as technology improved, would be used to greater effect later on in the war.

The other squadron aircraft involved in the attack had mixed fortunes. Only two returned unscathed to Woolfox and a third arrived badly shot-up. One landed at North Luffenham with failed brakes, narrowly missing a parked Hampden. Another landed at Wittering, thinking it was North Luffenham. Two more failed to return. Flying Officer Parsons and crew crash-landed at St Renan and, sadly, Flight Lieutenant Page and crew almost made it to the English coast only to drown before a rescue could recover them.

The squadron, like many others in Bomber Command during early February 1942, were kept on standby, loaded and ready to go should news be received that the German ships were at sea. Large numbers of mines were laid along the Dutch coast in the hope that the vessels would encounter them on a northerly route.

Bomber Command were becoming frustrated with waiting for the big ships to move but the anticipated day came on 12th February 1942. Operation *Fuller* was instigated. The squadron provided five Manchesters for the attack, even though some of the squadron aircraft had only landed at 09:15 that morning. The German ships had slipped away at night, and were travelling at high speed through the English Channel with many escort ships and protective fighter cover.

Bomber Command's efforts on the whole were a complete failure. The weather was terrible, with very few aircraft finding their quarry. Woolfox aircraft had mixed fortunes again – two returned without finding the target, two located the convoy, but a combination of flak and fighters prevented an attack, and the fifth crew made a bombing run on a battle cruiser from 450ft but missed the target. Several of the group returned to Woolfox peppered with holes from flak bursts.

The German ships all made it to the safety of German ports, although both the *Scharnhorst* and *Gneisenau* hit mines, which had been laid by 5 Group Hampdens. The sailing of these ships finally released Bomber Command from the effort-consuming and costly requirement to bomb them while they had been in French ports. Bomber Command had dropped 3,413 tons of bombs on these three ships in the preceding months and lost 127 aircraft in doing so. However, these raids had achieved some success, as both *Scharnhorst* and *Gneisenau* had been hit and badly damaged by bombs. This, and the constant threat of further damage, had prevented the ships from sailing from Brest on another Atlantic shipping raid, and had persuaded the Germans that they should be brought back to the greater protection of German ports.

Minelaying and participation in ever-bigger raids on German and French targets continued for the crews at Woolfox. Manchesters were still being lost on a regular basis, but there was light at the end of the tunnel for the squadron. 61 Squadron Conversion Flight was formed on 27th March 1942 with the purpose of converting crews onto the Lancaster.

On 5th May 1942, the squadron departed for Syerston in Nottinghamshire, and Woolfox returned to its original training role. 29 OTU was formed at North Luffenham and, as Woolfox was still a satellite, the Wellingtons from this unit made use of it.

June saw another new arrival: 1429 (Czech) OTU arrived from East Wretham in Norfolk. This unit's job was to train crews for 311 (Czech) Squadron based in Norfolk. The main party of 85 officers and men was flown in aboard the Flight's 12 Wellington Ics and three Airspeed Oxfords on 29th June. Their stay was short lived, as a movement order was received from Bomber Command. By 31st August, the unit had left for its new home at Church Broughton in Derbyshire as part of 93 Group.

The autumn of 1942 saw 29 OTU make use of the airfield again, but on 18th October Woolfox was closed for flying. The airfield was handed over to civil engineers to carry out some major changes. Instead of grass, three tarmac runways were

Avro Manchester Mk.Ia L7521 served 61 Squadron well and achieved over 300 flying hours before she was destroyed in a training accident at Waddington on 5th September 1942 when with 50 Squadron. (P C Birch.)

constructed, and a perimeter and 50 hardstandings were put in place. Four hangars, plus a collection of ancillary buildings, were also built. This all gave Woolfox a more permanent feel and on 7th June it became free of North Luffenham's control and was made a parent station in its own right within 3 Group.

An advance party from 1665 HCU (Heavy Conversion Unit) arrived on 4th June 1943 from Waterbeach. HCUs trained bomber crews for bomber operations. After completion of their course, the crews would be posted to a frontline squadron. 1665 HCU used the American airfield at Shipdam in Norfolk for some circuit training whilst Woolfox was being worked on. The move was complete by 5th June. The HCU brought with them sixteen Stirling Mk.L and IIIs. The Stirling was a popular aircraft in the air (apart from over the target, where its poor altitude attainment made it vulnerable to flak), but its weak point was take-off and landing. The aircraft had a habit of swinging heavily, and, if not corrected swiftly, this would result in the undercarriage collapsing. Several of the HCU's aircraft were severely damaged or written off in accidents of this type. The worst of these occurred on 5th July, when a Mk.I, BF339, started to swing on take-off. It ended up careering across the airfield out of control,

Only one Czechoslovakian unit was ever based at an airfield in Leicestershire and Rutland. 1429 (Czech) OTU stayed briefly at Woolfox Lodge in mid-1943 before moving on, with their Vickers Wellingtons, to Church Broughton in Derbyshire.

crossing the perimeter track and heading for the admin buildings. After striking a stationary vehicle, it continued for another 30 yards before colliding into buildings. Some of these were demolished, while others were damaged after the aircraft caught fire. BF339 was written off and it took a month to repair the damage caused to the admin site.

Changes were afoot again. The HCU was to stay for a total of only eight months. On 23rd January 1944, 1665 HCU left for Tilstock in Shropshire. As the demand for Stirling bomber crews subsided, there was an increase in demand to man Stirling Mk.IV glider tugs for 38 Group. This resulted in a change of role for the HCU.

Since May 1943, Woolfox had, like many other stations, been used for the storage of gliders. During May and June 1943, 32 Airspeed Horsas were delivered, towed and released by Whitley and Albemarle glider tugs over the airfield. The gliders were initially cared for by 29 OTU, but later, 33 Heavy Glider Maintenance Section, part of 2 Heavy Glider Maintenance Unit, would assume sole responsibility. All of Woolfox's Horsas would

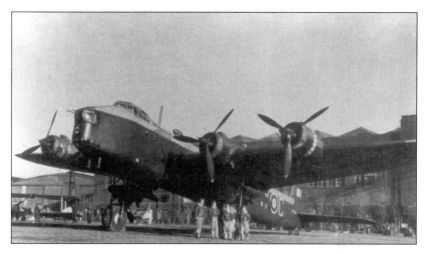

1665 HCU was equipped with the Short Stirling Mk.I. This aircraft, 'G-George', is pictured on a visit to Wittering. Air and ground crew of the 55th Fighter Squadron, 20th Fighter Group, USAAF, pose in front.

be handed over to the USAAF for use by the Troop Carrier Units.

After 1665 HCU left, the airfield was placed under Care and Maintenance, when the airfield received an unserviceable symbol. Work started on improving the airfield lighting system and installing sodium flare paths on two of the runways.

The airfield was still in a 'day use only' state when another operational squadron arrived. 218 (Gold Coast) Squadron came from Downham Market on 7th March 1944 with Wing Commander R M Fenwick-Wilson AFC in command.

Formed as a bomber squadron in the twilight years of the First World War, 218 Squadron had been a bomber unit ever since. Starting the Second World War briefly at Oakington in Cambridgeshire flying Blenheims, it then moved to Marham in Norfolk where it converted to the capable Wellington Ic followed by the Stirling, which would see it through the middle years of the war. A move to Downham Market, Norfolk in July 1943 followed and it was from here that Flight Sergeant Arthur Aaron was posthumously awarded the Victoria Cross after receiving appalling injuries while on a raid to Turin on 12/13th August 1943. The aircraft crash-landed in North Africa and Aaron died of his injuries nine hours later.

The difficulties with airfield lighting did not allow the unit to perform night operations until 9th April. The squadron was heavily involved in mine laying. Sorties ranged from the Baltic to the south of the Bay of Biscay. Leading up to the Allied invasion, other raids included railway yards at Chambly, Rouen and Lille.

At this time, 218 squadron was involved in training with a new blind bombing system called G-H. The system involved sending and receiving pulse signals to continuously measure distance and follow predetermined tracks with great precision. The first raid on which the squadron used G-H was the Chambly rail depot on 20/21st April. The raid was classed as a failure, as only

218 Squadron had a short but active time at Woolfox Lodge through the spring and summer months of 1944. A pensive looking Flying Officer Allen poses in front of a Short Stirling Mk.I 'Fante'. (Via P.H.T. Green.)

three out of fouteen aircraft managed to bomb, even with good weather and no enemy opposition. In its defence, the G-H system was in its infancy, and still being experimented with. It would go on to be used more effectively for the remainder of the war.

Chambly was again the target on the night of 1st/2nd May. G-H was used again with good results and accurate bombing. Unfortunately, the clear night sky favoured the German night-fighters. Two Stirlings failed to return and a third was badly mauled. EF184, a Stirling Mk.III captained by Pilot Officer Scammell, was attacked at least four times by Ju.88s. Damage was caused to the mainplane and tail unit, and the undercarriage would not lower. The flight engineer was killed and both mid-upper and tail gunners were wounded. Losing height constantly after the attack, Scammell, managed to achieve a successful belly-landing at the emergency airfield at Woodbridge in Suffolk.

With D-Day rapidly approaching, the squadron had been secretly training for a very special operation – Operation *Glimmer*. The object of the exercise was to create an imaginary convoy using 'Window'.

'Window' was a very early radio countermeasures weapon, and was the single most important device introduced by the RAF during the Second World War. It consisted of strips of metallised paper cut to a particular length and dropped from bomber aircraft in clumps to produce simulated responses on the enemy's radar screens. 'Window' was first used over Hamburg on the night of 24th/25th July 1943.

617 Squadron would fly a similar operation further down the coast, called Operation *Taxable*. The aircraft would fly very disciplined orbits and drop the foil strips to convince the German radar system that the invasion was in a different location. The 'Window' would look like a large collection of ships. On May 19th, HQ Bomber Command issued instructions to 218 Squadron to commence timed training flights. Six experienced senior crews with two reserves were selected. On May 20th, training commenced under the leadership of the squadron commander. Within the short space of eleven days, 119 training flights had been flown, and, furthermore, in that short period of time the squadron had reached the required standard of navigational and precision flying that would be required. Crews who operated during this period simply recorded in their log books, 'Special

251

Local Flying' or similar mundane entries. Little did these crews realise that they were ready to undertake arguably one of the most important operations of the war. The speed with which the squadron reached the stringent operational requirements confirms the very high standard of both the air and ground crews. It also testifies to the very special leadership qualities of the squadron's commanding officer, Wing Commander Fenwick-Wilson, A.F.C. June 1944 began with more training flights. Equipment tests were flown on June 2nd, 3rd and 4th, and 28 flights were flown by the selected crews. The weather during this period was far from ideal; low cloud, heavy rain and visibility down to five miles was not encouraging. The squadron crews were, regardless of this, ready and eager to operate.

Eight Stirlings, two of which were in reserve, would be involved in the operation, each carrying a complement of thirteen: two pilots, three navigators, one wireless operator, one flight engineer, two airgunners, two Window droppers, plus two replacements. All the Stirlings had left Woolfox by 00:43 hours on the morning of 6th June 1944.

The plan was for the squadron, once airborne, to fly elongated orbits with the major axis of the orbit perpendicular to the coast. During each of the orbits 'Window' would be discharged at a rate of twelve bundles per minute. Very precise flying was needed to

A pair of 218 Squadron Short Stirling Mk.Is high above the clouds. The Stirling has received a lot of bad press over the years, but despite this it was popular with its crews and in the right hands could be flown like a fighter.

achieve the desired effect. The timing called for an advance of eighteen miles at a speed of seven knots. This involved the front-line aircraft totalling 23 orbits. To achieve the desired effect of a convoy steaming out from the coast, the second line of aircraft came in eight orbits later than the first, thus these were required to fly only eighteen orbits. The flying time for the first line was 2¾ hours, and for the second line 1¾ hours. There were three aircraft in each line. These complicated orbits would, if the 'Window' were discharged on schedule, produce an imaginary convoy, which in turn would be picked up by the German Freya radar.

German reaction to *Glimmer* was almost instant. Searchlights came on and guns opened fire on the non-existent convoy. Night-fighters and E-boats were also diverted to the area but searched in vain. Throughout the mission, as far as 218 were concerned, everything went without a hitch, and the Stirlings returned safely to Woolfox between 05:02 and 05:12 hours.

A signal was later received from the Commander-in-Chief Bomber Command, Sir Arthur T Harris, which congratulated the squadron on its success. In a later report, he said that it was considered that both *Glimmer* and *Taxable* had 'contributed very materially to tactical surprise'.

From July 1944 onwards, the squadron began to receive the Avro Lancaster, with nine on strength by the end of the month. During this transition period, 3 Lancaster Finishing School (LFS) from Feltwell in Norfolk made use of Woolfox for circuits.

The Stirling would soldier on for a few more weeks, mainly involved in the continuous mining operations. The final raid from Woolfox was on 2nd August, ten Stirlings attacking a V-1 site in daylight at Mont Candon.

Two days later, 218 Squadron moved to Methwold, to complete a move which had started in July with the departure of 'B' Flight. 3 LFS used the circuit for a few more weeks, finishing the training of the 'C' Flight crews.

The station was under care and maintenance once again, with tar spraying of the runways and perimeter tracks being carried out. A new Motor Transport (MT) shed was built, and general preparations were being made for another new arrival.

Woolfox now became Station 478, having been transferred to the USAAF on 1st September. The 9th Troop Carrier Command Substitution Unit and 62nd Station Complement Squadron occupied the station for just over six weeks and, although some preparation was made, no American flying units moved in. The plan was to use Woolfox as a base for a troop carrier group, but it was not required, as the Americans had left by 18th October. Woolfox was situated in the heart of the Northern Carrier Group airfields. Cottesmore was one of them and its close proximity may have had a bearing on this decision.

RAF control had been resumed by 20th October. The station returned to 7 Group as a substation of 73 Base, North Luffenham. Ten days later an advance party from 1651 HCU arrived from Wratting Common in Cambridgeshire. The HCU was also going through the steady process of converting from Stirlings to Lancasters. The majority of these arrived in early November.

Typically of most HCUs of this period, the aircraft on strength were more varied than one might think. Apart from the usual Stirling Mk.IIIs, Lancaster Mk.Is and IIIs, of which it had 32 on strength by January 1945, the aircraft included a Beaufighter NF Mk.VI, Oxford Is, Hurricane IIcs and the odd Spitfire. The latter would be involved with fighter affiliation training, although the unit would exercise with 1426 (Enemy Aircraft Flight) at Collyweston as well. On one occasion, the Flight's Ju.88S-1 was used, and must have provided a realistic taster for the trainee crews of what operations involved.

Although the war was coming to an end, enemy intruder action still continued. On the night of 3rd/4th March 1945, two Lancasters, both on training exercises, were shot down near the airfield. There were a number of aircraft in the circuit at the time of the attack and the first warning that most of the crews got was when all the lights were doused. One aircraft came down on Cottesmore airfield (which was also under attack) while the second crashed in flames near Stretton. Out of fourteen aircrew, only one rear gunner survived.

With the end of the war in Europe, VE Day was celebrated with some gusto. A Nissen hut was burnt down as a result of over-exuberance and as a result fire crews were occupied throughout the night. A wise CO also took the precaution of placing a guard on the aircraft. It was possible that some adventurous soul might have decided to celebrate by taking an unauthorised flip. Many of the trainees thought that they would be dispatched to the Far East to take part in the final onslaught on Japan.

The last permanent flying unit to be based at Woolfox Lodge was 1651 HCU which operated the Avro Lancaster Mk.I and Mk.III until July 1945. This group was probably taken after the war, judging the number of happy faces. (J Hardman.)

The demand for bomber crews diminished almost overnight, which led, in turn, to a rapid decline of the many units which had been responsible for their training. This soon became evident at Woolfox. Flying training ceased at the end of June and on 13th July 1651 HCU was disbanded. The unit had lost ten aircraft during their short stay at Woolfox. The price of training was always high.

Post-war, the station was used as a German POW camp and was also taken over as an Equipment Dispersal Depot. The huts were converted in the late 1940s for use by ex-servicemen and their families. Others housed displaced persons, many of them Ukranians. From 1951 to 1953 the airfield was reactivated for use by Flying Training Command. 7 FTS Harvards and later Balliols from Cottesmore were seen performing circuits during this period.

The military had a final use for the old airfield. It would now house 62 (SAM) Squadron with Bloodhound I missiles. The site was still controlled by North Luffenham, which was the Tactical Control Centre.

The control tower at Woolfox Lodge was built to a night fighter station specification, even though it was never planned to receive any such kind of unit. It survives in reasonable condition, as it was converted into living accommodation many years ago, but today it is used by a local farmer as a store. (Author.)

By 1964, however, the missiles had gone, and in September 1966 the airfield was auctioned off to various sources. Today, the general layout of the airfield is undisturbed. Most of the runways and dispersals are still intact. The old Bloodhound site is close to the A1 and several derelict buildings are visible. Few Second World War buildings remain, although the control tower still stands defiant on the edge of the airfield and is in reasonable condition.

19

WYMESWOLD

National Grid Reference SK586224; 3½ miles ENE of Loughborough

An aviation enthusiast lucky enough to have been around in the 1950s would have had a treat at Wymeswold. From glamorous RAF fighter jets like the Meteor, Vampire and Hunter to rare machines like the Attacker and Avro Ashton, Wymeswold had it all. Admittedly, during the Second World War, like many other Leicestershire airfields, it played its part in aircrew training for bombers and transports, but post war the airfield went from strength to strength.

Air Ministry officials first selected a site for the new airfield in 1941. It was between the villages of Hoton and Wymeswold, 3½ miles north-east of Loughborough. The bulk of the airfield's technical and domestic sites were constructed on the eastern side, near to the village of Hoton. This name was not selected for the airfield, however, the reason being to avoid confusion with Hooton Park, which was many miles away in Cheshire.

Wymeswold was built to a standard three-runway design, the main runway running parallel with the Hoton–Wymeswold road. Construction began in mid-1941 and when the airfield officially opened on 16th May 1942 it was in a part-finished state. The airfield was originally intended for use as part of 7 Group Bomber Command, but was quickly changed to 92 Group. It was now home to the newly formed 28 Operational Training Unit (OTU), which was dedicated to training night bomber crews for front-line operations.

28 OTU was equipped with the Vickers Wellington Ic. Many of them had seen better days, having already served on operational

squadrons and also on other OTUs. Initially the unit was equipped with 27 Wellingtons and a pair of Westland Lysander target tugs. This was only half strength for an OTU; by the end of the year it would be almost double in size.

Initial efforts by personnel posted into Wymeswold were to ensure that the station was operational. The airfield was far from complete and maximum effort was therefore put into getting it into flying condition. On 1st June 1942, Wymeswold received its new station commander, Group Captain J R Bell DFC, who remained there until after the war's end.

28 OTU was ready for operations on 4th August 1942. The first course arrived and 'A' Flight, with twelve aircraft, was formed a few days later. Practice bombing ranges, at Clifton Pastures for daylight and Misson (South Yorkshire) for night, were allocated to the unit. Air to air firing practice took place on the Holbeach range, along with 14 OTU from Cottesmore. The Lysander III target tugs were also shared with 14 OTU. 'B' Flight was not activated until 11th September, when the training courses gained momentum.

During 1942, the USAAF started to arrive in neighbouring

The Westland Lysander served many OTUs in the target towing role until it was replaced by the Miles Martinet.

Northamptonshire. The result of operating over a strange country and possessing poor maps, an unscheduled arrival was recorded on 11th August. Five Boeing B-17F 'Flying Fortresses' were landed at Wymeswold, mistaking it for Grafton Underwood. The aircraft belonged to the 351st Bomb Squadron of the 301st Bomb Group; supplied with better maps, and slightly embarrassed, they left again.

As busy as the OTU was, the first flying accident to happen on station involved a 409 Squadron aircraft. A Beaufighter Mk. VIf, X8198, from Coleby Grange, south of Lincoln experienced an engine failure at 10,000ft. The pilot selected Wymeswold for his forced landing. Approaching the main runway downwind, the Beaufighter came in too fast and overturned. It was written off, but the two crew on board escaped with only minor injuries. The first of many accidents involving OTU aircraft did not fall to a Wellington as expected. De Havilland Moth Minor AW151 was one of only 26 aircraft that had been impressed into service at the start of the war. All OTUs were equipped with a variety of extra aircraft, gained from various sources. AW151 had been passed between a number of units before transferring to Wymeswold. On 13th September 1942, it landed heavily and its undercarriage collapsed. It held the dubious distinction of becoming the first aircraft written off by 28 OTU.

In February 1942, Bomber Command received a new commander in Chief. Air Marshall Arthur 'Butch' Harris brought Bomber Command out of the Dark Ages. He rapidly turned an almost ineffectual Command into a well-equipped fighting force. This all came at a high price for the crews. The 30 months preceding Harris' arrival saw Bomber Command drop 90,000 tons of bombs, with the loss of over 7,000 aircrew. Harris had raised these figures by the end of the war to 850,000 tons of bombs dropped and the alarming loss of over 55,000 aircrew. The aircrew losses were not confined to front-line squadrons – with the introduction of '1,000 bomber' raids in May 1942, Harris called upon OTU crews to take part as well. Instructors and senior pupils flew these raids, and, although having been formed only three months earlier, 28 OTU's turn came on the night of 10th/11th September.

Three Wellingtons from 'A' Flight took part in a raid on Düsseldorf. The force totalled 479 aircraft and all three 28 OTU

259

aircraft arrived back at Wymeswold unscathed. Three nights later, two more aircraft took part in a raid to Bremen. Fifteen Wellingtons were among the losses incurred that night; thankfully 28 OTU's aircraft were not among these statistics. The OTU's participation in the bombing campaign ended on the night of the 16th/17th September with a raid on Essen. The bombing was scattered, but turned out to be one of the most successful attacks on this difficult target. Over 10% of the force of 369 aircraft were shot down, 21 of them Wellingtons. Once again, though, the two aircraft supplied by 28 OTU returned to Wymeswold. This time, however, both aircraft suffered from flak damage, and the navigator from one of the aircraft was wounded in the neck and hand.

The first fatal accident took place on 7th October 1942 and involved one of the OTU's war-weary Wellington Ics. Warrant Officer Gee, Sergeant Barker and Flight Sergeant Jones were carrying out dual and right hand seat flying exercises. The aircraft was witnessed jettisoning fuel shortly before it crashed at Woodhouse Eaves, south of Loughborough.

During the period between the end of October and the beginning of November, more Wellingtons arrived on station. Sufficient aircraft arrived to form 'C' Flight on 31st October. By now 40 Wellingtons, two Lysanders and a single Boulton Paul Defiant started to make the airfield a bit congested. Even with this amount of aircraft, the OTU was still only at three-quarter strength. Castle Donington had been allocated as a satellite airfield for Wymeswold, and its timely opening on 1st January 1943 did not come too soon. 'C' Flight moved into Castle Donington on 2nd January, and this meant that the split system of training could be initiated. Conversion training was carried out at Castle Donington, while Wymeswold's 'A' and 'B' Flights would continue to carry out operational training.

28 OTU had reached its full quota of aircraft by the end of January 1943. In total 54 Wellingtons were now on the books, with the odd Oxford, Tiger Moth, Master, and Anson. The Gunnery Flight, which operated and maintained the two Lysanders, had more purpose built replacements arriving in March 1943. Miles Martinets replaced the Lysander, and the new aircraft improved the efficiency of Target Tug operations dramatically.

Wymeswold's responsibilities increased on 25th March, when several bombing ranges came under the airfield's control, including Mowsley in Leicestershire and Grandborough in Warwickshire. Two more ranges were under construction at Ragdale in Leicestershire and Wardley near Uppingham in Rutland, and these also came under Wymeswold's charge.

A new unit arrived from Finningley, in Yorkshire, on 23rd April 1943. 1521 Blind Approach Training Flight was equipped with eight Airspeed Oxford Is. The unit's job was to teach pilots the art of using Standard Beam Approach equipment. The forerunner of the modern Instrument Landing System, on poor visibility days the BAT Flight aircraft would be the only machines flying.

The most common way of aircrews gaining experience of flying over enemy territory was to carry out 'Nickel' raids. This involved leaflet dropping, and all OTU units and crews were expected to take part in them. The enormous amount of paper dropped during these raids is reflected in the fact that a separate building was constructed to hold it all.

Flying Officer R Lacerbe RCAF and crew flew one of sixteen aircraft involved in leaflet dropping on the night of 3rd/4th June 1943. Their objective was various towns along the coast of the

The Martinet first arrived at Wymeswold in the spring of 1943 but, with the takeover of Transport Command, disappeared when 28 OTU was disbanded in October 1944. (Via author.)

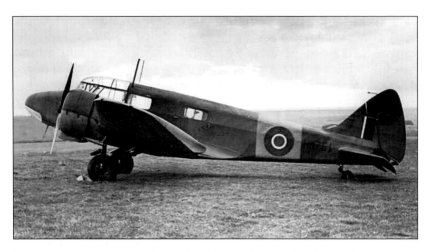

*One of the most common aircraft in RAF service was the Airspeed Oxford.
Used for a multitude of tasks, Oxfords operated for over two years at
Wymeswold with 1521 BATF. (Via author.)*

Bay of Biscay. A separate mine-laying raid along the coast was
also being carried out that night, and the OTU crews hoped that
they would attract the enemy fighters operating along the coast.
Lacerbe was unlucky that night – a Junkers Ju88-C6, based at
Bordeaux, was on patrol in the area. A running battle
commenced; driving their Wellington south, they eventually
shook the Junkers off, but were critically low on fuel. Neutral
Portugal was drawing closer, so there was no choice but to head
for it. Lacerbe ordered his crew to bail out over the Portuguese
town of Espinho. Lacerbe followed a few moments later after
directing the ailing bomber out to sea. The 28 OTU crew were
very lucky and, after being interned by the local authorities,
returned to England several months later.

Airfield work and modifications caused minimal disruption to
the OTU's training programme. But during April and June, both
of the OTU Flights at Wymeswold had to take up temporary
residence elsewhere while runway, perimeter and general
airfield lighting was fitted. Their first move was to Castle
Donington for a week; a second move was to Ossington in
Nottinghamshire. The latter gave 297 Squadron, flying
Armstrong Whitworth Whitleys, an opportunity to practise

towing their gliders fully-loaded. All of the ground and support staff, complete with equipment, were towed out of Wymeswold in Airspeed Horsa gliders. This method of movement meant that the OTU Flights lost virtually no flying hours because of the temporary move and the exercise gave the tug-and-glider pilots valuable experience, as they would later be carrying airborne troops into battle.

The flights returned to Wymeswold three weeks later and continued operational training throughout the summer months. The tired old Wellington Ic continued service in 1943, but a replacement was on the horizon by November. To the untrained eye, the new aircraft were just Wellingtons. But these were Mk.IIIs and Mk.Xs, with more power and better reliability; the OTU's accident rate suddenly took a downward turn. Good as this news was, the OTU was not fully converted to the new marks until the end of March 1944. Equipment improved still further for the Gunnery Flight during May 1944 as well. The Martinets had performed a sterling service, but had become obsolete and were replaced by Hawker Hurricane IIcs.

The airfield's runways were in dire need of attention at the beginning of June 1944. This meant another station closure and move for 'A' and 'B' Flights. This time, the unit's aircraft went on detachment to Bircotes in Yorkshire, departing on 20th June. Back at Wymeswold the contractors completed the repairs very

A Wellington Mk.X of 28 OTU sits on a snow-covered Wymeswold.

efficiently, and the Flights were back there by 24th July.

Visiting aircraft had frequently been seen at Wymeswold from the time that it opened. Halifaxes and Lancasters were a common sight. Ratcliffe's ferry pilots would collect Lancasters from Wymeswold, as their airfield was far too small for such a type. As operations built up, a separate site was constructed to cope with visiting aircrew and accommodation, and meals could be prepared with very little notice. Operational aircraft had been arriving singly since the beginning of 1943, but there was an influx on 5th August 1944, when bad weather caused hundreds of Lancasters and Halifaxes to divert from their east coast bases. 28 Lancasters and one Halifax arrived at Wymeswold that night; eighteen of the Lancasters were from 166 Squadron at Kirmington, North Lincolnshire.

The war took on a different pattern as the Allies steadily made headway across Europe. The demand for bomber crews subsided rapidly, and a reorganization of airfields and units would be needed. A signal received at Wymeswold on 1st October indicated that 28 OTU was to be disbanded and that Wymeswold would be transferred to 44 Group, Transport Command.

Transport Command took over Wymeswold in late 1944, and for the next three years the Douglas Dakota was the main aircraft operated. KP251 'NU-G' is a Mk.IV of 1382 (T) CU and served out its RAF service with 240 OCU at North Luffenham until August 1954. (A.J. Jackson Collection.)

On 10th October 1944, 28 OTU disbanded and was replaced by 108 (Transport) OTU, formed on the same day. The unit was to be equipped with the venerable Douglas Dakota, and the first aircraft arrived on 19th October. Castle Donington was still under Wymeswold's charge, and conversion training on the Dakota was carried out there. Once this was complete the training continued at the parent unit. Long hours of day and night flying were carried out, as well as intensive navigation practice. Staging- post procedure was a large element of this part of the crew's course and was important enough for part of the station to be made into a replica of one of the RAF's Transport Command Staging Posts, complete with briefing rooms and passenger, freight and messing areas.

By the end of 1944, 108 OTU was fully equipped with 40 Dakota I, III and IVs. Ground crews adapted very quickly to the American equipment needed to keep the Dakotas flying, which was reflected in the fact that the aircraft's serviceability record was over 90%. 108 OTU's accident rate was marred only twice by fatal accidents, both occurring in January 1945.

The first happened on 10th January, when Dakota IV KJ835 took off in a snowstorm. Unfortunately, the aircraft crashed near the railway line between Barrow on Soar and Sileby, killing the crew of three instantly. The second incident also involved a Dakota IV and happened as it was flying a long-distance navigation exercise over North Wales. No trace was ever found of the crew or aircraft, and it was presumed that the Dakota had come down in the Irish Sea.

With the war at an end in Europe the training of new aircrews at most units came to an abrupt halt. This was not the case at Wymeswold; as the war in the Far East still ploughed on, transport crews were still in demand. The OTU also flew many trips over north-western Germany to show ground crew the effects of the Allied bombing campaign. The 'Ruhr Tours' contributed greatly to the unit's flying hours. They achieved nearly 3,000 total hours in July alone.

A new title for the resident unit was devised on 10th August 1945. 108 (T) OTU became 1382 (Transport) Conversion Unit, (T)CU, retaining the Douglas Dakota. The (T)CU remained at Wymeswold until 10th Dec 1947, when it was moved to North Luffenham. This left Wymeswold in a state of Care and

Maintenance, and the station was effectively closed down. It was then transferred to 38 Group Transport Command on 5th January 1948 and it looked as if Wymeswold would take the path of many other wartime airfields. However, on 30th September, the airfield became part of 64 Group, Reserve Command and the future looked more promising.

Wymeswold was made active again in February 1949, and on 3rd April it became a fighter station for the first time. 504 Squadron (County of Nottingham) Royal Auxiliary Air Force arrived from Hucknall with Supermarine Spitfire F.22s. A few months later, the squadron made RAF history by becoming the first auxiliary unit to receive the Gloster Meteor F.4. A change of group occurred for the final time on 1st April 1950, when it came under the control of 12 Group Fighter Command.

A smaller company joined 504 Squadron on 15th July 1954. Auster AOP.6 observation aircraft of 1969 Flight, 664 (AOP) Squadron arrived, and were flown by Royal Artillery Officers.

Rolls Royce was carrying out trials on the Supermarine Attacker at Hucknall in Nottinghamshire, but Hucknall's grass runway was totally inadequate for trialling the tail-dragging jet. A decision was made to lay a concrete runway at Hucknall; so while this was happening, the entire Rolls Royce test team moved into Wymeswold. Their aircraft included a pair of Avro Ashtons, a Canberra B.2, Hunter F.1 and F.6. Rolls Royce were at Wymeswold from January 1955 to February 1956.

Detachments of three front-line RAF Squadrons made their presence felt at Wymeswold during the mid 1950s. 56, 257 and 263 Squadrons all visited with Hunters and the odd Vampire T.11.

It was announced in January 1957 that all of the RAF's auxiliary squadrons were to be disbanded. This was the beginning of the end for Wymeswold, but one last important event was to take place at the airfield. On Sunday 3rd March 1957, the airfield hosted the consecration and presentation of the 504 Squadron standard. After ceremonies were over, the new standard was placed in St Mary's Parish Church, Wymeswold, where it remains today.

One week later, on 10th March 1957, both 504 Squadron and 1969 Flight were disbanded. Wymeswold was then placed under Care and Maintenance for the final time, remaining under military control.

The airfield appears almost complete and all three runways remain in reasonable condition. The old technical site is on the left hand side and many buildings survive, being put to good use by several businesses. (Taken looking west.) (J Molyneux.)

The RAF may have been finished with Wymeswold, but many military aircraft would use the airfield for years to come. In early 1958, Field Aircraft Services moved their operation there from Tollerton in Nottinghamshire. They had won a large contract to overhaul the Royal Canadian Air Force aircraft operating in Europe. Types included Canadair Sabres, Silver Star and CF-100 Canucks. USAF contracts were won as well. Douglas SC-54 and R5D-1 were added to the list of aircraft maintained by Field Aircraft Services.

As military contracts expired, Field took on civilian maintenance. British European Airways Vickers Viscounts received overhauls, along with DC-3s and even the odd ex-military Lockheed Hudson. Syerston in Nottinghamshire had gained Wymeswold as a satellite airfield several years earlier, which provided 2 Flying Training School with extra airspace to practise circuits and bumps. Percival Provosts and, later, Hunting Jet Provosts, used the airfield on many occasions.

Wymeswold's control tower remains standing, but is a shell of its former self. (J Molyneux.)

Field Aircraft Services moved out of Wymeswold in April 1969 to the new East Midlands airport. The RAF made one last visit between 18th and 20th May 1970. Six Hawker Siddeley Harrier GR.1s of 1 Squadron, Wittering used part of the airfield during a mobility and deployment exercise.

Since then, the old airfield has been threatened with being used as a site for landfill, a nuclear waste dump and a 3,000-home town. It remains virtually complete today as an industrial estate, with a host of businesses using the remaining buildings and hangars for their trade. Large areas of runway and perimeter track still remain, along with the control tower, which still stands, minus its windows – a shell of its former self.

20

CIVILIANS AT WAR

When Neville Chamberlain made his famous announcement on 3rd September 1939, informing the nation that it was now at war with Germany, it did not come as a great surprise to the people of Leicestershire and Rutland. Air Raid Precaution (ARP) wardens had already been mobilised on 1st September, after German troops had crossed the Polish border. Blackout regulations were in place and a State of Emergency was in force, prompting many people to panic-buy essential supplies from local shops. Strict rationing would bring an end to this and would continue for many years after the end of the war.

The people of Rutland had been ready for the start of war througout the summer of 1939. An extensive blackout exercise, organised by the county's senior ARP officer, Major J D Joyce, had taken place on 5th July. RAF bombers from Cottesmore simulated the potential German attackers, and a blackout of Oakham was in force from midnight to 2 am. Several buildings in the town had been staged as bombed, and the local fire brigade had been kept busy all night. The exercise had been classed as a success with no accidents reported, as a result of operating with limited lighting.

The blackout undoubtedly had the greatest initial effect on the nation as a whole; travelling at night became so dangerous that most people wisely chose to stay indoors. Buses and trains were allowed to operate with only a single bulb, and all other vehicles had their headlights covered, with just a small slit for the beam to shine through. These regulations, combined with no street lighting, led to an alarming increase in road accidents. A high

An ARP exercise was held in Leicester during September 1938 and this young lady was a member of the John Bull Rubber Company's decontamination squad.

number of casualties also resulted from people falling down steps and bumping into various obstacles.

From lessons learned from the First World War, the Government was convinced that the Germans would use gas against Britain. In 1938, over 38 million gas masks were issued and people were advised to carry them everywhere they went. The masks were contained in a brown cardboard box tied with string and they were a familiar sight in the early months of the war, but by mid-1940 hardly anyone carried them, as there seemed to be little chance of the envisaged gas attacks coming.

Rationing was introduced from January 1940, and with it came the daily chore of dealing with ration cards, joining queues and chasing items that, only a few months earlier, had been easy to purchase. Butter, sugar, bacon and ham were the first items to be rationed, but potatoes, bread, fish and offal were in plentiful supply, and so these items became the main part of the diet.

'Dig for Victory' was the Government's campaign to encourage people to turn their gardens into vegetable patches and, indeed, the addition of fresh vegetables to dinner plates made life more bearable. The armed forces also took part in the 'Dig for Victory' campaign, even though they had no orders to do so. Often making use of good agricultural land, airfields lent themselves to the production of large areas of vegetables. The airmen stationed at Saltby, for example, were so successful at this that it almost became self sufficient and often traded its own produce for other items.

Another feature that was to change thousands of people's gardens was the distribution of personal air raid shelters. The most common type was the Anderson, named after the Home Secretary, Sir John Anderson. They were issued free to any household that earned less than £250 per year and they could provide protection from blast and flying shrapnel from falling bombs, but not from a direct hit! Easy to construct, they were made of curved steel which was bolted together and dug into the ground and then covered with at least three feet of soil. They were cold, small and prone to flooding but, from June 1940, saved many lives.

The authorities now prepared to receive their share of the planned 3.5 million evacuees that were to leave the country's major cities. However, only 1.5 million families actually joined the scheme. The first part of this vast operation was code-named 'Pied Piper' and involved many hundreds of thousands of pregnant mothers, children, teachers and helpers who were moved into the country. Both Leicestershire and Rutland had their fair share. Many returned to the big cities when they realised that living in the country held the same dangers: three out of four children were back home by the spring of 1940.

On 14th May 1940, Sir Anthony Eden, the Secretary of State for War, made a 'call to arms' broadcast, which highlighted the threat of a German invasion. With the vast majority of able-bodied men already serving in the forces, Eden announced the formation of a new home defence force called the Local Defence Volunteers (LDV). Within a day, over a quarter of a million men had enrolled in the LDV and by July this had risen to over one million. Initially ribbed as *Look, Duck and Vanish*, the LDV was renamed by Winston Churchill on 23rd July 1940 and became the Home Guard.

The Home Guard were initially poorly equipped, their only arms being a variety of garden and farm implements and the occasional shot gun. Uniforms and weapons had improved by 1941 and the introduction of standard army battledress, along with the issue of rifles shipped over from Canada, gave the Home Guard a more businesslike appearance. Although they were never taken seriously by other regular army units, had Hitler invaded there is no doubt that the Home Guard would have put up a staunch defence.

The period leading up to the fall of France in mid-1940 was called the 'Phoney War', and civilians of Britain were, for the first time, about to experience war at first hand. The many training exercises that the Observer Corps, Civil Defence wardens, First Aid parties and firemen had received would now be put to the test.

Leicester first received the attentions of the Luftwaffe at 10:15 hours on 21st August 1940, when at least eight High Explosive (HE) bombs were dropped along Cavendish Road, falling short of the intended target of the city's power station and gas works. The lone German aircraft was presumed to have been lost and took his opportunity. Six were killed and 24 injured. Bombs also fell on 14th September in the Humberstone area at St Ives Road and incendiaries were dropped in South Wigston, Oadby and all around Stoughton. A great deal of damage was caused, but the most serious attack on the city occurred on the night of the 19th/20th November 1940, when Leicester experienced its own Blitz. The German raiders were Heinkel He.IIIs of Luftflotte 2 and 3 which, in previous weeks, had been concentrating all their efforts on London. The majority of Heinkels carried a bomb load of HE bombs and incendiaries weighing at 4,410 lbs, while at least a dozen aircraft also carried lethal, 1,000kg parachute mines. At approximately 20:00 hours, approaching from the north-west to confuse ground defences, the first of three phases of the aerial bombardment began. The bombing was indiscriminate throughout the city centre and by 22:45 hours had reached its peak, but not before the worst incident of the raid occurred in a densely populated part of the city. Several HE bombs fell into Highfield and Titchbourne Streets, killing 41 people instantly and injuring many.

The final part of the raid struck the city at 01:15 hours and, by now, many fires were raging, providing easy markers for the last wave of German bombers. The 'All Clear' was eventually sounded at 04:00 hours. Like all Blitz-type attacks, the residential areas had suffered more than the strategically important

At 10:15 am on 21st August 1940, Leicester received its first bombs of the Second World War. A single German bomber dropped its lethal cargo across Cavendish Street, killing six and injuring 24 civilians.

One hundred and eight civilians were killed in a long indiscriminate raid on Leicester during the night of 19th/20th November 1940. This is a view of Highfield and Severn Street, a trailer ambulance lies wrecked in the foreground.

industrial targets: 108 people had been killed, 203 injured and over 5,000 homes and factories had been either destroyed or severely damaged. It was by far the worst raid to be inflicted on the city during the entire war.

Leicester fortunately never suffered the same level of bombing that was inflicted on the industrial Midlands, such as Coventry and Birmingham, and only sporadic raids followed. The last to be directed on the city was on 30th July 1942, when, once again, the Oadby and Wigston districts had incendiaries directed at them. Both counties were affected by the raids on the Midlands, as both Leicester and Rutland were usually traversed on their way to, or from, the target, so many bombs were jettisoned or dropped on these alternative targets.

A successful interception by the British of the German radio beam system, called 'Y' Verfahren, resulted in Leicestershire, rather than the intended target of Nottingham, being heavily bombed on 8th May 1941. On this night Sheffield, Derby and Nottingham were the major targets selected to be attacked.

Sheffield was to receive the main attack, but the first crews to arrive reported very poor visibility and the main force was redirected to bomb Hull.

The result of the German bombers following the distorted beam was that the remainder of the force bombed Nottingham thinking that it was Derby and the crews who were supposed to be bombing Nottingham, actually attacked the Vale of Belvoir! Hundreds of HE bombs and thousands of incendiaries rained down on the Vale but, incredibly, apart from a few blown-out windows and dislodged tiles, the only victims were two chickens.

Because of the severity and intensity of the German air attacks against targets in the Midlands, which was heavily involved in aircraft production, many civilian firms were employed in Leicestershire to manufacture aircraft components. Activity ranged from full aircraft production at Desford and Bitteswell to the equally important task of producing undercarriage units. For this, five dispersed factories were used, three in Leicester, one in Hinckley and one in Coalville, all concentrating on manufacturing Spitfire main- and tail-wheel undercarriages. By the war's end, the total units amounted to 28,567, enough to equip every Spitfire and Seafire produced, with several thousand to spare!

Lancaster components were also built in Leicester – ailerons, fuselage sections and wing outer trailing edges were built at the Leicester Corporation Bus and Tram Depot on Abbey Park Road. Noses, central fuselage and outer wings for the Lancaster were constructed in Briton Road at the Leicester Bus Garage. Freeman, Hardy and Willis produced fuselage floor assemblies and instrument panels and D Henderson & Sons made a huge variety of components in their works on St Saviours Road. Component parts for both Spitfire and Lancaster did not have to travel very far before reaching the main assembly lines. Over 1,000 Spitfires were assembled and flown from Desford and 1,329 Lancasters were produced by Armstrong Whitworth Aircraft at Bitteswell. This totalled nearly 20% of all Lancasters built.

Aircraft production was not confined to Leicester. At Loughborough, several hundred civilians were employed for the repair and modification of the Douglas Boston and Havoc, and many more on the de Havilland Dominie final assembly line at the Brush works. Taylorcraft at Rearsby were involved in full production of their Auster and repairing Hawker Hurricanes,

Hawker Typhoons and de Havilland Tiger Moths. When the war ended in 1945, the demand for military aircraft and their components dramatically declined, forcing the many Leicestershire employers to make thousands of aircraft workers redundant.

The people of Leicestershire and Rutland were given the chance to contribute to the war effort in another way when Lord Beaverbrook, who was in charge of the Ministry of Aircraft Production, suggested 'Buy a Spitfire'. Five thousand pounds was the amount needed to produce a Spitfire or Hurricane, and the donor was given the privilege of individually naming the aircraft. On 13th August 1940, the Leicester and County Spitfire fund was launched. Within eight days, a cheque for £5,000 was received from a local businessmen in an effort to get the scheme underway. Many individual funds were set up in both counties and the profile of the campaign was raised by setting up various captured German aircraft, including Messerschmitt Me.109s and Junkers Ju.88s, and charging people to view the machines. Seventeen Spitfires and one Hurricane were put into the air by the money-raising efforts of the Leicestershire people. Efforts were no less encouraging in Rutland when a War Weapons Week was held in May 1941. With a target of £60,000, in a short space of time over £140,000 was raised, the major part of it going towards aircraft production. The county had a Spitfire of its own, named *Stamford*. Although named after the Lincolnshire town, most of the cash raised for the fighter came from neighbouring Rutland. Also worthy of mention was the Rutland War Ship Week, which raised an incredible £191,414 14s 6d, which amounted to £9 12s 6d per head of population and enabled the small county to adopt a destroyer, *HMS Cottesmore*. Another £225,000 was raised by the people of Rutland in May 1943, during the 'Wings for Victory' campaign. This enabled the county to purchase five Avro Lancasters and make a valuable contribution towards the eventual defeat of Nazi Germany.

Economically the war brought many advantages to local and national business alike. The construction of so many airfields in such a short space of time brought lucrative contracts to the big construction companies, and also a large amount of work to smaller firms and individuals. For example, many local people specifically bought lorries and went to work transporting various items, including wood, sand and gravel, to help in the construction of the airfields. Although most airfields were constructed in an average of ten months, the Air Ministry paid well and many people reaped the rewards. Once a new airfield was opened, the influx of airmen would come as quite a shock to the local villagers, as the average population of an RAF station was approximately 2,000 people. The most obvious trader to benefit from this was the local publican, whose premises during the war years could range from a beer barrel set up inside a house to a fully equipped pub.

A fully operational airfield also brought its dangers to the locals, the main threat during the early war years being from German bombing; however, later on, an individual had much more chance of being struck by a crashing British aircraft. Several aircraft were unlucky enough to crash into neighbouring villages – this was most likely to happen during circuit training – but generally this was a rare event and every effort was made not to overfly densely populated areas. That said, the test pilot based at Loughborough used to like to make a show of flying low over the town, and in this case a blind eye seems to have been turned.

The Americans arrived quite late in Leicestershire and Rutland, compared with many eastern counties. Soldiers of the 82nd Airborne Division made Leicestershire their home; the majority of their camps were centred around Leicester, although they did have a large camp at Ashwell near Oakham in Rutland as well. On arrival in Britain, the American servicemen were issued with a pamphlet called *Over There*, which gave them information about the British people. The pamphlet contained many dos and don'ts, with more emphasis on the latter. One of the don'ts was NEVER criticize the King and Queen!

Friction was unavoidable, especially at places like Cottesmore where the American airmen were initially under the command of the RAF, whose senior officers did not take to the relaxed attitude of the Americans. But generally, they were popular with both military and civilians alike and their generosity, especially to local charities and deprived children, quickly removed any resentment that was first felt upon their arrival. The many thousands of American airmen who served at Cottesmore during the Second World War have nothing but happy memories of their stay in England.

When the Allies invaded mainland Europe on 6th June 1944, life on the Home Front began to improve. The nation could now

Memorial stone in front of Cottesmore's Station HQ in recognition of all the American units that served there during the Second World War. (J Molyneux.)

taste victory, the national press claiming that the war would be over by Christmas. Instead, German attacks on Britain took on a new form, in the shape of pilotless flying bombs called V-1s, or 'Doodlebugs' because of their distinctive engine note. Although only one V-1 actually fell in Leicestershire, the county was affected by another mass evacuation from London as a result of the new threat, but nearly all the evacuees had returned by September 1944.

The blackout restrictions were partially lifted in October 1944 and the Home Guard was disbanded on 1st November. When the war ended on 8th May 1945 in Europe the day was called 'Victory-in-Europe' (VE) Day and was treated as a holiday. The 'People's War' had come to an end, Churchill announcing, 'This is your victory.'

His Majesty King George VI, as he had done the day war broke out, addressed the nation on the 8th May: 'Armed or unarmed, men and women, you have fought, striven and endured to your utmost.' Over 65,000 British civilians had been killed and another 86,000 wounded fighting the 'People's War' on the home front.

APPENDIX

A breakdown of all RAF and USAAF Units and their aircraft that were stationed at the Leicestershire and Rutland airfields during the Second World War.

Bitteswell

18 OTU Wellington Ic and IV.
29 OTU Wellington III and X.
105 OTU Wellington X and Dakota III.

Bottesford

1524 BATF Oxford I.
207 Squadron Manchester I and Ia, Lancaster I.
207 CF Lancaster I and Manchester I and Ia.
90 Squadron Stirling I.
467 (RAAF) Squadron Lancaster I and III.
30 HGMU Horsa I.
436th TCG C-47.
440th TCG C-47.
1668 HCU Lancaster I, II, III and X, Hurricane IIc, Spitfire V and Beaufighter VI.
1321 BDTF Hurricane IIc.
7 Gp. Comm Flt Oxford II, Dominie I, Proctor III and Magister I.
Station Flight Oxford II, Tiger Moth I and II.

Braunstone

7 EFTS Tiger Moth I and II

Bruntingthorpe

29 OTU Wellington III and X, Anson I, Oxford I and II, Defiant I, Spitfire V, Tiger Moth II, Martinet TT.I, Hurricane IIc, Master II and Lysander IIIa.
1683 BDTF Tomahawk I and IIa.
Power Jets Limited Lancaster II, Wellington II/VI, Meteor F.1.

Castle Donington

28 OTU Wellington Ic, III and X.
108 (T)OTU Wellington X, Dakota III and IV.

Cottesmore

35 Squadron Wellesley I, Battle I.
185 Squadron Hampden I, Hereford I, Anson I.
207 Squadron Wellesley I, Battle I, Anson I.
106 Squadron Hampden I, Anson I.
14 OTU Anson I, Hampden I, Hereford I, Wellington I, Ia, Ic and II, Oxford I and II, Defiant I, Tiger Moth I, Martinet TT.I and Lysander III.
9th AF TCC. 50th TCW. 9th AF TCC Pathfinder School C-47 and C-53.
316th TCG C-47, C-53, C-109, CG-4A and C-46.

Desford

7 E&RFTS, 7 EFTS Tiger Moth I and II, Hart, Hind, Audax and Magister I.
3 CANS. 3 AONS Anson I.

Leicester East

196 Squadron Stirling III and IV.

620 Squadron Stirling III and IV.
190 Squadron Stirling IV.
93 Gp (Screened) Pilots School Wellington III.
107 OTU Dakota III.
1333 (TS) CU Dakota III, Horsa I and II.
Glider Pick-Up Training Flight Dakota III, CG-4A.

Market Harborough

14 OTU Wellington Ic, III and X, Oxford I, Hurricane IIc, Martinet TT.I and Master II.
1683 BDTF Tomahawk I, Hurricane IIc.

Melton Mowbray

4 OAPU Boston III, Wellington XIII.
306 FTU Boston III.
304 FTU Oxford I, Beaufighter I, VI and X, Beaufort I and II, Mosquito VI and XIII, Marauder I, Stirling III, Wellington X, XI and XIII.
1 FCP. 4 APU. 12 FU Oxford I, Anson I, Lancaster I, III and X, York I, Beaufighter X, Corsair IV, Liberator VI, Dominie I, Mosquito VI, XIX and XXX, Hellcat II, Halifax III, Hurricane IIc, Hudson I, Master II, Harvard III Mustang III and IV, Stirling IV and V, Warwick I and III, Spitfire V and IX, Vengeance IV and Lysander I.
1341 (SD) Flight Halifax III.
1588 and 1589 (Heavy Freighter) Flight Stirling V.

North Luffenham

17 EFTS Tiger Moth II.
61 Squadron Hampden I, Manchester I.
144 Squadron Hampden I.
408 (Goose) RCAF Squadron Hampden I.
29 OTU Wellington I and III, Anson I, Defiant I, Tiger Moth I and II, Whitley V.

General Aircraft Glider Assembly and Modification Unit
Hamilcar.
HGMU Whitley, Albemarle I, Horsa.
1653 HCU Lancaster I and III, Oxford I, Beaufighter VI,
Mosquito XIX, Hurricane II, Spitfire I and V.

Nuneaton

18 OTU Wellington Ic.
1513 BATF Oxford I.
105 OTU Wellington X.
1381 (T) CU Wellington Ic and X, Hurricane II, Dakota III.
250th Field Artillery Battalion, **US Army** L-4H Grasshopper.

Ratcliffe

6 FPP (ATA). 6 FP (ATA) Anson I, Tiger Moth II, Dominie I,
Argus I and II.

Saltby

14 OTU Hampden I, Wellington I.
2 HGMU Horsa I.
32 GMS Horsa I.
314th TCG C-47, C-53, C-46 and C-109.
1665 HCU Stirling I and III, Halifax III, Spitfire V.
349th TCG C-46.

Woolfox Lodge

14 OTU Hampden I.
29 OTU Wellington I.
61 Squadron Manchester I and Ia, Lancaster I.
61 CF Manchester I, Lancaster I.
33 HGMS Horsa.
1665 HCU Stirling I.

1429 (Czech) OTU Wellington I and Ic.
218 Squadron Stirling I and III.
3 LFS Lancaster I and III.
21 HGMU Horsa.
1651 HCU Lancaster I and III, Spitfire V.

Wymeswold

28 OTU Wellington Ic, III and X, Moth Minor, Lysander III, Martinet I, Master II, Hurricane II, Anson I, Tutor and Defiant I.
1521 BATF Oxford I.
108 (T) OTU Wellington X and Dakota III.
1382 (T) CU Dakota III and IV, Magister I.

BIBLIOGRAPHY

PRO Air 29/688 (Bitteswell, Leicester East, Wymeswold)
PRO Air 29/672 (Bruntingthorpe)
PRO Air 29/479 (Market Harborough)
PRO Air 28/529 (Melton Mowbray)
PRO Air 28/679 (Saltby)
PRO Air 28/440 (Leicester East)
PRO Air 29/857 (Bottesford)
PRO Air 29/617 (Desford)
PRO Air 2/10659 (Leicester East)
PRO Air 29/472 (Melton Mowbray)
PRO Air 29/857 (North Luffenham)
RAF Bomber Command OTU Losses, Vol. 7 – W R Chorley – Midland Counties.
RAF Bomber Command Losses, Vol. 1 to 6 – W R Chorley – Midland Counties.
The Bomber Command War Diaries –– Middlebrook and Everett – Midland Publishing.
Fields of Deception – Colin Dobinson – Methuen
UK Airfields of the Ninth Then and Now – Roger Freemann – After the Battle.
Wings Over Rutland – John Rennison – Speigl Press, 1980.
RAF Flying Training and Support Units – Sturtivant, Hamlin & Halley.
Action Stations 2 – Bruce Barrymore Halpenny – PSL.
Support and Strike – John Hamlin – GMS.
The Bomber Command Handbook – Jonathon Falconer – Sutton.
Aviation in Leicester and Rutland – Roy Bonser – Midland Counties.
Valor Without Arms – Michael N. Ingrisano – Merriam Press.
Birds Eye Wartime Leicestershire 1939–1954 – Terence Cartwright-TCC Publications.
The British Bomber – Francis K Mason – Putman.
Aircraft of the Royal Air Force – Owen Thetford – Putman.

INDEX

RAF Units

Squadrons

Other Units

107 (T) OTU 144–149
108 (T) OTU 85, 265
204 Advanced Flying School 120
240 Operational Conversion Unit 27, 199
256 MU 60
304 Ferry Training Unit [FTU] 175
306 FTU 174
1321 Bomber Defence Training Flight [BDTF] 57
1333 (Transport Support) Conversion Unit 149
1381 (T) CU 206–207
1513 Beam Approach Training Flight [BATF] 30, 204
1521 BATF 183–84
1651 Heavy Conversion Unit [HCU] 254–255
1653 HCU 197, 198, 199
1665 HCU 18, 234, 236, 247–248
1668 HCU 56, 120
1683 BDTF 74–75, 77, 166, 167
Bombing Analysis School 78
Heavy Glider Conversion Unit 194–196, 199
Power Jets Unit 33, 79–80

American Units
9th Air Force Troop Carrier Command 12, 22–26, 227
250th Field Artillery Battalion 204–205
314th Troop Carrier Group [TCG] 227–234
316th TCG 109–120
349th TCG 235–236
436th TCG 54–55
440th TCG 56

Australian Squadrons
467 (RAAF) 21, 47–54 *passim*

Canadian Squadrons
408 (Goose) 188–189
410 200
439 200
441 200

Czechoslovakian Units
1429 (Czech) OTU 246

Polish Units
18 (Polish) OTU 20, 28–30